T0335049

Scholarly Reprint Series

The Scholarly Reprint Series has been
established to bring back into print
valuable titles from the University of
Toronto Press backlist for which a
small but continuing demand is known
to exist. Special techniques (including
some developed by the University of
Toronto Press Printing Department)
have made it possible to reissue these
works in uniform case bindings in runs
as short as 50 copies. The cost is not
low, but prices are far below what
would have to be charged for such
short-run reprints by normal methods.

The Scholarly Reprint Series has
proved a valuable help to scholars and
librarians, particularly those building
new collections. We invite nominations
of titles for reissue in this form, and
look forward to the day when, with this
series and other technological developments, the label 'out of print' will
virtually disappear from our backlist.

ESSAYS IN
POLITICAL ECONOMY

IN HONOUR OF E. J. URWICK

EDITED BY H. A. INNIS

WITH AN INTRODUCTION BY
THE HON. AND REV. H. J. CODY

THE UNIVERSITY OF TORONTO PRESS
1938

POLITICAL ECONOMY SERIES, No. 1

PUBLISHED BY

THE UNIVERSITY OF TORONTO PRESS
AND
THE MAURICE CODY FOUNDATION

SCHOLARLY REPRINT SERIES EDITION 1978
Reprinted 2017
ISBN 978-1-4875-9192-2 (paper)

TABLE OF CONTENTS

INTRODUCTION

THIS volume of essays in Political Science is a tribute to the character and work of Professor Edward Johns Urwick who in June, 1937, retired under the age limit from the chair of Political Economy in the University of Toronto. It is the first volume of a series in Political Economy to be published by the Maurice Cody Foundation and the University of Toronto Press. It includes articles written by colleagues of Professor Urwick in the Department of Political Economy on subjects in which they had special interest, and articles which are summaries of work done by holders of the Maurice Cody Fellowship since its establishment in 1928. By a happy coincidence, this volume is issued fifty years after the chair in Political Economy was founded.

No more appropriate commemoration of a great teacher's services could be devised than the writing of a book on various phases of the subject to whose study he has devoted his energy and power of research. Professor Urwick is "worthy for whom we should do this". He was born in Cheshire, England, in 1867, almost on the birthday of the Canadian Confederation, the son of an eminent Congregational minister, the Rev. Dr. William Urwick. He was educated at Uppingham Public School, raised to heights of fame by its great Headmaster, Edward Ihring. Thence he passed to Oxford, winning a first class in *Literae Humaniores* in 1890 and taking his M.A. in 1892. From early manhood, he was deeply interested in the welfare of the people. From 1899 to 1902, he was sub-warden of Toynbee Hall—that pioneer social settlement in East London—under the leadership of the Rev. Samuel A. Barnett (afterwards Canon of Westminster Abbey). When Canon Barnett died in 1913, full of years and of honour, Mr. Urwick was one of the pall-bearers at the funeral. Something of what Professor Urwick was to the ideals and efforts of London social workers may be learned from the pages of Mrs. Barnett's Life of her husband. He was Director of the London School of Sociology from 1902 to 1910 and Professor of Social Philosophy in the University of London from 1912 to 1922. He was elected Vice-President of the Sociological Society of England and had the practical experience gained by serving as a Poor Law Guardian from 1896 to 1902, and as a member of the Port of London

Immigration Board from 1897 to 1903. His pen was busy in those years. He published successively *Studies of Boy Life in Great Cities* (1903); *Luxury and Waste* (1906); *A Philosophy of Social Progress* (1909), and in the same year, *The Message of Social Progress*. The last book he wrote in England was *The Message of Plato* (1920) in which he maintained that the great Greek philosopher was influenced by currents of Indian thought.

Professor Urwick retired from his academic work in England and came to Canada in 1924 mainly, I believe, to give his sons a start in this new country. He had not been long in Toronto before Professor R. M. MacIver induced him to be a Special Lecturer in the Department of Political Economy and this he was from 1925 to 1927. When Professor MacIver left this University for a chair in Columbia University, Professor Urwick was appointed as his successor. From 1927 to 1937 he graced the chair of Political Economy and was made Head of the whole Department of Economics and Political Science. Indeed, Commerce and Finance, and at first Law, were included in the broad sweep of his supervision. When illness compelled Professor J. A. Dale to retire from the directorate of the Department of Social Science, Professor Urwick assumed these additional duties.

In 1927 he published one more book *The Social Good*. I think it one of the best, sanest, and most constructive books ever written on this subject. I highly prize my copy of it, as it was sent me by him and was accompanied by one of his characteristically gracious and modest letters. The essentials of happiness he sets forth as: Work; Strong Interests; the Companionship of People whom one likes and who also likes one, and therefore, constant reciprocity of service; an Ideal to live for; and Immunity from severe physical hindrances, as well as from too great care and anxiety. It would be hard to improve on this list, especially as each ingredient is set forth against a fundamentally religious background. The conclusion of his whole argument deserves quotation: "Every step in social progress has for its condition—its only condition—some extension of social sympathy in the form of a projection of your and my will beyond the limits of self-interest or narrow group-interest, inspired by a pattern of goodness acceptable to both you and me in our best moments. And no progress can be made on any other terms." He wrote once of his former chief, Canon Barnett, a word of appreciation which I think may well be applied to himself: "Another characteristic added both to his power and to his lovableness. He was always young, and met every change of condition, every new combination of circumstances, with the vigor, freshness and elasticity of youth. He was not afraid, therefore, to be inconsistent. He was a progressive as naturally as some people are conservative."

I wish to pay my own tribute of warm appreciation for his services both to this University and to this community. He toiled hard at his work; he was accessible to his students; he was a wise counsellor to his colleagues; he was no remote academician but a brother lending a helping hand to the manifold social welfare activities of this city. Though he is now a Professor Emeritus, he is still giving lectures in Sociology and as Chairman of the Welfare Council of Toronto he is still supplying wise leadership to the manifold efforts made by earnest men and women to promote the Social Good in our land. May this tribute of Essays in Political Economy cheer him in his continuing tasks and assure him that he is still held high in our esteem and affection!

As I have already said, the publication of this volume is made possible by the generous support of the Maurice Cody Research Fellowships and Scholarships Fund. After my dear and only child, Henry Maurice Cody, a graduate of this University and a barrister at Osgoode Hall, met what seemed to be an untimely death in 1927 by drowning, on his holidays, in a Northern Ontario river, a group of his friends, under the leadership of Senator the Hon. Sir Edward Kemp, K.C.M.G., determined to commemorate his name in connection with his *Alma Mater*. A substantial sum, about $50,000, was raised to provide for an annual research fellowship and for two undergraduate scholarships to be awarded on a special examination. The intention of the Founders was that the field of study should be economic rather than historical; that investigation should be made, in a broad and scientific spirit, into the economic development of Canada; and that special studies should be made of those urgent problems which are confronting this growing Dominion. That the results of these studies should be available for all, publication of the Fellowship theses in whole or in part is absolutely necessary. The Committee, appointed under the original trust, has, therefore, made provision to include in this volume summaries of the investigations carried out by the Maurice Cody Fellows. These researches have extended over a wide field.

In 1929 the first fellowship was awarded to Dr. S. A. Saunders and his work has been published as follows: *The Economic Welfare of the Maritime Provinces* (Wolfville, 1932); "The Maritime Provinces" (*The Canadian Economy and Its Problems*, Toronto, 1934, pp. 127-33); "Memorandum on Municipal Finance" (*Appendices, Report of the Royal Commission, Provincial Economic Inquiry, Nova Scotia*, 1934); "Comments upon *Report of the Royal Commission, Provincial Economic Inquiry, Nova Scotia*" (*Commerce Journal Annual Review*, March, 1935); *The Modern World, Political and Economic*, in collaboration with Dr. R. A. MacKay (Toronto, 1935); "The Reciprocity Treaty of 1854: A Regional Study" (*Canadian Journal of Economics and Political Science*, vol. II, Feb., 1936); "The Maritime Provinces and the National Policy" (*Dalhousie Review*, vol. XVI, April, 1936); "The Maritime Provinces and the Reciprocity Treaty" (*Dalhousie Review*, vol. XIV, Oct., 1934); "A Note on the Dairy Industry in the Maritime Provinces" (*The Dairy Industry in Canada*, ed. H. A. Innis, Toronto, 1937, pp. 283-4); "Forest Industries in the Maritime Provinces" (*The Lumber Industry in Canada*, Toronto, 1938). Miss A. L. Chapman was appointed in 1930 and her article in this volume is a summary of a Master's thesis, "The Economic Effects of Tariffs on the Canadian Dairy Industry". Mr. O. J. McDiarmid and Mr. Leo Warshaw were appointed in 1932. Mr. McDiarmid completed a Master's thesis on Canadian tariff policy and trade agreements at the University of Toronto, and secured his Doctor's degree at Harvard University on a thesis in the same field. His article is the result of this special work. Mr. Warshaw completed a Master's thesis on the economic forces leading to a centralized federation in Canada, and it is the basis of his article. Miss Betty Ratz was appointed in 1933 and her published work includes the article on labour in the *Encyclopedia of Canada*, articles on aviation and mineral development (*Bank of Nova Scotia Monthly*, June, 1936), "Historical Background of Forest Industries in Canada" (*ibid.*, June, 1937), "Wheat and the Canadian Empire" (*ibid.*, Nov., 1937), and "The United Front in Toronto 1872" (*New Frontier*, June, 1936). Mr. F. W. Burton was appointed in 1934 to work on the subject,

"The Role of Wheat in Canadian Economic History". He has published "Wheat in Canadian History" (*Canadian Journal of Economics and Political Science,* vol. III, May, 1937), "The Business Cycle and the Problem of Economic Policy" (*Canadian Economy and Its Problems,* Toronto, 1934, pp. 143-58), "The Wheat Supply of New France" (*Transactions of the Royal Society of Canada,* May, 1936), and an article on the grain trade in the *Encyclopedia of Canada.* These provide a background for his article in this volume. Mr. W. T. Easterbrook was appointed in 1935 to pursue investigations in the field of rural credit in Canada. He has published an article on rural credit in the *Encyclopedia of Canada* and on "Agricultural Debt Adjustment" in the *Canadian Journal of Economics and Political Science,* Aug., 1936. His volume on the *History of Agricultural Credit* is in the press. Mr. Douglas Woods was appointed in 1936 to study the problem of conservation in Canada, with special relation to forests. When publication completes investigation, the aims of those who established the Maurice Cody Foundation will be realized.

In this year 1938 we are celebrating the establishment of the first chair of Political Economy in the University of Toronto. I was present as an undergraduate at the inaugural lecture given by Professor William James Ashley, and vividly remember his deliberate utterance, the cautious and well-based enunciations of his views. A man of his type, never a mere doctrinaire, always in touch with history and with the actualities of the present, was the ideal incumbent of this new chair. He gave weight and authority to a subject scarcely regarded then as possessing much scientific value. Professor Ashley went to Harvard in 1892 and later on to Birmingham, where he organized and vindicated the first Faculty of Commerce in that University. He was followed in the chair at Toronto by James Mavor (1894-1923); R. M. MacIver (1924-7); and E. J. Urwick (1927-37). This original broad department has been the parent of other flourishing specialized departments, such as Law, Sociology, Social Science, and Geography.

From this department a steady stream of post-graduate students has flowed to the important British and American universities, and men well trained in the principles of Political Economy have entered the public life of this country. Among them were the Rt. Hon.

Mackenzie King, Prime Minister of Canada, the Hon. Howard Ferguson, formerly Premier of Ontario, Sir Edward Beatty, President of the Canadian Pacific Railway, S. J. Maclean of the Railway Commission, and W. H. Moore, formerly Chairman of the Tariff Board of Canada.

The Social Sciences are to-day demanding an increasing share of attention in all universities; and research in them is as vitally important to the nation as is research in the field of the Physical Sciences. Our relations to one another are as worthy of accurate and sympathetic consideration as are our relations to the material universe. I look for marked developments in this field of our university work.

Not long ago Sir Josiah Stamp, a great man of practical affairs and a well-disciplined economist, felt constrained to give a public answer to the complaint that economists do more harm than good. It is often asserted that they disagree among themselves; that they never consistently say the same thing; and that they never can tell you what is going to happen, or if they do make a forecast, their prediction is falsified by the event. Sir Josiah maintains that one reason for these complaints is that the title economist is claimed by many people who have never undergone any discipline in economic thought but who "excogitate by the light of nature what beforehand they want to think". In every science there is a generally-accepted book of knowledge covering perhaps ninety per cent of the field, while over the remaining ten per cent a healthy unrest prevails. Economics is not singular in this respect. The trained economist collects facts and tries to group them so as to discover principles and tendencies. But he knows how complex is economic life and how misleading a "simple statement" in economics may be; he knows that he cannot make things too easy for people and that short cuts to prosperity are at bottom uneconomic; in consequence of his warnings he is often unpopular. "Without the economist", says Sir Josiah, "we would have debased coinage, unwise banking, crazy credit, unsound public finance, trade crises all the time, tariffs ruining the productive power of the world under the guise of promoting the interests of little bits of it. In fact, every generation would respect every economic folly that short-sighted mercantile selfishness or blown-out cloudy idealism has committed through the ages." This is his answer to the question: "Does the economist do more harm than good?" It is adequate.

We do need more economists with better training; more money spent on economic research; a closer contact between abstract conceptions and the world of facts; better co-ordination and more constructive mutual criticism of views before the giving of public advice; and a fairer hearing when a considered economic pronouncement is made.

I trust that the essays and studies in this volume will demonstrate that some economists at least do more good than harm, and make a real contribution to the exposition and the solution of Canadian problems in politics, business, and finance.

H. J. CODY

President's Office,
University of Toronto,
January, 1938.

SOME ASPECTS OF CORPORATIONS

C. A. ASHLEY

THE proportion of the world's business which is conducted by companies with limited liability has increased rapidly. In 1837 Lord Brougham, urging the House of Lords to reject a bill, said that limited liability was "contrary to the whole genius and spirit of English law, contrary to the genius and spirit of the Constitution",[1] and it was not until 1855 that it became a matter of general right,[2] although it had for many years been granted by Charter or by Act of Parliament to individual companies. In 1932 it was estimated that 94 per cent of manufacturing in the United States was carried on by corporations.[3] Parallel with this growth there has been a great increase in the size of big companies, and this has been so striking in its effects as to produce recently a large body of literature on imperfect competition. Some of the implications of the rapid revolution which has taken place have, however, often been overlooked, and misconceptions of some aspects of corporations are common.

In a recent article[4] Mr. J. M. Cassels puts forward four fundamental assumptions generally accepted by orthodox economists and shows how one of these, free atomistic competition, must be modified as a result of the concentration of activity in large companies. The first assumption to which he refers, "that, in their business activities, men are motivated almost entirely by the desire of each to maximize his own individual economic gain", appears still to be acceptable to him and to most economists although Messrs. Berle and Means, who have supplied so many facts proving that competition is imperfect, have also written: "Just what motives are effective to-day, in so far as control is concerned, must be a matter of conjecture. But it

[1]B. C. Hunt, *The Development of the Business Corporation in England, 1860-1867* (Cambridge, Mass., 1936), p. 84.

[2]*Ibid.*, p. 89.

[3]A. A. Berle and G. C. Means, *The Modern Corporation and Private Property* (New York, 1934), p. 14.

[4]"Monopolistic Competition and Economic Realism" (*Canadian Journal of Economics and Political Science*, vol. III, Aug., 1937).

is probable that more could be learned regarding them by studying the motives of an Alexander the Great, seeking new worlds to conquer, than by considering the motives of a petty tradesman of the days of Adam Smith."[5]

Two points arise from this. First, the law has endowed companies with certain of the attributes of an individual, but the law has not been able to give to a company the capacity to be influenced by motives. Its actions, although legally those of an individual, must be decided upon by another individual. Does the economist assume that a company acts in a manner calculated to maximize its profits or those of the individual making the decision? The former is manifestly untenable and the latter leads to complications which have yet to be explored, although the majority of commercial transactions are probably involved. The personal profit of the management does not necessarily coincide with profit for the company; the best interests of the shareholders (*i.e.*, of the company) may be diametrically opposed to the best interests of the management. The management may seek direct personal profit or they may divert profits from one company to another in which their interest is larger; use profits for unprofitable expansion of the company; continue operating the company when liquidation would be best for the shareholders.

Secondly, the motives of the management may not be chiefly profit, and if they are already wealthy, profit may fade into insignificance. Increased power, which may be sought for self-glorification or for political reasons, becomes the main incentive. "It is also desirable to notice that, in fostering the existence of corporations, the state is sponsoring the creation of economic power in highly concentrated form. Indeed, in many instances the state is making possible the establishment of organizations which . . . practically exercise sovereign powers."[6] No one who has any knowledge of the activities of Kreuger would suggest that the motives for any transaction of one unit in his group of companies were even probably the maximizing of profit for that unit. He came near to exercising sovereign powers, and it appears likely that his companies were used for supplying direct subsidies for political groups in various countries.[7] The effects of the power motive are of particular importance

[5]Berle and Means, *The Modern Corporation and Private Property*, p. 350.
[6]S. H. Slichter, *Modern Economic Society* (New York, 1931), p. 152.
[7]M. Georg, *The Case of Ivar Kreuger* (London, 1933), *passim.*

in labour relations, for the management of a company, actuated by powerful prejudice or by pride, can reject arrangements which would be in the interests of the company without suffering themselves; management salaries do not cease during a strike or lock-out.

The management of a company are seldom displaced, and they have a security of income and of alternative opportunity through nepotism which may leave them indifferent for long periods to the welfare of the company. As long ago as 1854, Herbert Spencer wrote:

As devised by Act of Parliament, the administrations of our public companies are almost purely democratic. The representative system is carried out in them with scarcely a check. Shareholders elect their directors, directors their chairman; there is an annual retirement of a certain proportion of the board, giving facilities for superseding them; and by this means, the whole ruling body may be changed in periods varying from three to five years. Yet, not only are the characteristic vices of our political state reproduced in each of these mercantile corporations—some even in intenser degree,—but the very form of government, whilst remaining nominally democratic, is substantially so remodelled as to become a miniature of our national constitution. The direction, ceasing to fulfill its theory as a deliberative body whose members possess like powers, falls under the control of some one member of superior cunning, will, or wealth, to whom the majority become so subordinate, that the decision on every question depends on the course he takes. Proprietors, instead of constantly exercising their franchise, allow it to become on all ordinary occasions a dead letter; retiring directors are so habitually re-elected without opposition, and have so great a power of insuring their own re-election when opposed, that the board becomes practically a close body; and it is only when the misgovernment grows extreme enough to produce a revolutionary agitation among the shareholders that any change can be effected.[8]

With the wide distribution of shares and the latest methods used by directors, this is an understatement at the present time. So helpless have shareholders become that in capital reorganizations they frequently appoint as a "protective committee" the very people in whom they foolishly placed their trust when the company was promoted.[9] And yet many people assure us that the rights of shareholders are so strong that there is no need to regulate the activities of directors in the interests of investors or the general public.

The necessity for some state interference in the promotion, operation, and (in England) reorganization of companies has gradually

[8]Hunt, *The Development of the Business Corporation in England*, p. 135.
[9]F. I. Shaffner, *The Problem of Investment* (New York, 1936), ch. xii.

been realized, but the principle of *caveat emptor* is still generally thought to be sound, and the state still regards most company affairs as a domestic matter and is unwilling to intrude unless invited by a member of the family. The Companies Act requires certain things to be done and prohibits others, but, in Canada, it appears that the state is loathe to take action if it knows of breaches of the Act, except under pressure from shareholders. The vast influence of companies on the economy as a whole is dawning but slowly on our minds, and legislation lags sadly behind the ingenuity of corporation lawyers. "Meanwhile the contrivances of the law for the defence of the public against them plod with heavy steps some way in the rear. . . ."[10]

The method by which a board of directors becomes self-perpetuating has been indicated above. In most companies two or three directors spend a considerable part of their time on the affairs of the company; the rest are appointed for various reasons. Although few people expect all the directors of a company to spend their whole time in the interests of the company, some sort of responsibility for its conduct, some knowledge of its affairs, might reasonably be expected. Possibly a large proportion of part-time directors are honest and give some protection to the public, but the tradition of accepting the honour and fees associated with a seat on the board in the spirit in which it is usually offered is bad. "This passive uprightness is an important asset: but it does not always compensate for the indolence and blindness of directors, who are accomplices in wrong-doing in this sense that they receive their fees, and yet plead ignorance of matters which a sense of their duty should have caused them to investigate. The Law courts of England, in spite of great recent improvements, appear still to treat this form of wrong-doing too indulgently."[11]

One of the commonest of the passive type of director is the "prestige" director. In England the nobility and retired officers of the services are used as ornaments, and an impecunious aristocrat with a resounding title may gather from directorships enough to maintain some semblance of the state to which he has been called. In Canada this type of director is drawn largely from established captains of industry, which is a more pernicious habit, for investors

[10]A. Marshall, *Industry and Trade* (ed. 3, London, 1920), p. 332.
[11]*Ibid.*, p. 321.

believe that men with records of success are actively participating in the management of a company when this is not the case. When mention was made in the House of Commons at Ottawa of the number of boards on which certain men served, Mr. R. B. Bennett, who was prime minister at the time, March 1, 1934, said: "They control the companies they head but in the case of others I know they often do not attend the directors' meetings."

Other directors are appointed solely for the purpose of introducing business or of establishing connections with financial companies, and this may frequently result in an interference with the ordinary operations of the market and in a division of loyalties which involves a breach of trust. Yet other directors are appointed on a reciprocal basis which may amount to nothing more than "You appoint me and I will appoint you and we shall both be a thousand a year better off". The whole question of Guinea-Pig Directors is effectively dealt with by Mr. Samuel.[12]

The question of divided loyalties, which has been mentioned above, is sometimes acute. When a company issues bonds, it chooses the trustee for the bondholders and, in Canada, a trust company is usually appointed. Now the directors of trust companies are very often directors of banks, and directors of banks are much sought after to adorn the boards of industrial companies; or, alternatively, important directors of industrial companies are appointed to directorships of banks. How is it possible for a man to act in a position of trust first as a company director, secondly as the banker holding that company's account, and thirdly as trustee for the bondholders of the company? In times of stress the three interests he represents are inevitably in conflict, and the only solution to his difficulties appears to be to think mainly of his own interests; but because of the impersonal nature of companies and particularly of trust companies, few people are aware of this. In some large companies three or four directors may be in this position.

The annual accounts of public companies are sent to shareholders and are filed (if Dominion incorporation) with the secretary of state. In addition, the large public companies advertise their balance sheets in the newspapers. Private companies are under no obligation to publish their accounts in any way and some private companies are

---

[12]H. B. Samuel, *Shareholders' Money* (London, 1933), ch. v.

so large as to be dominant in their respective fields, and it is most undesirable that such an anomaly should persist.

It would, however, be a mistake to suppose that the published accounts of companies give valuable information in a useful form, and probably more people are deceived than are enlightened by them. Sir W. McLintock, a chartered accountant, giving evidence before a committee appointed by the Board of Trade in England, remarked that many balance sheets are "models of obscurity".[13] The Dominion Companies Act now requires balance sheets to give certain information and some of the obscurity has passed away, but, in spite of this, balance sheets are still far from satisfactory. Professor Smails writes: "The balance sheet is, in fact, a highly technical statement intelligible only to those who are thoroughly versed in accounting convention and procedure, and yet by an unfortunate historical accident it is the one accounting statement which has been made accessible to everyone."[14]

It should be added that Professor Smails was writing of an idealized state of affairs, for there are many reasons why a balance sheet, although intelligible, may be entirely misleading, even to an expert accountant, unless he has facilities for considerable research into the affairs of the company. Unfortunately it is true that the majority of company managers are not concerned with publishing accounts which, by the application of accounting conventions, will disclose a true picture of the affairs of the company. Their motives are various: perfunctory satisfaction of legal requirements; a wish for reflected glory; maintenance of their positions; formation of public opinion; *etc.* Sometimes the accounts of companies are deliberately designed to deceive; sometimes the management think they are acting honestly in the best interests of shareholders; hundreds of directors would be shocked beyond measure at the suggestion that they should attempt to disclose the "true" condition of a company year by year.

At an annual meeting of Tube Investments, Limited, Mr. Arthur Chamberlain (cousin of two ex-chancellors of the Exchequer) said that the directors did not bring all the profits into the balance sheet,

[13]*Ibid.,* p. 241.
[14]*Canadian Journal of Economics and Political Science,* vol. III, Aug., 1937, p. 454.

but only so much as they considered would make "a pretty balance sheet". He continued: "I do, however, make one concession to exactitude. If the real earnings of the year are larger than those of the preceding one the figure shown in the balance sheet will be larger, and if they are smaller the balance sheet figure will also be smaller. The increase or decrease will only be a pointer, it will have no actual relation to the real figure." The *Accountant,* reporting this speech, commented as follows: "The kind of candour which prompts the chairman of a public meeting to tell his shareholders that the accounts contain 'one concession to exactitude' is, in our view, misplaced candour which could be transferred with advantage to the balance sheet itself."[15] Later, at a meeting of Roneo, Limited, Mr. Chamberlain said: "There are hundreds, if not thousands of bad directors, and if there are thousands of bad directors there are tens of thousands of bad shareholders—foolish creatures, short-sighted, ignorant, and easy-going shareholders, most of whom ought to go to prison for neglect of their duties. As long as you shareholders neglect your duties so long will bad management flourish."[16] Surely ignorance of shareholders of the manipulation of accounts by eminent business men hardly calls for a prison sentence!

Secret reserves are one of the commonest means of concealing the truth; they are also one of the most difficult to deal with because they are used habitually by banks and other financial institutions to which the rest of the business world tends to look for a lead. The only justification of their use by banks is that, if the public knew the truth, panics would be frequent, and this is hardly complimentary either to the public or to the bankers. What, in any case, could be more ridiculous than for the president of a bank at the annual meeting to give a long lecture on the course of business, comforting or admonishing, while presenting a set of accounts that have been "cooked" to conceal the effect of the course of business? The Macmillan Report (p. 156) strongly condemned "window-dressing"; a similar method of deception used each week by the English banks.

The management of industrial and commercial companies are not faced by the necessity of avoiding general panic in the public interest and at the cost of their honesty. Their deliberate deceit is sometimes

[15]*The Accountant,* vol. XCIII, Dec., 1935, p. 812.
[16]Reported in *ibid.,* vol. XCV, Nov., 1936, p. 643.

explained by them as being in the best interests of shareholders, partly through concealing the truth from competitors, but the real explanation is more often that the management have interests other than those of the shareholders at heart and believe that shareholders who wish for accurate information are impertinent: ". . . directors seem to have been governed to a large extent, in the selection of information to be made public, by a paternal notion that they knew best what shareholders ought to want. Protests of shareholders have in practice served only to confirm directors in their opinion of the unfitness of shareholders to make decisions which directors were always perfectly willing to make for them."[17] Unfortunately, the significance of reserves is seldom fully understood by bankers and financial journals, and these encourage the management to build up what they believe to be a sound position. The operations of large companies are of public interest, and investors and investigators are placed in a hopeless position when published accounts are meaningless. Speaking before a meeting of auditors, Sir Josiah Stamp said, ". . . Your modern fetish of a 'safe' or 'sound' balance sheet, which lies in almost every line . . .".[18] In spite of this, few auditors find difficulty in giving a "clean" report, certifying that a balance sheet "gives a true and correct view of the affairs of the company" when they know this to be entirely untrue.

Apart altogether from the usual types of secret reserves there are many other ways in which the management can, within wide limits, fix the apparent operating results of a company to suit their own ends, although careful study of accounts such as those now required of companies with Dominion charters may disclose the manipulation. Such are variations in the method of calculating depreciation, and the setting up and utilization of specific reserves against investment losses. "Again it often happens that those who control a company want to shake the public out, and acquire a yet greater control of it. They then charge expensive improvements to income account; and prepare a balance sheet, which will show that little or no dividend can be paid: and meanwhile they make large sales of the stock by concealed routes. When the price of the stock

[17]Hunt, *The Development of the Business Corporation in England*, p. 139.
[18]Reported in *The Accountant*, vol. LXXXVI, June, 1932, p. 776.

has thus been lowered, they quietly buy all that they have sold, and a great deal more."[19]

More stringent regulation of directors and auditors may do something to reduce the abuses which are rampant, but the best method of attacking them is the standardization of accounts, and publicity enforced at frequent intervals. "In any event such corporations should be required to follow a standardized method of accounting. . . ."[20] "Reliable market information, however, is needed not only by business men but also by investors, wage earners, and consumers. Investors must not be compelled to buy securities largely on the basis of balance sheets and income statements which are often next to worthless. Investment bankers cannot be relied upon for information concerning securities because, like all merchants, they are bound to puff their own wares."[21]

When attention is drawn to nefarious business practices, business men will say that the vast majority of companies are managed honestly and that it is undesirable to regulate all merely to prevent occasional abuse. Anyone who has read even part of the evidence that has been given before various investigating committees and commissions during the past ten years will be convinced that abuse is very widespread, and that it is to be found often in companies of so large a size that the repercussions are considerable.

The regulation of business to prevent abuses does not mean government interference in the details of business transactions. It means acknowledgement of responsibility for individual actions of the management;[22] recognition that directors are servants of, and trustees for, the shareholders; standardization of accounts; monthly statements of volume of business; raising auditors to the position of public officers (and changing their habits to fit their position). We are asked to believe that the effects would be so deleterious that business would languish and no man with any ability would run the risk of managing a company. An optimistic sceptic may doubt whether the prevention of gross abuses of trust will cause grass to

[19]Marshall, *Industry and Trade*, p. 337.

[20]Columbia University Commission, *Economic Reconstruction* (New York, 1934), p. 63.

[21]Slichter, *Modern Economic Society*, p. 854.

[22]*Cf.* Woodrow Wilson, quoted in W. Z. Ripley, *Main Street and Wall Street* (Boston, 1927), ch. i.

grow in our main streets; whether no capable business man will work unless he has a completely free hand and can avoid all personal responsibility; and whether a little humility would not become a company director as well as arrogance.

OVERHEAD COSTS, TIME PROBLEMS, AND PRICES

I. M. BISS

I N the literature of economics, theoretical, historical, and descriptive of various industries, few terms have been more variously used than "overhead costs". Though most of the variations are made upon a common theme of costs incurred in the provision of productive capacity which is, for some reason, incapable of adjustment to the exigencies of demand, they embrace widely divergent types of situation which are not always clearly distinguished. One distinction is fundamental. (*a*) Some costs of this type arise out of the use of *indivisible* productive equipment (in the widest sense, including both tangible and intangible elements in the whole apparatus of production) with a capacity which cannot be perfectly adapted to all ranges of output even at the time of its installation. The average cost per unit of its output must necessarily be greater for some outputs than for others. Such equipment may be either durable or ephemeral in character. (*b*) Other costs of this type arise out of the use of productive equipment with a capacity which lasts for a considerable period of time so that perfect adjustment to changes of demand can only be made at the time of installation or organization, or after a lapse of time sufficient for the equipment to wear out. A second, underlying theme can sometimes be disentangled, that of joint, inseparable costs of joint products.

The capacity of a plant may be inflexible through time because durable equipment has been installed and does not wear out at once; because productive activity has been undertaken and materials, labour, and capital applied to particular uses at some time in advance of the realization of returns; or because certain resources cannot rapidly be disbanded and reassembled. Indeed it may be necessary to keep a certain combination intact if productive capacity is to be maintained unimpaired. Such inflexibility of capacity over a period of weeks or months or years may create either of two types of situation in which capacity cannot be perfectly adjusted to demand. (1) Durable equipment may have been installed, and materials and labour applied in the expectation of continuous production on the scale to which these investments were adapted. Demand may falsify expectations by falling off permanently or for the time being, or by failing to expand in accordance with expectations, and for a time adjustment to the unforeseen change is impossible. (2) It may be technically necessary to use equipment which is durable and resources incapable of reorganization at will (or, if not necessary, more economical to do so than to carry on production with any of the more flexible types of equipment that are available), even though it is known that demand fluctuates in a definite and uncontrollable manner, so that there must be recurrent intervals of unused capacity. In this paper an attempt is made to review the price analysis appropriate to each of these two contrasting types of situation.

I

If all equipment came into being and was used up instantly in a single act of production, or if it was all completely versatile, the briefest interval of time would be a "long run" in the Marshallian sense of a period of sufficient duration to allow a completely free reconstruction of a concern's plant and personnel to any desired capacity. But typically the long-lived constructions and appliances of modern industry and of transport and power systems consist of localized changes in natural features (as in the case of power dams or the road beds of railways) or are otherwise specialized in their productive capacities, so that they can neither be sold for, nor applied to, any but their designed use without extra outlays being required. During the "short run" of their lifetime, which may vary from a period of hours in the case of some appliances to decades in the case of others, their productive capacity must be taken as given in any decisions as to output policy, and money invested in them in advance must be regarded as a "sunk cost", irrevocable, and therefore irrelevant to future price policy, until the plant wears out and the question of replacement comes up in a new "long run".[1] The over-

---

[1] If the equipment is unspecialized and has alternative opportunities open to it, no matter how durable it may be its use in any one line of production involves a sacrifice of possible revenue from other applications, and this loss must be included among the avoidable costs. Thus as long as the water powers developed by pulp and paper mills could only be used to drive their own grinders and machinery they were prepared during a depression to quote prices which

head "cost" of such non-salable, specialized equipment as lasts longer than the interval covered by the "short run" is, paradoxically, not a cost in the "short run" at all. In the provision of this equipment a portion of the unspecialized resources of the economy has already been committed to the form of appliances, information, materials, and other productive apparatus with given, narrowly defined productive powers. Expenditures made in the past on its account cannot now be modified by any alteration of price or output policy, nor can its specific productive powers be changed unless additional expenses are incurred. The entrepreneur is concerned only with further outlays on such additional means of production as must be combined with it in larger or smaller proportions if production is to be carried on, and which could be avoided in whole or in part if production were abandoned or cut down. Such outlays constitute the avoidable costs,[2] which are the only true costs in the "short run".

The specific relationship of these avoidable costs to "short run" price depends upon the type of competition prevailing in the market or markets in which the product is sold.

(1) Under conditions of pure competition, in the "short run" as in the "long run", the entrepreneur will be prepared to continue pro-

"left the power side out of the question". The dam was built and the money invested there could not be recovered, so the manufacturer was content to let the mill go on operating provided there was a "profit on the raw material and labour". The introduction of transmission lines and growing demand for electricity changed this. The power could now be turned into electrical energy and sold elsewhere. "Power (locked up on the bank of some stream) has in many cases been given away by manufacturers in order to sell their goods, but hereafter power must be reckoned in the cost of finishing the article just as is labour, or coal, or raw material." See *Pulp and Paper Magazine,* vol. VI, March, 1908, p. 70. A similar situation exists in respect of material and labour which are committed to a particular type of production in anticipation of a long postponed return. A change in the conditions of demand may falsify expectations, but adjustments to the altered demand must be made without reference to expenditures made in the past. The only possibility of avoiding loss lies in the exploitation of such alternative opportunities as may be available. If a farmer's fields are already sown, to consider what expenditures he made in sowing them will not help him to a wise decision as to whether they should be reaped.

[2]These are Marshall's "prime costs" (*The Principles of Economics,* ed. 8, London, 1930, pp. 359-60, 373-7, 419-24) and Professor J. M. Clark's "direct" or "out of pocket" costs (*Studies in the Economics of Overhead Costs,* Chicago, 1923, pp. 38-40).

duction if, but only if, he is at least able to cover all his costs. Since in the "short run" these include only the avoidable costs,[3] it will be worth while continuing production as long as total revenue is even slightly in excess of their sum total. But the shorter the "run" the smaller must be the aggregate of the avoidable costs for any given output, as a larger proportion of the whole apparatus of production is available for use without any further outlay being required on its account. Replacements and maintenance of only those more perishable materials and appliances that are used up and wear out in the brief interval in question will be included among these avoidable costs. The longer the "short" run the larger will be the proportion of the whole plant that will have to be replaced if production is to continue at a given rate, and the larger, therefore, the total of avoidable costs for any given output. Finally, in the longest "run" of all even the most durable equipment wears out and the most intractable elements in the plant become capable of reorganization. This is the new "long run", in which, again, outlays on every productive agent used, whether durable or ephemeral, must be included in the sum total of expenditures that must be covered to justify continued production.

But in the "short run" no less than in the "long run", the entrepreneur is concerned not merely to cover his costs but to secure the greatest possible excess of total revenue over total costs. If production has been organized on a scale suited to a given demand situation, with the equipment appropriate to that scale, and then demand unexpectedly[4] falls off, apparently for good, it becomes necessary to make readjustments in policy if this end is to be attained. Under conditions of pure competition, the firm produces but a negligible fraction of the whole output of a standardized commodity. Since to charge any higher price would debar it from making any sales at all, it must, once the period of transition is over, simply

---

[3]While the more spectacular cases of "overhead costs" occur among large, oligopolistic producers, even firms operating under conditions approximating to pure competition may be faced with problems of durable and continuous (though, except on a very small scale, not indivisible) productive equipment. The prairie wheat farmer uses specialized, durable equipment. He cultivates and seeds his land in anticipation of returns. In each case there is a "sunk cost".

[4]Much the same analysis applies when, even though changes in demand are anticipated, their timing, duration, and intensity are unpredictable.

accept the new conditions of demand, as expressed in the lower market price, and get the best results open to it by so adjusting output that any larger scale of production would give a marginal avoidable cost greater than the marginal revenue, and any smaller scale of production would give a marginal avoidable cost less than marginal revenue. Only if this most profitable possible output does not bring in a revenue sufficient to cover total avoidable costs will existing firms abandon production. Until even its most durable equipment wears out or the market price drops below its lowest average avoidable cost, each one will continue to produce, but the longer the time that elapses after the fall in demand the larger will be the proportion of its equipment which will need renewal, and the higher, therefore, the lowest average avoidable cost and the minimum below which price cannot fall. Conversely, the shorter the period the lower will this minimum be, and the further price may fall without compelling cessation of production. The shorter the "run" the less elastic must be the whole supply of the commodity. As price falls individual firms will meet the situation by the slight reduction of output necessary to bring marginal avoidable costs for the period in question into line with the new marginal revenue, and the price will come to rest as close to the lowest average avoidable costs as is necessary to allow the absorption of the sum of their outputs in the new conditions of demand. In the "long run" some firms[5] will not renew worn out equipment and the aggregate of the outputs of all surviving firms will contract to the new "long run" level apposite to the new conditions of demand. If, in the limiting case, these conditions are such that every possible output has a demand price lower than the lowest average cost of each of the group of firms which would be required to produce it, then in the "long run" all production will cease. If

[5]In an industry subject to constant (or uniform) costs of production, it is hard to see why some firms should drop out and not all the others as in terms of the usual analysis there appears to be no perceptible difference in their "long run" cost conditions. Perhaps this is a case in which there is no necessary tendency to equilibrium, but rather alternating crises of over- and under-production; perhaps there are differences in the conditions of the different firms which are important from the point of view of the process of change from one state of equilibrium to another, though not from the point of view of permanent production once the scale of output is established. Differences in the temporary liquidity of firms, or in their alertness in apprehending new conditions and making adjustments to them, provide possible examples.

that output of the commodity as a whole which commands a demand price equal to the lowest average cost of each of the group of firms which is required to produce it, is smaller than the old equilibrium output, which is likely to be the case, then the new equilibrium output of the commodity will be smaller, though that of the surviving firms is likely to return to the original level, at least in the most probable[6] conditions of constant (or uniform) costs for the production of the commodity as a whole.

If the unexpected change in the conditions of demand is believed to be transient, the situation is complicated by the fact that even without any prospect of immediate returns, it may be necessary to maintain the durable equipment and keep together a certain proportion of the executive staff, foremen, skilled, and otherwise indispensable,[7] workers if the original "long run" capacity is to be available in the future when the demand is expected to revive. These necessities add in part to the "short run" avoidable costs, and in part detract from them. If use of the durable plant during the "short run" wears it out faster than it would wear out or become obsolete as a result of the mere passage of time, then that extra wear and tear must be included among the avoidable costs, since a potential source of revenue is being exhausted in production in the "short run". On the other hand, "short run" revenue possibilities may not justify either the provision of depreciation reserves and outlays on the maintenance of plant against the ravages of time, nor the upkeep of even a skeleton staff on the scale dictated by the supposed requirements of the future. Such expenditures are made without reference to current production. They would not be affected by any modifications of immediate price and output policy. They are incurred in anticipation of future production and must be looked on as costs "sunk" in relation to that projected output, and not at all as costs avoidable in the "short run". Since, however, their expenditure implies the provision of equipment available without further outlay for use in the "short run", it may permit production in the "short run" at a lower

[6]See P. Sraffa, "The Laws of Return under Competitive Conditions" (*Economic Journal,* vol. XXXVI, Dec., 1926). It is, of course, true that as the problem of durable equipment assumes a greater importance conditions of pure competition are correspondingly less likely to be realized.

[7]Such as the pump crew in a mine.

total avoidable cost, and so indirectly influence the "short run" price and output policy.

(2) A firm catering to a distinct market of its own, whether under conditions of monopoly or of impure competition, will similarly be concerned with the relationship of price to average avoidable costs, and of marginal revenue to marginal avoidable costs, but, in contrast with the firm operating under conditions of pure competition which must sell at the going price or forgo production altogether, it may set any one of a wide range of alternative prices. It is therefore concerned not merely with the problem of selecting the best output in view of the market price, but the best *combination* of price and output.

Since the demand in its individual market for the firm's product is less than infinitely elastic, it imposes limitations upon the amount that can be sold at each price. There may exist other markets, insulated from this one by barriers to resale and movements of customers. In these even the highest demand price is relatively low, and the demand is more elastic, perhaps infinitely elastic. In such markets additional quantities of the product may be disposed of at a lower price, as when goods are "dumped" beyond tariff barriers in foreign markets in which the demand may be very nearly completely elastic. Whether such possibilities are worth adopting depends on whether the marginal avoidable cost of the simple monopoly output is as low as the highest marginal revenue obtainable in the market in which the demand is the more elastic of the two.[8] If this condition is fulfilled it pays any monopolist to discriminate regardless of whether the "run" is short or long, of whether there are any "overhead costs" or not.[9] It is more likely to be realized in the

[8]This section is based on a simple short run adaptation of the long run analysis in Mrs. Robinson's *Economics of Imperfect Competition* (London, 1933), pp. 179-202. It should be noted that, as Professor Pigou (*The Economics of Welfare*, ed. 3, London, 1929, p. 286) and Mrs. Robinson (*op. cit.*, p. 188 *ff.*) have shown, the simple monopoly output is not necessarily smaller than the discriminating monopoly output. The latter will, however, be larger when the simple monopoly price is too high to allow any sales in the weaker market, while the discriminating firm will sell in both (*ibid.*, p. 190). Even in other cases Mrs. Robinson's analysis suggests that a larger output is more likely with discrimination than without it (*ibid.*, p. 201).

[9]Historically there seems to have been an association between the phenomenon of "overhead costs" and the practice and theory of discrimination. "But

"short run" than in the "long run" for the same firm and the same markets. This is because in the "long run" the marginal costs which must be balanced against the marginal revenue include the extra cost of the *whole* of the equipment needed to produce the extra output to be sold on the basis of price differentiation, since in the "long run" the durable and persistent elements of productive capacity are perfectly adjustable to the scale of production required (unless, indeed, these elements are characterized by indivisibility as well as durability and persistence). It may happen, then, that the "long run" equilibrium is satisfied by sales in a single, relatively high priced market, without its being worth while to take advantage of any opportunity for discriminating that may exist.   Then demand falls off unexpectedly. For the time being, there is on hand productive equipment designed to produce an output substantially in excess of possible sales at the old price under the new conditions of demand.   This excess capacity persists until existing equipment wears out, if the new equilibrium output is smaller than the original output, or until demand revives. In these circumstances the marginal avoidable cost of larger outputs, at least up to the full designed capacity of the plant, will be very low, and the shorter the "run" and the more durable and persistent the equipment the lower it will be. This relatively low marginal avoidable cost may well be as low as the marginal revenue to be derived from some volume of sales in the low-priced market in which demand is relatively elastic, even though the "long run" marginal cost is consistently above marginal revenue in this market from any volume of sales. Under these conditions a firm will practise discrimination in favour of temporary customers, such as that practised by the Hydro-

---

it was the railroad itself that first brought the notion of overhead costs into real prominence with economists.   When railroads were new, their rates were commonly uniform or nearly so, based on weight and distance, and were uniformly high.   Soon it was discovered that additional traffic could be carried at little or no additional cost and that reduced rates, if confined to classes of traffic not already moving, would increase the net earnings of the company" (Clark, *Economics of Overhead Costs*, p. 9).   Though the possibilities of discrimination were thus revealed in an industry peculiarly beset by "overhead costs" arising from the use of equipment both durable and indivisible, discrimination is profitable to any firm no matter how ephemeral and divisible its equipment may be, if it caters to one imperfectly competitive market, and has access to other effectively insulated markets in which the elasticity of demand is different.

Electric Power Commission of Ontario in disposing of large quantities of "surplus power" at special low rates to pulp and paper mills for use in steam generators.[10]

Besides making price adjustments, a firm catering to its own market or markets may be able to modify the demand schedule for its product by appropriate adaptations of the quality of its goods, of the incidental services or subsidiary commodities which it offers to its customers, or of the expenditures which it makes on high-pressure salesmanship[11] and on "developmental" policies. The added cost of improvements in quality, supplementary services, sales effort, and "developmental" policies must be added to the marginal cost of production and weighed against marginal revenue for any given output. Since in the "short run" the marginal avoidable cost of production is low for at least some ranges of output smaller than the designed capacity of the plant, there may be greater scope for incurring such subsidiary outlays, but this is unlikely unless the "short" run in question covers a period of months or even of years. It may take time for an improvement in quality to modify consumers' buying habits; it may take time to organize supplementary services; it may take time to plan and execute an advertising campaign; and it may take a very long time indeed to carry through a "developmental" policy involving the establishment of new enterprises or "sending good money after bad" in constructing still further durable equipment to open up more uses for that already in existence. If a substantial part of the equipment has a high degree of continuity, so that a temporary recession of demand cannot be met by a complete readjustment of capacity, even if it bids fair to last for many years; or if it is highly durable, so that an extinct demand may long be survived by the apparatus originally designed to meet it, then "short run" crises of excess capacity may last for so long that it is worth while adopting policies of this type which require many years for the realization of their full effects. If a company operating a smelter faces exhaustion of the mines which it serves, it may prospect for new ore bodies

[10]See the *Annual Report of the Hydro-Electric Power Commission of Ontario for 1934*, pp. xiii-xiv.

[11]See Edward Chamberlin, *The Theory of Monopolistic Competition* (Cambridge, Mass., 1933), pp. 71-176. Discrimination may take the form of differences in quality, or in supplementary services as well as in price, but such cases are not here discussed.

and start new mines. A hydro-electric company in the same circumstances may start a pulp and paper mill, or install steam boilers for customers at its own expense. The particular combination of policies which it pays to adopt is that which gives the maximum possible excess of total revenue over total avoidable costs of production, of quality variation, of sales effort, of supplementary services, and of "developmental" activities all together, subject always to the essential condition that total revenue must at least equal the aggregate of avoidable costs of production and of building up demand.

(3) Under conditions of duopoly and oligopoly (whether combined with production for a distinct market or not) the firm must qualify this simple consideration of the relation between current revenue and avoidable costs by taking into account an especially dangerous possibility of "spoiling the market".[12] An attempt to maintain sales in the face of a falling demand by reducing price would probably be the signal for disastrous competitive price cutting, which would force down the demand schedules for the products of all the rivals to a level lower than that which first set the process in motion. Such firms will, therefore, be disposed to let well enough alone and, if they can, maintain, even in the face of substantial unused capacity, the "long run" equilibrium price. This individual disposition may be bolstered up by tacit or explicit understandings as to minimum prices, or at least conformity with pricing systems devised to minimize the danger of undercutting, such as the basing point system in the steel, cement, and other industries.[13] If discrimination is practicable it may be possible to get round this difficulty by maintaining the customary price or the new "long run" equilibrium price in the central market, which is in danger of being spoiled, and isolate price reductions in subsidiary private markets, where they need not lead to a declaration of any general price war.[14]

[12]See Marshall, *Principles of Economics*, pp. 360 and 376-7. There are, of course, other ways in which the market may be "spoilt", such as a change in consumer's dispositions when they have experienced a lower price, but the reflex effect of a price cut upon rivals' policy is probably the most important type, and it must be taken into account in "long" as well as in "short run" decisions by oligopolistic producers.

[13]I am indebted to Professor J. M. Clark for this suggestion and for other data regarding the cement industry.

[14]The barriers to resale and customer movement need not here be natural ones; they are even more likely to be matters of agreement or convention.

The danger of "spoiling the market" appears to be less with competition in improvements in quality, supplementary services, and sales effort than in price competition, which seems to be giving ground increasingly in modern industry to these other types of inducement, especially in oligopolistic industries. Some "developmental" policies carry still less danger of general cut-throat competition as they are directed to building up a market exclusively tributary to one concern, but they may become violently competitive in cases which involve "raiding the territory" of other large concerns, as in the construction of rival lines by the Canadian Pacific and the Canadian National Railways to tap the same mining district, or the construction, in the early days in the absence of any "gentleman's agreement" or public utility commission control, of duplicate distribution lines in the same street by concerns competing in the sale of electricity within a single city.

II

The second type of overhead cost situation involving time problems is that in which, while demand is known to fluctuate in a regular and predictable manner, technical conditions compel the use of equipment which is either specialized, unsalable, and durable in character or which is incapable of being rapidly dissipated and re-assembled. Such equipment may be necessary if a certain product is to be obtained at all, or its use may render production so much more effective than production by any alternative means that it is worth while in spite of the irregularity of demand. To generate electricity it is necessary to have a generator, and, barring accidents, the most short-lived practicable generator would last for longer than a day; but the demand for electricity fluctuates within twenty-four hours on most systems from a "peak", when energy is needed all at once for lighting, motive power in industry and to drive street cars during the rush hours, and for cooking, to a "trough" late at night, when the majority of people are asleep and most factories dark and silent. To transport goods overland it is possible to use men, or pack animals,

---

Freight absorption by cement producers meeting the prices of rival base mills is a special case of such non-provocative discriminatory price reduction. Oligopolistic discrimination seems to be one type which is not based on a comparison of the relative elasticities of demand in two markets. *Cf.* Robinson, *Economics of Imperfect Competition,* p. 181 and p. 185.

or wagons, and in Canada, canoes on natural waterways. Each of these is a flexible method offering a possibility of rapid adjustment of capacity to meet even quick fluctuations in demand, but the cost of moving goods by caravans of human porters, by pack trains, or wagon trains, or by canoe is so great per ton mile that it is cheaper to build railroads and canals even though the unavoidable durability of some of their component parts makes it impossible to adjust their capacity to the seasonal and cyclical fluctuations in demand that must take place within their lifetime, creating a recurrent problem of unused capacity.

All firms subject to daily, seasonal, or cyclical fluctuations in demand, and using, none the less, equipment which outlasts successive waves of high and low demand, face such a problem. Storage may be possible, but storage is expensive, and in the public utility and transport industries (with rare exceptions, such as gas) it is impossible. In effect firms in these industries sell the services of their durable producing and distributing equipment.

Paradoxically such problems of unused capacity are "long run" problems, since they must be faced at the initial installation of the plant. The entrepreneur planning the construction of a railway or a power plant must from the beginning take into account the fact that no matter how large or how small he builds it, it will be impossible to avoid periods of complete or partial disuse during its lifetime, since demand cannot be prevented from falling off at recurrent intervals too brief to allow readjustment of the capacity of the durable plant. In a few rare cases in which one group of possible customers has a steady demand and another a highly fluctuating demand, he may be able to build it only just big enough to handle the continuous minimum or "base" load, excluding the demand of the irregular consumers. Ordinarily this is impossible. If the entrepreneur's product is to be of any use at all to potential consumers, it must be available to them when they require it, and they require different quantities at different times.[15] He must be prepared to meet their

[15]In technical language the load factor of their demand is less than 100 per cent. In some cases technical or geographical limitations will make it impossible for the plant to operate continuously at full capacity. If stream flow fluctuates a hydro-electric plant may be forced to produce at less than designed capacity in low water periods. In this case the capacity factor is used to represent the proportion of unused capacity involved.

peak demand as well as their minimum demand, and he will therefore have to adjust his "long run" price and output policy with due
allowance for interludes of complete or semi-idleness.

There may be no alternative to charging the same price per unit
of output to all purchasers regardless of whether their demand adds
to the peak or helps fill up the trough of the wave of fluctuating
demand.   If this is so he must take as the basis of his calculations
a period of at least as long as the interval from peak to peak of that
type of demand fluctuation that has the greatest amplitude.   The
"standard burden rate" used in charging overhead costs to each unit
of output in such seasonal industries as the automobile industry is
in part a device to enable this to be done.   The plant will not be built
unless total revenue taken in in slack periods and in busy periods
together promises at least to cover total costs including depreciation
on the whole equipment and a return on the money invested in it
equal to the highest that could be obtained in any alternative investment.   It remains to decide which particular scale and capacity will
be most profitable.   If all potential consumers' demands fluctuate in
the same way with the peak and the trough at the same time, the load
factor of the whole plant is the same regardless of what price is
charged and what the amount sold may be.   Marginal revenue then
falls off with an increase in output simply because the demand price
is lower.   More commonly as a larger average output is offered for
sale new types of consumers will have to be induced to buy.   Their
demand may have a relatively low load factor so that the load factor
of the whole system becomes worse.   More probably the differences
in the timing of the fluctuations in their demand will cancel out some
of the fluctuations in the demands of the consumers of the smaller
average output, so that the load factor of the system as a whole is
raised.[16]   In these cases the drop in the marginal revenue associated
with the enlarged average output will be exaggerated or checked as
the case may be by the change in the load factor.   In either case the
greatest possible excess of total revenue over total costs is obtained
for that output which gives marginal revenue per unit of installed
plant capacity through the whole period of the longest fluctuation in
demand, equal to the marginal cost per unit of installed plant capacity
for the same period.   Sometimes, indeed, a company is able to charge

[16]In technical language the "diversity factor" has improved.

for its product on the basis of the plant capacity which must be held continuously at the disposal of each customer, even though he may use it for only a part of the time. Power contracts basing the monthly or annual charge on the consumer's installed capacity or peak load fall into this category. In such cases the problem of a capacity rigid in relation to fluctuating demands is transferred to the consumer. The company is really selling units of plant capacity and not units of product.

Few rate structures have the simplicity of a uniform rate per unit either of output or capacity. An energy charge as well as a minimum or service charge is usually made to the consumer of electricity. The service charge and the energy charge alike may be different to different classes of consumers and for different rates of consumption. Penalties may be imposed for a low load factor and rewards offered for a high one. These and other complexities in the rate structure are partly discrimination in the ordinary theoretical sense, but they are partly price differentiation of one of two other types frequently called discrimination, but having, apparently, a fundamentally different basis.[17]

(a) Different rates may be charged to different classes of consumers not because it pays to charge higher prices in markets insulated against the *movement of consumers or units of demand* into the lower priced markets but in order deliberately to provoke such movements. (Insulation against resale is as necessary in this case as in the other.) If by this means the load factor is raised so that the same total output can be handled by a smaller plant and the consequent reduction in revenue is more than offset by the reduction in total costs of production, there is a gain.

[17]Cf. Pigou, *Economics of Welfare*, pp. 275-8 and Robinson, *Economics of Imperfect Competition*, p. 179. It is not clear that such theoretical writers use the term "discrimination" in these secondary senses, though other writers have done so, for example Professor Clark (*Economics of Overhead Costs*, p. 426) : "The same device may be used as a means of marking off a class of customers, merely because they will stand a higher toll. The United States Commerce Commission has refused to permit railroads to make discriminations *on this ground alone*" (my italics). Compare also p. 23, and p. 281; but contrast p. 103, where it is stated, with reference to a case of joint production, that "this is not discrimination". I am indebted to Mr. V. F. Coe of the University of Toronto, who drew my attention to the distinction between these two subsidiary types of price differentiation.

(*b*) Even if, by such means, demand is made as regular as is technically possible, or if it cannot be made more regular without a sacrifice of revenue greater than the incidental reduction of total costs, or even if charges are made on a peak load basis for the full capacity of the plant, there still remain predictable, recurrent surpluses of capacity as long as uncontrollable fluctuations of demand persist. Then, if there exist yet other markets insulated not only against resale but also against *the transfer of customers and units of demand,* special rates may be given for business which can be handled entirely in off-peak periods, supply being terminable "at will", as with electrical energy to be used for heating water or generating steam. This need not involve any increase in the scale of the generating plant beyond that which would be required to meet peak load demands in the high price markets, but merely use of the same capacity at times when it would otherwise be idle.   The Marshallian joint product analysis[18] is, therefore, more appropriate to the situation than the Robinson analysis in terms of marginal aggregate revenue and marginal cost for the whole output sold in both markets.   The total demand for plant capacity can be interpreted as consisting of the demand for its product or services during peak periods plus the demand for its products or services during off-peak periods.[19] In the case of a central electric station, for example, the aggregate demand price for plant capacity of each possible scale may be obtained by adding the average revenue obtainable per unit of plant capacity from sales of off-peak power, to that obtainable from sales of peak-load power.   Average differential costs peculiar to each class of business, such as outlay on extra billing or additional transmission lines, must be deducted from the gross demand price.   Then the *net* marginal aggregate revenue from both sources together can be calculated.   The best possible results are obtainable from plants organized on a scale such that marginal net aggregate revenue per unit of plant capacity is equal to marginal cost per unit of plant capacity. The price charged for a kilowatt hour of electrical energy is then the

[18]Marshall, *Principles of Economics,* pp. 388-99.

[19]There may, of course, be intermediate classes of business between the two extremes of business at the time of full peak load and at times of minimum load. Each of these could be dealt with as a separate joint product, but as there is no change in principle only the simplest case of two classes of business is discussed.

average revenue from the whole possible output of each class of such energy per unit of plant capacity, divided by the number of kilowatt hours of energy of each class produced per unit of plant capacity. The scale of the plant is likely to be somewhat larger than the scale that would be most profitable if price differentiation, and so off-peak sales, were impossible, just as a larger scale of operations is likely to be rendered possible by a chance to sell any by-product.

Price differentiation designed either to raise the primary load factor or to stimulate custom for potential output in intervals of un-used capacity is a permanent part of the "long run" price structure not merely a temporary, "short run" expedient, since it is planned in advance to meet predictable recessions in demand.

To sum up: fluctuations of demand in relation to productive equipment, the capacity of which is incapable of adjustment to meet them, create specific pricing problems. Expenditures incurred in making available such unadjustable capacity are undertaken on the basis of calculations as to the prospects of its use and returns from it, over the whole period of its inflexibility. If the changes in demand are imperfectly foreseen allowance cannot be made for them in ad-vance. If, and when, they do occur consideration of the "long run" expenditures which have been incurred on entirely irrelevant grounds, does not help towards a decision as to the appropriate adaptations of price, output, and sales-building policy. Only the avoidable "short run" costs are relevant. When recessions of demand can be fore-seen, allowance is made for them in the "long run" in calculating the prospects of profit from an investment in long-lived equipment before it is undertaken. Both such unexpected and expected, but uncon-trollable, fluctuations in demand involve the possibility of production for discontinuous intervals of time at a very low total avoidable cost and, for some ranges of output, at a very low marginal avoidable cost, so that the downward limits set by cost of production to a fall in price, and to the possibility of price differentiation are much lower than in the "long run".

ADAM SMITH ON VALUE

V. W. BLADEN

" **I**T is the fate of all great books to get boiled down and served up
cold in text books, which purport to tell exactly what the great
book comes to, as though a man's conclusions were worth very much
apart from the way in which he arrived at them.   We must all have
had the experience, after reading even appreciative books about great
authors, of going back to the authors themselves and finding how
much more there is in them than their commentators had led us to
expect." These words of A. D. Lindsay, in the introduction to his
Karl Marx's Capital,[1] are directly applicable to Adam Smith's *Wealth
of Nations*.   The object of this paper is not to boil the *Wealth of
Nations* down once more, but rather to plead for a careful re-reading
of the book itself.   In particular it is suggested that attention should
be concentrated on what Adam Smith was trying to do, on what
questions he was trying to answer, rather than on considering what
his followers made of him, or what questions modern economists
think he should have asked.   Before proceeding there is one other
quotation from A. D. Lindsay, equally applicable to Karl Marx and
to Adam Smith, which should form part of this introduction:

The original thinker is too much occupied in trying to express the creative
thought which is welling up in him to trouble himself about getting it all
straightened out.   There are always parts of his work which he has taken
over as they stood from other people.   There are always bits of dead wood in
a great man's work.   The really tidy and consistent thinkers are the average
minded disciples, who make a neat and orderly system out of their master's
work, in which the inconsistencies are explained away, and much of what
makes the man worth reading explained away along with them.   For, unfortunately, it is much easier to make a tidy pattern out of dead wood than
out of growing shoots.

Bearing this in mind we shall not be worried by the inconsistency of
isolated statements, but shall look for the consistency of the system
as a whole.[2]   We shall also remember that in the infancy of a science

[1]London, 1925.

[2]*Cf.* F. H. Knight, "The Ricardian Theory of Production and Distribution"
(*Canadian Journal of Economics and Political Science*, vol. I, Feb., 1935, p. 7).

terminology is loose and ill defined; we shall not be surprised, therefore, to find the same word used in several different senses.[3]

"The first sentences of the 'Introduction and Plan of the Work'
hold out great hope of a systematic theory of production. . . . But
Smith's performance falls far short of his promise . . . after three
luminous but short chapters . . . he slips from the subject, by way
of a discussion of the origin and use of money, back into the theory
of prices which had been evolved in his lectures on Police."[4] This
judgment of Cannan on the theory of production in Adam Smith is
a clue to his judgment on the theory of value. It will be here argued
that chapter v, and the greater part of chapter xi, of the *Wealth of
Nations,* which discuss the "real price" of things, are essentially a
continuation of the theory of production. They are concerned with
the "improvement in the productive powers of labour". It will further
be argued that chapter vii on the "Natural and Market Price of
Commodities" is also an essential part of the theory of production,
for the main concern there, and throughout the book, is with the
appropriate direction of production. The *Wealth of Nations* is most
closely related to Professor Pigou's *Economics of Welfare.* The
interest lies not in why prices are what they are, but in what is the
best distribution of resources.[5] In other words, the theory of value is

After making a statement in the text that "the classical economists give no
picture of a system of prices", he adds in a footnote: "Let it be observed here,
once and for all, that general negative statements are to be taken subject to
interpretation. They mean that the 'system expounded' by the writer does not
take account of the facts in question. . . . Such general negative statements
are in no wise disproved by citing particular passages in which the fact or
principle in question is, or seems to be recognized."

[3]See L. M. Fraser, *Economic Thought and Language* (London, 1937).
Notice n. 3 on p. 119: "Bailey's strictures on Ricardo seem to me wholly
justified provided that it be assumed that Ricardo always meant—or thought
he meant—by 'value' *exchange* value. I cannot believe this."

[4]Edwin Cannan, *A Review of Economic Theory* (London, 1929), p. 53.

[5]Professor F. H. Knight appears to contradict this view in the sentence
quoted in n. 2, above. But in the second part of his article in the May number
of the *Journal* he qualifies this statement and does more justice to Adam
Smith: ". . . the discussions of value theory give, in connection with natural
price, a fair indication of the general nature of the organisation mechanism
and process under price competition, but . . . the chapters on distribution ignore
this reasoning. . . . It is in Smith that we find much the clearest view of the
organisation process" (p. 173). With these statements we are in complete
agreement.

an essential part of the case for laissez-faire. This is obvious if book
IV is read along with chapter vii.

Unfortunately Adam Smith stated his plan of attack on the problem of value in the following way: "In order to investigate the principles which regulate the exchangeable value of commodities, I shall
endeavour to shew, First, what is the real measure of this exchangeable value; or, wherein consists the real price of all commodities"
(p. 28).[6] Taking him at his word, chapter v on "Real and Nominal
Price" is part of the treatment of exchange value. There is, then,
justification for those who have been misled. But a study of this
chapter along with the parts of chapter xi in which the concepts are
put to use seems to make it clear that the system is concerned with
quite other things. Amidst great confusion there seems to be a clear
purpose: (1) to get below the veil of money to the real process, men
working and commanding the work of others; (2) to find a measure
of the ease or difficulty of producing goods, a measure of changes in
productive efficiency, a measure of changes in "real costs". The
study by G. T. Jones on *Increasing Return*[7] is a modern example
of this line of investigation; comparison of that study with the *Wealth
of Nations* should conduce to a better understanding of Adam Smith.

In the "Introduction and Plan of the Work" the part of labour
in production is stressed. "The annual labour of every nation is the
fund which originally supplies it with all the necessaries and conveniencies of life" (p. lvii). Again, in the beginning of chapter v,
Adam Smith says: "Labour was the first price, the original purchase
money that was paid for all things" (p. 30). When considering the
aggregate income of any society this view of labour cost is generally
satisfactory. Thus Professor Knight says:

To the question what anything costs we may give many kinds of answer. In
the field of economics proper two propositions may be put forward as true and
important in untangling truth and error in the theory of price. The first is
that the cost in general, to an individual or society, of securing an income in
the sense of his (or its) total aggregate of satisfactions does consist of the
"pain" (or sacrifice of "pleasure", if there is any difference, or both) involved
in production in an exhaustive sense. . . . The other principle is that with
reference to a money income or economic income as a part of the total flow

---

[6]Numbers in brackets after a quotation refer to pages in the Modern
Library edition of the *Wealth of Nations* ed. by Edwin Cannan (New York,
1937).

[7]Cambridge, 1933.

of satisfactions, if the aggregate of this part is a fixed magnitude and the actual range of choice under consideration involves only its detailed composition, then the "real cost" of any particular small increment of the money income is the sacrifice of the competing increment which was actually given up in order to get the one in question.[8]

The correctness of this second principle must also be recognized; but it may be pointed out that in this case "cost" is used in the sense relevant to the problem of economical choice. It may be argued that it would be of interest to know something about changes in the "labour cost" of particular commodities at different times as the technique of production improved; and one may note that such changes in "labour cost" will affect the "cost" in Professor Knight's sense, since an improvement in the technique of production (or a lowering of the "labour cost") of one commodity will mean that that commodity can be produced with the displacement of fewer alternative products.

Most of the misunderstanding of the theory of value in Adam Smith results from a failure to understand his use of the phrase "real price". Most modern economists assume that he must have been intending to explain market price, and that he gave two inconsistent explanations, one in his chapter on "real and nominal price", the other in his chapter on "natural and market price". This is definitely stated by Professors Gide and Rist: "Hitherto the 'real' price has signified the price that is based upon labour. Now the 'natural' price is defined as the price of goods valued at their cost of production. The change of name is not of any great significance. What Smith was in search of on both occasions was that true value which always kept in hiding behind the fluctuations of market prices. It is the same problem, but with a new solution."[9] It cannot be too strongly stated that it was not the *same* problem. When Adam Smith

---

[8]F. H. Knight, "Professor Fisher's Interest Theory: A Case in Point" (*Journal of Political Economy*, vol. XXXIX, April, 1931, p. 185). *Cf.* H. J. Davenport, *Value and Distribution* (Chicago, 1908), p. 9: "And so, while, socially speaking, the labor-fund-purchase idea is a cost doctrine of the labor sort, it is such by the very fact that it is social in character and treats the whole product as a unit purchased by the whole of the labor applied."

[9]C. Gide and C. Rist, *A History of Economic Doctrines* (trans. into English by R. Richards, New York), p. 78. See also p. 76: "two different but equally erroneous solutions [of the problem of value] have been successively adopted by him, but he has never actually decided between them."

says, "at all times and places that is dear which is difficult to come at, or which costs much labour to acquire; and that cheap which is to be had easily, or with very little labour" (p. 33), he is not explaining why things are dear or cheap, he is defining what dear and cheap mean. "The real price of everything . . . is the toil and trouble of acquiring it" (p. 30); again this is definition not explanation. Only if "real price" is so defined do his comparisons of the real price of particular commodities at different times make sense. If he had been using price as a synonym for value in the strict sense in which it has come to be used by economists, Adam Smith would be liable to all the strictures of Samuel Bailey.[10] "It is essential to value, that there should be two objects brought into comparison. It cannot be predicated of one thing considered alone, and without reference to another thing. . . . Value denotes consequently nothing positive or intrinsic, but merely the relation in which two objects stand to each other as exchangeable commodities." You cannot compare the value of wheat in 1700 with its value in 1800; you can only compare its value in 1700 with the value of other commodities in 1700, and its value in 1800 with the value of other commodities in 1800. But Adam Smith was discussing "real price" not "value"; he was concerned with the historical question: are things in general, and particular things, easier "to come at"?

It became necessary for Adam Smith, in this inquiry into real price, to defend duration of labour as a test of ease or difficulty of acquiring a good, so he says: "Equal quantities of labour, at all times and places, may be said to be of equal value to the labourer. In his ordinary state of health, strength and spirits; in the ordinary degree of his skill and dexterity, he must always lay down the same portion of his ease, his liberty, and his happiness. The price which he pays must always be the same, whatever may be the quantity of goods which he receives in return for it. Of these, indeed, it may sometimes purchase a greater and sometimes a smaller quantity; but it is their value which varies, not that of the labour which purchases them" (p. 33). In this quotation the word value is again used in an extremely loose way; but the meaning is reasonably clear—"it is their

[10]*A Critical Dissertation on the Nature, Measures and Causes of Value* (London, 1825; no. 7 in the series of reprints of scarce tracts in economics and political science published by the London School of Economics, 1931), p. 4. See above, n. 3.

value [*i.e.*, real price] which varies, not that [*i.e.*, the disutility] of
the labour". Only by assuming that he must have used the word
value "correctly" is it possible to justify the criticism of Samuel
Bailey on Malthus and, indirectly, on Adam Smith: "He [Malthus]
maintains, after Adam Smith, that labour is always of the same
value; that is, according to his own definition, always retains the
same power of commanding other objects in exchange; and yet, in
the same treatise, he speaks of the labourer earning a greater or
smaller quantity of money or necessaries, and insists that it is not
the value of the labour which varies, but the value of the money or
the necessaries. As if produce or money could change in value
relatively to labour, without labour changing in value relatively to
produce or money."[11] It would be legitimate to criticize the loose
use of the word value; it does not seem legitimate, or useful, to make
nonsense of an author's work by assuming that he has used a word
in one sense only, when he has quite clearly used it in three or four
different ones.

From the point of view of society as a whole, or of any isolated,
self-sufficient peasant, the concept of the "real price" of anything as
"the toil and trouble of acquiring it" is a simple and reasonable one.
There is, however, difficulty in applying it to individuals in a society
where the division of labour has gone far, and where most production
is for sale and not for use. Of the majority of us it is not unreason-
able to say that "what is bought with money . . . is purchased by
labour, as much as what we acquire by the toil of our own body" (p.
30). But this ignores property incomes; and also it means that the
quantity of goods that we can purchase with our labour depends on
how much labour we can command as well as on how efficient that
labour is. So Adam Smith turned his attention to "labour command".[12] "Every man is rich or poor according to the degree in
which he can afford to enjoy the necessaries, conveniencies, and

[11]*Ibid.*, p. 25. *Cf.* Cannan, *A Review of Economic Theory*, p. 166.

[12]Professor Paul Douglas sees here one more "theory of value". "There
are . . . the outlines of two very different theories . . . namely, the labor-
jelly or labor-cost theory, and the labor-command theory. . . . The labor-jelly
theory declares that the value of an object is determined by the quantity of
labor units required to produce it, while the labor-command theory declares that
the value of an object is determined by the amount of labor which can be
purchased with it" (*Adam Smith, 1776-1926*, Chicago, 1928, p. 88).

amusements of human life. But after the division of labour has once
thoroughly taken place, it is but a very small part of these with which
a man's own labour can supply him. The far greater part he must
derive from the labour of other people, and he must be rich or poor
according to the quantity of that labour which he can command. . . .
The value of any commodity, therefore, . . . is equal to the quantity
of labour which it enables him to purchase or command" (p. 30).
The usual connection between the "real price" of an object and its
"labour command" is not examined with any care, but Adam Smith's
view can be deduced from a sentence about the effect of the discovery
of the abundant silver mines of America. "As it cost less labour to
bring those metals from the mine to the market, so when they were
brought thither they could purchase or command less labour" (p. 32).
At first sight this suggests that Adam Smith accepted the labour
theory of value as applicable not only to "a nation of hunters" but
also to "the advanced state of society" in which he lived. That he
did not accept this theory of value is clear from his statement to the
contrary: "Neither is the quantity of labour commonly employed in
acquiring or producing any commodity, the only circumstance which
can regulate the quantity which it ought commonly to purchase,
command, or exchange for" (p. 49). It should also be clear from
the fact that he expounds an expenses of production theory in chapter vii. But he did assume that *changes* in the "real price" of commodities would produce *changes* in the "labour command" in the
same direction and of roughly the same magnitude. He assumed
that an improvement in efficiency in producing any one commodity
would cheapen that commodity not only to those who purchased it
directly by the toil of their own bodies but also to those who bought
it with money.[13] It also seems clear that he understood the mechanism

[13]*Cf.* John M. Cassels, "A Re-interpretation of Ricardo on Value" (*Quarterly Journal of Economics,* vol. XLIX, May, 1935) : "The difficulties which
have been encountered all along in finding a satisfactory interpretation of
Ricardo's Principles have been due not only to the intricacy of his reasoning
and the obscurity of his writing but also to the preconceived ideas with which
his readers have invariably approached his work. We have naturally expected
to find in the chapter on value in a book entitled The Principles of Political
Economy an explanation of *how* values are determined. . . . This, however,
was certainly not what Ricardo meant to give us. . . . When Ricardo wrote his
chapter on value he was concerned not with the ratios of exchange which might
exist at any one time but with the changes in those ratios which might take

by which this result would be achieved: things which are easier "to come at" will become more plentiful and, unless the demand is increasing equally rapidly, the price will fall. Certainly he did not ignore demand: "If by the general progress of improvement the demand [for silver] . . . should increase, while at the same time the supply did not increase in the same proportion, the value of silver would gradually rise" (p. 176).

"Who has sixpence is sovereign (to the length of sixpence) over all men; commands cooks to feed him, philosophers to teach him, kings to mount guard over him—to the length of sixpence" (Thomas Carlyle). This view of the real economic process as one of men working and commanding the work of others was of great importance in the development of classical, and later of socialist, theory but, curiously enough, though used in the discussion of value, it was not applied very clearly in the *Wealth of Nations* to the problem of distribution. It is implied in chapter vi: "in this state of things the whole produce of labour does not always belong to the labourer" (p. 49). But in "An Early Draft of the Wealth of Nations" recently discovered by Professor W. R. Scott, and published in his *Adam Smith, as Student and Professor,*[14] there is an admirably clear exposition of this view. He is trying to explain the "causes of public opulence":

It cannot be very difficult to explain how it comes about that the rich and the powerful should, in a Civilized society, be better provided with the conveniencies and necessaries of life than it is possible for any person to provide himself in a savage and solitary state. It is very easy to conceive that the person who can at all times direct the labours of thousands to his own purposes, should be better provided with whatever he has occasion for, than he who depends upon his own industry only. But how it comes about that the labourer and the peasant should likewise be better provided, is not, perhaps, so easily understood. In a Civilized Society the poor provide both for themselves and for the enormous luxury of their Superiors. The rent, which goes to support the vanity of the slothful Landlord, is all earned by the industry of the peasant. The monied man indulges himself in every sort of ignoble and sordid sensuality,

place between two periods of time. . . . So engrossing, indeed, was his interest in this question of the *'variations in relative value'* that those very words or their equivalents occur no less than 200 times in this one short chapter, an average of 7 times on every page."

[14]Glasgow, 1937. See pp. 325-8. *Cf.* review by C. R. Fay of Professor Scott's book in *Canadian Journal of Economics and Political Science,* vol. IV, Feb., 1938.

at the expence of the merchant and the Tradesman, to whom he lends out his
stock at interest. All the indolent and frivolous retainers upon a Court, are,
in the same manner, fed cloathed and lodged by the labour of those who pay
the taxes which support them. . . .

In a Society of an hundred thousand families, there will perhaps be one
hundred who don't labour at all, and who yet, either by violence, or by the
more orderly oppression of law, employ a greater part of the labour of the
society than any other ten thousand in it. The division of what remains too,
after this enormous defalcation, is by no means made in proportion to the
labour of each individual. On the contrary those who labour most get least.
The opulent merchant, who spends a great part of his time in luxury and
entertainments, enjoys a much greater proportion of the profits of his traffic,
than all the Clerks and Accountants who do the business. These last, again,
enjoying a great deal of leisure, and suffering scarce any other hardship
besides the confinement of attendance, enjoy a much greater share of the
produce, than three times an equal number of artizans, who, under their
direction, labour much more severely and assiduously. The artizan again,
tho' he works generally under cover, protected from the injuries of the weather,
at his ease and assisted by the convenience of innumerable machines, enjoys a
much greater share than the poor labourer who has the soil and the seasons
to struggle with, and, who while he affords the materials for supplying the
luxury of all the other members of the common wealth, and bears, as it were,
upon his shoulders the whole fabric of human society, seems himself to be
pressed down below ground by the weight, and to be buried out of sight in
the lowest foundations of the building. In the midst of so much oppressive
inequality in what manner shall we account for the superior affluence and
abundance commonly possessed even by this lowest and most despised member
of Civilized society, compared with what the most respected and active 'savage
can attain to.

The division of labour, by which each individual confines himself to a
particular branch of business, can alone account for that superior opulence which
takes place in civilized societies, and which, notwithstanding the inequality
of property, extends itself to the lowest member of the community.

It is not a very far cry from this to the description of exploitation
in volume I of Karl Marx's *Capital*, where the process is viewed as
one in which the working class has to give up part of its product to
the owners of property, or has to work part of the day for itself and
part of the day for the propertied class.[15]

[15]The continuity of exploitation, as the command by the few of part of
the labour of the many, through changing social forms is emphasized by Karl
Marx: "Wherever a part of society possesses the monopoly of the means of
production, the labourer free or not free, must add to the working time necessary for his own maintenance an extra working time in order to produce the
means of subsistence for the owners of the means of production, whether this
proprietor be the Athenian καλος καμαθος, Etruscan theocrat, civis Romanus,

It is one thing to insist that Adam Smith in his discussion of "real price" was concerned with variations in "real cost" over long periods of time, it is quite another thing to approve of his measurement of such changes, or even to agree that measurement is possible. Faced with the difficulty of measuring directly the amount of "toil and trouble" involved in producing any commodity, Adam Smith looked for some commodity which either had had a constant "real price", or had commanded a constant amount of labour, or both, over long periods of time. Silver was dismissed—"as it cost less labour . . . so . . . they could purchase or command less labour". Corn was selected as such a commodity, first on empirical grounds: "the rents which have been reserved in corn have preserved their value much better than those which have been reserved in money" (p. 34).[16] Theoretical support for choosing corn was found along two lines. First, he maintained that he who possesses corn, "the subsistence of the labourer", commands labour. "Equal quantities of corn, therefore, will, at distant times, be more nearly of the same value, or enable the possessor to purchase or command more nearly the same quantity of the labour of other people. They will do this, I say, more nearly than equal quantities of almost any other commodity; for even equal quantities of corn will not do it exactly. The subsistence of the labourer . . . is very different upon different occasions" (p. 35). Second, he later maintained that the "real price" of corn had been stable over long periods in spite of the agricultural revolution of the eighteenth century. "In every different stage of improvement, besides, the raising of equal quantities of corn in the same soil and climate, will, at an average, require nearly equal quantities of labour . . . the continual increase of the productive

Norman baron, American slave owner, Wallachian Boyard, modern landlord or capitalist" (*Capital*, Chicago, 1926, pp. 259-60).

[16]See Davenport, *Value and Distribution*, cap. xiii; *cf. Official Papers by Alfred Marshall*, ed. by J. M. Keynes (London, 1926), pp. 32-3: "I have found myself often unable to follow what was said because I could not make out how the word was used, when an appreciation of gold was contrasted with a fall of general (gold) prices. Therefore in order to make my position clear, I would like to say that when it is so contrasted, and used as denoting a rise in the real value of gold, I then regard it as measured by the increase in the power which gold has of purchasing labour of all kinds." See also the works of C. M. Walsh, especially *The Fundamental Problem in Monetary Science* (London, 1903).

powers of labour in an improving state of cultivation being more or less counterbalanced by the continually increasing price of cattle, the principal instruments of agriculture. Upon all these accounts, therefore, we may rest assured, that equal quantities of corn will, in every state of society, in every stage of improvement, more nearly represent . . . equal quantities of labour, than equal quantities of any other part of the rude produce of land" (p. 187). One must admit that the theoretical support for his choice of corn as a measure of changing real price is very weak. Perhaps the real trouble is that there is no measure of real price; certainly it is hard to feel any confidence in the measurements made by Mr. G. T. Jones.[17]

In the "Digression concerning the Variations in the Value of Silver during the Course of the Four last Centuries", which forms a large part of chapter xi, the word value is used as the equivalent of "real price", and changes in the "corn" price of silver are taken as measuring changes in its "real price". It is easy for a modern reader to assume that Adam Smith was discussing changes in the value, in the modern sense of general purchasing power, of money, and that his problem was an index number problem. When he suggests (pp. 185-6) that the high value of silver in ancient times was exaggerated through paying too much attention to certain parts of the "rude produce of land", such as cattle, poultry, and game of all kinds, it is natural to jump to the conclusion that he is worried over a problem of "weighting": the same conclusion occurs to the modern reader when he suggests that the "suspicion that the value of silver still continues to decrease" (pp. 216-7) is the result of paying too much attention to these same goods. When he says, in the first case, "this cheapness was not the effect of the high value of silver, but of the low value of those commodities" (p. 186), one may rise in arms, with Samuel Bailey, and say this is meaningless. But it is really made quite clear that value is there used in the sense of "real price", for he continues: "It was not because silver would in such times purchase or represent a greater quantity of labour, but because such commodities would purchase or represent a much smaller quantity than in times of more opulence and improvement. . . . Labour, it must always be remembered, and not any particular commodity or

---

[17]*Op. cit. Cf.* A. C. Pigou, "The Laws of Increasing and Decreasing Cost" (*Economic Journal*, vol. XXXVII, June, 1927).

set of commodities, is the real measure of the value both of silver and of all other commodities" (p. 186). Similarly on the later period: "Though such commodities, therefore, come to exchange for a greater quantity of silver than before, it will not from thence follow that silver has become really cheaper, or will purchase less labour than before, but that such commodities have become dearer, or will purchase more labour than before. It is not their nominal price only, but their real price which rises" (p. 217).

But while Adam Smith was concerned with changes in real price (labour cost and/or labour command), differences in the changes in real price as between different commodities will produce changes in the position of those commodities in the hierarchy of exchange values. His discussion, therefore, of the real price of silver, or cattle, does constitute a study of changing values such as Edwin Cannan asked for: "History tells us how certain values have changed; let theory tell us why such changes took place."[18] Strangely enough, Cannan gave no credit for this sort of work to Adam Smith; attention, therefore, is here drawn to two examples, viz., silver and cattle. That the value (labour command) of silver had not fallen as far as those who paid attention only to the increasing supply would have expected, was explained by "the gradual increase of the demand for silver".[19] (1) "The increasing produce of the agriculture and manufactures of Europe must necessarily have required a gradual increase in the quantity of silver coin to circulate it:[20] and the increasing number of wealthy individuals must have required the like increase in the

---

[18]A Review of Economic Theory, pp. 214-7; see also pp. 170-2.

[19]It is worth noting that in the Wealth of Nations the discussion of money is introduced by an explanation of why money is held, thus facilitating the use of the concept "demand for money". "Every prudent man . . . must have endeavoured to manage his affairs in such a manner as to have at all times by him . . . a certain quantity of some one commodity or other, such as he imagined few people would be likely to refuse in exchange for the produce of their industry" (pp. 22-3). The "Cambridge" rather than the "Fisher" equation is foreshadowed.

[20]It is surely not overgenerous to say that "without a change in the value of silver" (i.e., without a change in its labour command and presumably in its purchasing power) is understood. Similar generosity would lead one to doubt Professor Angell's judgment that Adam Smith "conceives of the 'channel of circulation' as being confined within rigid price walls" (The Theory of International Prices, Harvard, 1926, p. 34). The customary element in prices was probably still very important in the eighteenth century.

quantity of their plate and other ornaments of silver" (p. 202). (2) "America is itself a new market for the produce of its own silver mines; and as its advances in agriculture, industry and population, are much more rapid than those of the most thriving countries in Europe, its demands must increase much more rapidly" (p. 202). (3) "The East Indies is another market for the produce of the silver mines of America. . . . Tea, for example, was a drug very little used in Europe before the middle of the last century. At present the value of the tea annually imported by the English East India Company, for the use of their own countrymen, amounts to more than a million and a half a year. . . . The consumption of the porcelain of China, of the spiceries of the Moluccas, of the piece goods of Bengal . . . has increased very nearly in like proportion . . . the precious metals are a commodity which it always has been, and still continues to be, extremely advantageous to carry from Europe to India. There is scarce any commodity which brings a better price there" (pp. 205-6).[21] (4) Finally Adam Smith discussed "wear and tear", loss in transportation, and: "In the greater part of the governments of Asia, besides, the almost universal custom of concealing treasures in the bowels of the earth, of which the knowledge frequently dies with the greater quantity" (p. 208).[22]

Turning next to cattle:

in uncultivated countries, nature produces [cattle] with such profuse abundance that they are of little or no value . . . as cultivation advances [they] are therefore forced to give place to some more profitable produce. During a long period in the progress of improvement, the quantity of these is con-

---

[21]Some light on the drain to the east is thrown by the "Mandate" of the Chinese emperor to George III on the occasion of the Macartney Mission, 1793: "Our dynasty's majestic virtue has penetrated into every country under Heaven, and Kings of all nations have offered their costly tribute by land and sea. As your Ambassador can see for himself, we possess all things. I set no value on objects strange and ingenious and have no use for your country's manufactures" (quoted in Sir Frederick White's *China and Foreign Powers*, London, 1927). The east may have no use for European manufactures, but it had an almost insatiable desire for silver.

[22]In the face of this discussion of the market for silver, which could be supplemented from other parts of the "Digression", it is surprising that J. W. Angell should dismiss Adam Smith's " 'dynamic' formulation of the quantity theory in which the element of growth was included" as "rather parenthetical" and "never incorporated into his general reasoning on monetary problems". See *The Theory of International Prices*, p. 35.

tinually diminishing, while at the same time the demand for them is continually increasing. Their real value, therefore, the real quantity of labour which they will purchase or command, gradually rises, till at last it gets so high as to render them as profitable to produce as anything else which human industry can raise upon the most fertile and best cultivated land. When it has got so high it cannot well go higher. If it did more land and more industry would be employed to increase their quantity. . . . It had not got to this height in part of Scotland before the Union. Had the Scotch cattle been always confined to the market of Scotland . . . it is scarce possible, perhaps, that their price could ever have risen so high as to render it profitable to cultivate land for the sake of feeding them [pp. 219-20].

There follows a most interesting discussion of the effect on agriculture generally of this rise in the price of cattle: "the quantity of well-cultivated land must be in proportion to the quantity of manure which the farm itself produces; and this again must be in proportion to the stock of cattle which are maintained upon it. . . . Of all the commercial advantages, however, which Scotland has derived from the union with England, this rise in the price of cattle is, perhaps, the greatest" (pp. 221-2). A similar story is told of poultry, hogs, milk, butter, and cheese (pp. 224-8).

In addition to the theory of "real price", outlined in chapter v and used in chapter xi, Adam Smith outlines a theory of "natural and market price" in chapter vii. This constitutes his "theory of value" in the modern sense, and it includes a theory of short run "market" price and long run, normal or "natural", price of a very modern character. It is true that he saw no way through the paradox of utility: "Nothing is more useful than water; but it will purchase scarce anything. . . . A diamond, on the contrary, has scarce any value in use; but a very great quantity of goods can frequently be had in exchange for it" (p. 28). But this did not affect his theory; for the part played by demand in the determination of price is correctly stated and the whole book may be looked on as a plea for "consumer's sovereignty".[23] The part played by demand is different in the short run and the long run; in the short run demand determines the market price, in the long run the price is determined by the cost of production and demand determines the quantity produced.

[23]A convenient phrase coined by Professor W. H. Hutt, *Economists and the Public* (London, 1936). But see M. Dobb, *Political Economy and Capitalism* (London, 1937), p. 180, for the element of "authoritarianism" in the "valuations of the market under capitalism".

Cost of production is construed in terms of alternative opportunity.
There is in every society, or neighbourhood, an ordinary or average rate both
of wages and profit. . . . There is likewise . . . an ordinary or average rate
of rent. . . . These ordinary or average rates may be called the natural
rates. . . . When the price of any commodity is neither more nor less than
what is sufficient to pay the rent of the land, the wages of the labour, and the
profits of the stock . . . according to their natural rates, the commodity is
then sold for what may be called its natural price. . . . When the quantity of
any commodity . . . falls short of the effectual [*i.e.*, the effective demand at
the natural price], all those who are willing to pay the whole value of the rent,
wages, and profit . . . cannot be supplied with the quantity which they want.
A competition will immediately begin among them, and the market price will
rise. . . . The quantity of every commodity brought to market naturally suits
itself to the effectual demand. . . . If at any time it exceeds the effectual
demand, some of the component parts of its price must be paid below their
natural rate. If it is rent, the interest of the landlords will immediately prompt
them to withdraw a part of the land; and if it is wages or profit, the interest
of the labourers in the one case, and of their employers in the other, will
prompt them to withdraw a part of their labour or stock from this employment [pp. 55-7].[24]

A cost of production theory of this sort is satisfactory as a statement
of "particular equilibrium" under conditions of competition as long
as one can assume that cost will be constant for any variation of supply. Mr. Sraffa[25] has pointed out that "constant cost" must be assumed, for "increasing cost" involves conditions which make particular equilibrium analysis inappropriate and "decreasing cost" is
inconsistent with competition. The theory also provides an introduction to "general equilibrium" by drawing attention to one
condition, *viz.*, equality of earnings of each factor in its various

[24]There seems to be nothing in Professor Cannan's discussion of the effect
of a disease among coal miners, which is intended as a criticism of Adam Smith,
that does not follow from Adam Smith's own theory: "The price of coal could
not rise an atom if the same quantity of coal continued to be put on the market."
But who would deny this, certainly not Adam Smith. "If the numbers of
miners were reduced to one half, the price of coal would rise just the same if
the miners still employed did not get a penny more than they did before."
True, but Adam Smith would then be looking for the factor which was paid
"above its natural rate", and would be speculating on whether the conditions
of its supply were such that it could continue to be paid above its natural rate
for a long time. A study of the case of the "public mourning" (p. 59) gives
justification for these assertions as to what Adam Smith would say. See
A Review of Economic Theory, p. 171.

[25]P. Sraffa, "Laws of Returns under Competitive Conditions" (*Economic
Journal*, vol. XXXVI, Dec., 1926).

alternative employments. The theory is defective in that it fails to see that the "natural rates" of wages, profit, and rent are themselves simultaneously determined in the same process; moreover, it ignores the possibility of varying the proportion of the "factors" used in the production of any one commodity, and consequently fails to state as a second condition of equilibrium that the prices of the factors of production must be such as to induce no "substitution". For these developments economics waited nearly a hundred years; they, rather than the solution of the paradox of utility, or any supposed new attention to demand, are the real contributions of the "utility" theorists.

"But though the market price of every particular commodity is in this manner continually gravitating . . . towards the natural price, yet sometimes particular accidents, sometimes natural causes, and sometimes particular regulations of police, may, in many commodities, keep up the market price, for a long time together, a good deal above the natural price" (p. 59).[26] In this paper reference will be made only to one of the "natural causes" instances, *viz.*, French vineyards. "Some natural productions require such a singularity of soil and situation that all the land in a great country, which is fit for producing them, may not be sufficient to supply the effectual demand. The whole quantity brought to market, therefore, may be disposed of to those who are willing to give more than what is sufficient to pay the rent of the land . . . together with the wages of the labour, and the profits of the stock . . . according to their natural rates [*i.e.*, at the rates payable in their alternative occupations]. Such commodities may continue for whole centuries together to be sold at this high price; and . . . the rent of land is in this case . . . generally paid above its natural rate" (p. 61). In chapter xi this doctrine is illustrated: "good common wine, such as can be raised almost anywhere . . . and which has nothing to recommend it but its strength and wholesomeness" (p. 155) cannot long sell at a price which is more remunerative to landlords, farmers, or workers than ordinary farm produce. But from certain soils wine "derives a flavour which no culture or management can equal, it is supposed,

[26]One can, of course, make merry at this use of the word "natural". It would be more reasonable to say that the "natural" price of such commodities was high. But if the terminology is strange, the meaning is clear and the analysis sound.

upon any other. This flavour, real or imaginary, is sometimes
peculiar to the produce of a few vineyards" (p. 155). Such wines
sell permanently at high prices; "the difference is greater or less,
according as the fashionableness or scarcity of the wine render the
competition of the buyers more or less eager. Whatever it be, the
greater part of it goes to the rent of the landlord." One can only
regret that this discussion of "specific" factors was confined to land.
That it was not extended to labour can be explained by his belief in
the essential similarity of all men: "The difference in natural talents
in different men is, in reality, much less than we are aware of. . . .
The difference between . . . a philosopher and a common street
porter, for example, seems to arise not so much from nature, as from
habit, custom and education."

STAPLE PRODUCTION AND
CANADA'S EXTERNAL RELATIONS

F. W. BURTON

E CONOMICS and politics are now inextricably mingled, and it is now no longer possible, as it was in the age of laissez-faire theory, for economists to maintain the integrity of their science by a staunch contempt for all existing political institutions. The decline among economists of respect for laissez-faire is due partly to development within economic theory regarding such problems as monopoly, money, unemployment, and public finance; partly to recognition of the inadequacy of abstract theory alone; and partly to underlying trends of public policy toward socialism and national autarchy, which may be good or bad, but which drastically change in any case the data with which economists must deal.

In the world of new theories and new policies, Canada is found to occupy a vulnerable position. An unusually high degree of economic dependence upon other nations, indicated by a high per capita value of external trade, places her peculiarly at the mercy of the policies of foreign governments. Every further retreat of laissez-faire will accentuate Canada's vulnerability. Thus external policy is closely entangled with internal policy and with the welfare of Canadian producers. Canada's economic dependence upon foreigners originates in geographic facts. The cost to Canada of economic self-sufficiency would, therefore, be impossibly high, and tariff protection would be an extremely expensive solution for her problem. The geographic factors which compel Canada to rely upon external trade are: (1) natural resources great in quantity but specialized in kind; (2) high transport costs, internal and external.

Canada's resources fit her for the production in great volume of a variety of foods, raw materials, and products manufactured from them; they are her export staples, which need not be mentioned in detail. But Canada is weak in resources which are the basis of diversified industry. Cheap labour, the least specialized resource of all, is lacking and is not to be desired. Iron ore, coal, and oil are lacking in the chief industrial area; but power is afforded to many industries by hydro-electric plants. In agriculture, climate seriously limits the variety of available products; Indian corn is important only in southern Ontario.

Transport costs are high internally and externally. Most of the productive areas are remote from the sea. The St. Lawrence River, an important eastward outlet, has many disadvantages: only southward are the routes short and open, and this increases dependence upon the United States. Internally, the effects of such barriers as the Rocky Mountains and the Precambrian shield are obvious. The effects of high transport costs are many. Internal barriers encourage trade by each region with the United States rather than with other provinces. The high overhead costs of east-west routes diminish the elasticity of the national economy and intensify problems of depression; and they stimulate nationalist policies, aiming at internal economic expansion and the diversion of trade from north-south to east-west routes.[1]   Finally, transport costs, by raising the expenses of production, limit Canada to industries in which she is particularly favoured by her resources: a diversified industrial agglomeration can arise only in an area having cheap transportation, water routes being especially important.[2]

Much of what has been said seems not to apply to southern Ontario or to the St. Lawrence valley. These regions enjoy many advantages as centres of diversified industry—cheap transport by rail and water, hydro-electric power, and abundant raw materials of several kinds. Nevertheless they do not provide an adequate basis for the economic self-sufficiency of Canada. Lack of coal and iron ore is not their most serious disadvantage. The value of an industrial area depends largely upon its access to markets; and southern Ontario and southern Quebec would be much more valuable centres of industry, given access to the United States market. Confined as they are to the Canadian market, they suffer two disabilities: (1) the smallness of the national market which seriously handicaps decreasing-cost industries; (2) the high internal costs of transport which hamper

[1]H. A. Innis, *Problems of Staple Production in Canada* (Toronto, 1933), ch. ii; also "Unused Capacity as a Factor in Canadian Economic History" (*Canadian Journal of Economics and Political Science*, vol. II, Feb., 1936).

[2]On the relation between transport costs and international trade, see B. Ohlin, *Interregional and International Trade* (Cambridge, 1935), part III.

production of goods in one part of Canada for consumption in another part of Canada, and which also subdivide the national market into still smaller regional markets. The result is that, while Ontario and Quebec could advantageously supply many manufactured commodities to the United States, other parts of Canada could most advantageously buy many manufactures from the United States; hence, in spite of the industrialization of Ontario and Quebec, the cost to Canada of economic self-sufficiency remains high.

Canada's geography burdens her with a complex of economic problems, not all of which have been adequately explored by economic science. Equilibrium economics in the past has assumed a type of economy (which was perhaps formerly approximated in parts of Europe) possessing the following characteristics: (a) diversified and relatively mobile factors of production; (b) low transport costs; (c) emphasis on trade and on secondary production rather than on extractive industries; (d) ease of adjustment to changing conditions, due to the numerous alternative opportunities of the factors of production, and to a relatively small element of overhead cost; (e) a relatively large domestic market, making external disturbances of secondary importance; (f) progress by infinitesimal degrees rather than in the discontinuous kangaroo fashion of new countries. The initiation of new stages of development could thus take place without government intervention.

It is hardly necessary to show in detail that the Canadian economy largely contradicts these assumptions;[3] or to show the economic instability and the large field for government intervention which result from this. The object of this paper is to discuss certain respects in which economic conditions in Canada are dominated by relations with other countries (especially the United States and Great Britain), and in which Canadian economic policies may come into conflict with policies elsewhere. The topics to be discussed are: Canada's access to external markets, transportation and tariff policy in Canada, and (briefly) monetary policy and monopoly.

[3]H. A. Innis, works cited; also *Fur Trade in Canada* (New Haven, 1930), ch. vi; "Significant Factors in Canadian Economic History" (*Canadian Historical Review*, vol. XVIII, Dec., 1937; *The Canadian Economy and Its Problems* ed. by H. A. Innis and A. F. W. Plumptre (Toronto, 1934); and A. F. W. Plumptre, "The Nature of Political and Economic Development in the British Dominions" (*Canadian Journal of Economics and Political Science*, vol. III, Nov., 1937).

The need of external markets still, as throughout history, dominates the Canadian economy. Instability in foreign markets, due partly to economic fluctuation and partly to changes of government policy, has been the principal cause of economic instability in Canada. And in a long-run view, the Canadian economy has been moulded and inhibited by the restrictive policies of other countries. The opening of an inland fur trade *via* the St. Lawrence River began an economic and political connection, which still persists, between Canada and Western Europe. Alliance with France and later with Britain, and separation from the United States, have been the chief external influences upon the Canadian economy.

Mercantilist policies dominated, or attempted to dominate, the course of Canada's external trade under the French and early British Empires. But the policy of imperial self-sufficiency was defeated in both régimes by lack of balance between the resources of the various colonies: Canada's inadequate wheat supply, for example, compelled the Nova Scotia fisheries and the sugar-plantations of the British West Indies to depend upon the United States for bread.[4] Mercantilism contributed to Canadian development in the period 1815-47 by the imperial preference granted to Canadian wheat and timber. Development so stimulated was, however, precarious and unstable. It was precarious because the advance of free trade sentiment in Great Britain made the withdrawal of the preference inevitable. It was unstable, first, because narrow markets inevitably accentuate the effects of local fluctuations (Canadian timber producers were thus harnessed to the jolting chariot of Great Britain's booms and crises); and, second, because the fluctuation of British harvests, combined with the sliding-scale duties of the Corn Laws plus the cost of overseas transport, at times excluded Canadian wheat almost entirely from Great Britain, which in years of high prices took the greater part of Canada's export surplus.[5] Since Canada's wheat

[4]H. A. Innis, "Cape Breton and the French Regime" (*Transactions of the Royal Society of Canada*, vol. XXIX, sect. 2, 1935); G. S. Graham, *British Policy and Canada, 1763-1791* (London, 1930); F. W. Burton, "The Wheat Supply of New France" (*Transactions of the Royal Society of Canada*, vol. XXX, sect. 2, 1936).

[5]F. W. Burton, "Wheat in Canadian History" (*Canadian Journal of Economics and Political Science*, vol. III, May, 1937).

surplus was small in comparison with Britain's total demand, Corn
Law policy was determined with little reference to the Canadian
situation, and colonial preference was merely the tail of the Corn
Law kite. Hence the apparent betrayal of Canadian interests in the
repeal of the Corn Laws, and hence the ensuing economic and political
crisis in Canada.[6]

Reciprocity with the United States became the chief object of
Canadian commercial policy after the collapse of mercantilism. The
American market for agricultural produce became particularly desirable in the middle of the nineteenth century, since population in the
eastern states had begun to press upon subsistence, and the western
surplus was still small.[7] In the 1830's, poor wheat harvests in the
eastern states brought high prices and eliminated for the year 1837
the usual export surplus of the United States. The protective American tariff recently imposed on wheat contributed greatly to agrarian
unrest in Upper Canada at this time, especially as Canadian wheat
was simultaneously excluded by low prices from the British market.[8]
The annexation and reciprocity demands of 1848 showed growing
appreciation in Canada of the desirability of the United States market
as a substitute for the British. The period of the Reciprocity Treaty
(and afterward until the drastic tariff-raising which began in 1890)
demonstrated the ability of Canada to supply the United States with
a wide variety of commodities. Among agricultural products, wheat
turned out to be less important as an export than had been anticipated.
The wheat surplus of the western states began to flood the markets
of both America and Europe; but Canada exported to the United
States such commodities as barley, meat, wool, and timber, and the
resulting diversification of her economy lessened the impact of poor
harvests and low price for wheat.[9]

[6]G. N. Tucker, *The Canadian Commercial Revolution, 1845-1851* (New
Haven, 1936).

[7]W. Trimble, "Historical Aspects of Surplus Food Production of the
U.S.A., 1862-1902" (*Annual Report of the American Historical Association*,
1918, p. 223).

[8]*Upper Canada Journal of Assembly*, 1835, appendix, vol. I, "Three Reports
from the Select Committee on Trade and Commerce"; D. G. Creighton, "The
Economic Background of the Rebellions of 1837" (*Canadian Journal of
Economics and Political Science*, vol. III, Aug., 1937).

[9]D. C. Masters, *Reciprocity Treaty of 1854* (London, 1937).

Protective tariffs revived throughout the world in the later nineteenth century, as a result of intenser international competition both in industry and in agriculture, which followed the spread outward from Great Britain of railway-building and new techniques. As the American market was closed, production of staples revived in Canada —first, of cheese[10] and later of prairie wheat—for export to Britain and Western Europe. This meant a narrower range of Canadian exports and a less elastic national economy. On its wheat basis, Canada flourished in the relatively prosperous period 1898-1929, but the inherent instability of specialized staple production has been revealed in the intense depression of the Prairie Provinces as a result of drought, low prices, and economic autarchy on the continent of Europe.

No simple solution is apparent for the problem of instability in external wheat markets. Access to the United States market free enough to solve the problem of Canadian agriculture, is most unlikely to be attained, in spite of the efforts of well-educated diplomats, without the drastic step of annexation. This was one of the principal arguments for annexation used by enlightened non-patriots in Canada in the post-Confederation period. Annexation to the United States would involve an institutional revolution in Canada, and is certainly not a practical political issue at present. It seems conceivable, however, that some future collapse in the old world markets for Canada's staple exports might force Canada to seek annexation, in order that diversified production for the American market might replace staple production for Europe and avert economic ruin and social chaos. This is a grim conception.

Imperial preferential tariffs, which have been much advocated and moderately achieved, can be praised only by the faintness of the damns. A prerequisite of the revival of colonial preference by Great Britain was the availability of adequate food supplies from the Dominions.[11] This was achieved in the twentieth century; but in the case of wheat at least, Empire production has so far outrun Empire consumption that an imperial protective tariff, in becoming

[10]H. A. Innis (ed.), *The Dairy Industry in Canada* (Toronto, 1937).
[11]Joseph Pope, *Correspondence of Sir J. A. Macdonald* (Toronto, 1921), pp. 448-9, Letter of Sir John A. Macdonald to James Edgecombe, July 4, 1889.

possible, has become ineffective. The maintenance of a wheat economy in Canada depends upon large sales to the continent of Europe. So far as imperial preferential tariffs are effective, they are, of course, subject to the recognized anti-tariff arguments. But, in fact, local economic nationalism within the Empire greatly diminishes their importance. The most injurious economic effects of the Ottawa Agreements of 1932 fell upon certain foreign countries.[12] But far worse than the economic are likely to be the psychological effects of an imperial protective system. Foreign distrust of the British Empire, usually perceptible, is gravely increased; and colour has been added to the colonial demands of Central European powers. And in the British character, an exclusive tariff policy intensifies two ugly features, from which it also largely springs: (1) the short-sighted avaricious provincialism of the Dominions; (2) the satanic vainglory of successful imperialism. The greatest argument against imperial preference is thus a moral one.

Protective tariffs have been advocated in recent years as a device for rectifying an unfavourable balance of trade, or for increasing national self-sufficiency in order to facilitate the management of money. Whatever advantages such policies may have, they could more suitably be applied by individual British countries than by the Empire as a whole; and in view of the high cost of self-sufficiency to Canada, it would seem inadvisable in her case to carry these policies very far.

High transport costs (to change the subject) being an important feature of the Canadian economy, the development of inland routes and the fixing of charges have at all periods been fundamental influences upon Canada's welfare and progress. The problem is also interwoven with those of Canada's external relations, economic and political, with Great Britain and with the United States. The role played by the St. Lawrence River in Canada's national development is familiar. The influence of the St. Lawrence began with the fur trade, and was maintained chiefly by the pressure of overhead costs upon both public and private interests, until the present consummation of an overbuilt transcontinental railway system, intended to support a heavy east-west trade centring in the St. Lawrence route. From

[12]C. R. Fay, *Imperial Economy* (Oxford, 1934), ch. vi.

the economic point of view, this is perhaps the dominant theme of Canadian history.[13]

The period 1815-50 was perhaps of particular importance in Canadian history, as determining future development in many fundamental ways. The struggle for improvement of the St. Lawrence route went, at this period, hand in hand with the struggle for external markets, for immigrants, and for self-government.[14] Development of the St. Lawrence was demanded both by the commercial class of Canada and by the more enlightened of the Upper Canada wheat producers, but for different reasons, the merchants seeking a larger volume of trade for the St. Lawrence, the wheat producers seeking cheap transportation for their export surplus. These two motives sometimes clashed.

The burden of transport costs upon the Upper Canada wheat producer is suggested by a reasonable estimate in 1842 of 26s. 2d. per quarter (sterling) as the cost of transport of wheat from Hamilton, Upper Canada, to London.[15] This figure suggests that transport costs were at least as important as the sliding-scale duties of the Corn Laws (with colonial preference) in intensifying the effect on the Upper Canada producer of a fall in wheat prices in Great Britain.

Upper Canada farmers demanded only cheap transport and a fair farm price for wheat, and were quite prepared to sell to the United States or to use United States routes, if their objects could thus be attained. The influence of the Lower Canada merchants and of the

[13]H. A. Innis, works cited; Tucker, *The Canadian Commercial Revolution*; H. A. Innis and A. R. M. Lower, *Select Documents in Canadian Economic History, 1783-1885* (Toronto, 1933); R. G. Trotter, *Canadian Federation* (Toronto, 1934); W. T. Jackman, *Economic Principles of Transportation* (Toronto, 1935); D. A. MacGibbon, "Economic Aspects of Proposed St. Lawrence Shipway" (*Queen's University Bulletin of Departments of History and Economics,* no. 58, 1929), and *Canadian Grain Trade* (Toronto, 1932), chs. ix, x, and appendix.

[14]*Upper Canada Journals of Assembly,* 1821, Report of Select Committee on Internal Resources (in *Ontario Archives Report,* 1913, pp. 428-35, 472, 499); Innis and Lower, *Select Documents in Canadian Economic History, 1783-1885,* part I; *Upper Canada Journals of Assembly,* 1835, appendix, vol. I, First Report (of three) of Committee on Trade and Commerce; *ibid.,* 1836, pp. 167-72, Resolutions of Upper Canada Assembly on Trade and Commerce.

[15]*Canada Journals of Assembly,* 1842, appendix W, Memorial of Mount Cashell and petitioners.

provincial and imperial governments brought the decision that Canada should improve its own St. Lawrence route. In spite of the sums of money spent to this end, the more rapid improvement of the United States routes, combined with the superiority of New York over Montreal as a terminus for ocean routes, caused the diversion to American routes of the bulk of Canada's export trade by 1850. However, a large absolute increase in Montreal's trade began late in the nineteenth century, as a result of several factors: the development of the ocean steamship made river ports more acceptable; and the channel of the St. Lawrence was improved for their accommodation; but most important was the settling of the Canadian prairies, and the linking of them with Montreal by transcontinental railways; the industrialization of Ontario and Quebec, and the mining and forest industries, were also factors.

While the port of Montreal has thus become one of the principal ports of the continent, one may question whether the St. Lawrence route, viewed geographically and technically, is of sufficient value to justify the important role which it has played in Canadian economic and political history. In comparison with New York, Montreal has both advantages and disadvantages: it is more readily accessible from the interior of the continent, but its position in relation to the Atlantic Ocean is much inferior. These geographic facts are reflected in the structure of inland and ocean freight rates, the former favouring Montreal, the latter New York.[16] Handicaps tending to raise ocean rates at Montreal are high insurance rates and the raising of overhead costs by the winter closing of the river. New York has more varied liner connections and a more elastic supply of tramp steamers. Montreal's destiny, then, is to serve as the principal outlet to Europe of the wheat of the eastern Prairie Provinces; and as the regional port of Ontario and Quebec, which involves a heavy import trade in such bulk commodities as coal and oil, to supply the industrial region

[16]*Proceedings of Committee of Canadian Parliament on Ocean Rates, 1925,* pp. 348-9. To show the persistence of geographic influences through history, see Isaac Weld, *Travels through the States of North America and the Provinces of Upper and Lower Canada* (London, 1797), vol. II, p. 62; *Imperial Blue Books,* 1848, no. 405, Memorandum of Canadian Executive Council on Effect of Navigation Laws on Trade of St. Lawrence, Inland Rates, Montreal; *Canada Journals of Assembly,* appendix no. 2, 1858, Report of Select Committee on Great Lakes Trade, Treaties, Tariffs, *etc.* (Merritt).

of Eastern Canada. Montreal was not naturally fitted to become, as it hoped, the great *entrepôt* for the interior of North America; this position fell inevitably to New York, through its overwhelming advantages as a port.

What, then, is one to think of the historic trend of Canadian policy, which has emphasized east-west traffic centring on the St. Lawrence? This trend has been stimulated in several respects by Canada's external relations: (1) tariff barriers between Canada and the United States have strangled the easy north-south routes; (2) trade directed toward the British market by early mercantilist and later protective policies has provided a basis for the improvement of east-west routes; (3) construction of east-west routes has been aided financially by the British government in the canal age, and by the Canadian government in the railway age; (4) defence was a motive in the development of Canadian routes, at least in the case of the Intercolonial Railway.

Private interest combined with naïve patriotism has been the driving force in Canadian transport development. The mixture of nationalism with boom-psychology was a world-wide phenomenon in the later railway age. Nation-building and empire-building, in the old world as in the new, proceeded in step with railway building, industrialization, and the advance of economic frontiers.[17] Optimistic nationalism, increasingly triumphant in Canada from Confederation until the Great War, gave Canada her overdeveloped railway system, with its accumulating debt.

The Canadian tariff is related closely to the problem of transportation. This was pointed out in 1859 by A. T. Galt, who justified recent increases in Canadian tariff rates, as a method of paying for the new transportation facilities which lowered the cost of trade between Canada and Great Britain.[18] This argument is weakened to some extent by the fact that canal and railway construction in the United States, preceding similar construction in Canada, had provided outlets for the produce of Upper Canada, with which the St.

[17]The attractive naïveté of the period is well exemplified in G. M. Grant, *Ocean to Ocean* (Toronto, 1877).

[18]*Canada Sessional Papers*, 1860, no. 38, Report of A. T. Galt in reply to Sheffield Chamber of Commerce; also Innis, *Problems of Staple Production in Canada*, ch. ii.

Lawrence route was unable for many years to compete, even after being improved.

Does the tariff at present aid the Canadian railways? One could answer this question only by estimating the effect of the tariff upon the volume and direction of Canadian trade. Probably this effect, for good or evil, is less than many people believe, the course of trade being determined chiefly by such factors as the distribution of natural resources, the volume of exports, the location of external markets, and the overhead costs of railroad transport. No doubt the tariff results in a considerable decrease in imports from the United States, a less drastic decrease in imports from Great Britain, and some increase in purchases of manufactures from Ontario and Quebec by inhabitants of other provinces. The probable effect on the traffic seems to be a small increase in east-west traffic, a great decrease in north-south traffic, and (due to the general burden of restriction of trade) some decrease in local traffic. It seems unlikely that the tariff benefits the railways much. The suggestion that the tariff may benefit the western farmer by increasing railway traffic and making possible a lowering of freight rates for agricultural products, is a complex case of the heresy that tariff protection granted to a decreasing-cost industry may make possible a lower price for its product than under free trade, a result which would appear only under very unusual conditions.[19]

The fact remains that Canadian development depended upon the provision of canals and railways; and that these have been provided through the support of government revenues raised through the tariff. One can only comment that a tariff is a crude and pernicious way of raising revenue; and that it is unfortunate that Canada's policies of tariff protection and railway building were carried so far during the era of optimistic nationalism.

Monetary policy has become a burning issue not once or twice in the history of North America. Usually the issue has been raised by the farmers of the western frontier, as a result of depressed prices. This was so in the time of Andrew Jackson and William Lyon Mackenzie, and in the time of William Jennings Bryan, and is so again in the time of Roosevelt and Aberhart. Academic opinion, which

[19]Beveridge *et al.*, *Tariffs, the Case Examined* (London, 1932).

was against the farmers in the nineteenth century, is now on the whole in sympathy with them.

Since it is the prices of raw materials which fall farthest during depression, countries specializing in extractive industry face the dismal alternative at such times of deflation or depreciation; and monetary policy becomes essentially a compromise between these possibilities. For Canada more than for most countries, the objective of monetary policy which is usually emphasized—the stabilization of the general price-level—is a meaningless abstraction. What concerns Canada is the maintenance, at simultaneous optimum points, of two different ratios: (1) the foreign exchange rate of the Canadian dollar, and (2) the ratio between the prices of export staples and of goods manufactured for domestic consumption. No simple principle can be laid down, such as the maintenance of the gold standard or of a sterling standard. Justice to staple producers appears to demand some degree of depreciation during depression; and the criterion must be the greatest good to the greatest number of economic interests.[20] Problems of monetary policy resulting from the recent depression led to the formation of a Canadian central bank, an institution thought unnecessary in the era of a "natural" gold standard. Co-operation with the central banks of Great Britain and the United States will be necessary in the stabilization of exchange rates, and perhaps ultimately in international price stabilization policies.

Monopoly and imperfect competition are now recognized to have opened an immense new field for government regulatory policies.[21] This is, moreover, a problem of uncertain limits, expanding readily into the inclusive question of the structure of society, and the potentialities of Socialism or Fascism. Government efforts to check monopolistic tendencies have accomplished little up to the present, while some forms of government regulation have actually encouraged these tendencies. What interests us here is the international repercussions of monopoly, and the exposed position of Canada in this respect.

Those who suffer by the growth of monopoly fall into two groups: (1) producers in industries in which competition is still relatively

[20]A. F. W. Plumptre, "Canadian Monetary Policy" (*The Canadian Economy and Its Problems*, p. 159).

[21]J. M. Cassels, "Monopolistic Competition and Economic Realism" (*Canadian Journal of Economics and Political Science*, vol. III, Aug., 1937).

atomistic; agriculture on the whole falls into this class, as international competition prevents the influencing of prices even by large
co-operative organizations; (2) producers in extractive industries;
although competition is frequently imperfect (*e.g.*, in mining or
newsprint) heavy overhead costs make restriction of output and
stabilization of prices more difficult than in secondary industry.

It is evident that Canada, which specializes in agriculture and
extractive industry, is as usual in a vulnerable position. While
Canadian producers for export are likely to find difficulty in restricting output to maintain prices, the foreign producers of Canadian
imports (at least of those imports which come chiefly from a single
country) may find the process of restriction easier. This is precisely
the reverse of the "dumping" problem. We may repeat that every
encroachment upon laissez-faire, whether by government or by private
monopoly, increases Canada's vulnerability. What is likely to be
Canada's fate in some future world of planned economies?

In conclusion, we see the Canadian economy entangled in problems which cannot be solved by Canada's unaided efforts. Canada
occupies an exposed position because of her dependence upon foreigners and the tendency of larger and more self-sufficient countries to
solve their own problems at her expense. From what external
sources may Canada hope for co-operation?

The British Empire, a system of effectively co-operating governments, is perhaps the most favourable factor in the situation. But
too much must not be expected of it. The imperial connection has
to some extent distorted Canada's economy by emphasizing staple
production and east-west trade. Moreover, the present British
Empire, with its mental diversity and its multitudinous external relations, is adapted neither to self-sufficiency nor to centralized economic
planning.

The United States, with its isolationist tradition, has not usually
been found a co-operative nation, and change in this respect is likely
to be slow. The huge change of annexation, however, is at least of
theoretical interest. Annexation is Canada's principal taboo; it is
never mentioned in public, as tigers are never mentioned in countries
in which most of the people are ultimately eaten by tigers. But there
are two important arguments for annexation: (1) the desirability
of the United States market; and (2) the weakness of Canada as

a unit for economic regulation and planning, if planning is to be her fate. Annexation may then be a suitable long-run objective, at least for the English-speaking provinces of Canada; but within the measurable future the question will not become practical, except in circumstances too dire to be considered.

Since no drastic change in her external relations seems likely to prove productive, the best policy for Canada is eclecticism, liberalism, and moderation, observing whatever truth remains in laissez-faire economics, and approaching the problems of government intervention with the utmost co-operation obtainable from foreign countries.

THE TARIFF AND CANADIAN BUTTER

AGATHA CHAPMAN

CANADA has imposed a duty on butter ever since before Confederation. At the time of Confederation the duty was 4 cents per pound, and under the General Tariff it remained at that figure until 1930. In 1897 the British Preferential Tariff was created, allowing duties ⅛ lower, and from 1898 on ¼ lower, than under the General Tariff. Thus butter could be imported under the Preferential Tariff, which applied to Great Britain and to any British country giving Canada similar treatment, by paying duty at the rate of 3 cents per pound. New Zealand was included in this schedule in 1904. In 1907 an additional schedule was created, the Intermediate Tariff, applicable to any foreign country which had been on the General Tariff and which had given Canada certain benefits. However, the rate on butter remained under this schedule the same as that under the General Tariff, 4 cents per pound.

In 1925 the Australian Treaty was signed, giving mutual concessions in regard to tariffs. Among the privileges accorded by Canada was the reduction of the duty on butter to 1 cent per pound. However, any possible effect of this change in rate was nullified by the Patterson scheme which came into operation in Australia a few months after the signing of the treaty, and gave an export bounty on butter. The Canadian anti-dumping clause[1] came into operation against Australian butter, imposing an extra duty equal to the difference between the export price and the price in Australia, provided that the duty did not exceed 15 per cent ad valorem. This did not apply to butter shipped on consignment, but apparently the Australian exporters did not take much advantage of that fact.

The treaty was more influential in its effect upon the butter trade with New Zealand. From October 1, 1925, its privileges were extended to New Zealand by order-in-council and, since there was no equivalent of the Patterson scheme in operation in New Zealand, the dumping duty could not be brought into effect.

[1]See J. Viner, *Dumping, a Problem in International Trade* (Chicago, 1923).

At first opposition to this arrangement was slight but, as imports of butter from New Zealand increased, hostility was fanned by propaganda against the treaty, and was intensified by the general depression, beginning in the fall of 1929. On April 12, 1930, New Zealand was given the required six months' notice of termination of the agreement, and it came to an end on October 12, 1930. Tariff protection generally was increased as a result of the depression: on May 30, 1930, the Liberal government raised the rates on butter to 4 cents per pound under the British Preferential Tariff, 6 cents per pound under the Intermediate Tariff, and 7 cents per pound under the General Tariff. During the election of 1930 the Conservatives made considerable political use of the point that harm had been done to Canadian farmers through the terms of the Australian Treaty. Even the raising of the duty rates in May, 1930, and the rescinding of the agreement with New Zealand were regarded as inadequate by the Conservatives, and on September 16, 1930, it was announced that the rates had been raised to 8 cents per pound under the British Preferential Tariff, 12 cents per pound under the Intermediate Tariff, and 14 cents per pound under the General Tariff.

Canadian butter producers began to fear that shipments on consignment from Australia would increase as they could still enter Canada at a duty of 1 cent per pound. Alarm on this account was removed by an agreement in December, 1930, whereby Australian butter was not to be released to the trade in Canada at a price under 32 cents per pound. This agreement held until the revision of the Australian Treaty on August 3, 1931, when the rate on Australian butter was increased to 5 cents per pound; this rate was extended to New Zealand on May 24, 1932.

While this has been the history of the tariff on butter, it is difficult to ascribe to the tariff changes their proper influence on the industry. The conditions which affect the production of butter and, through their influence on production, the price, are so complex and so varied that it is almost impossible to point to any clear-cut result and to state that it was brought about by a change in tariff rates. It may be well to outline some of these conditions.

First, butter production must compete with other types of farming. Since there is a large amount of land which can be used either for dairy farming or for the production of some other type of farm commodity, it is evident that the demand for, and price of, these other commodities will have an influence upon the output of dairy products. Much of the land suitable for other types of agriculture, such as grain growing, would not be adaptable to dairy farming, but there are large areas—for example, much of the land used for vegetables and fruit—where dairying can well be interchanged with other enterprises according to the relative price level of the various products. In York County in the vicinity of Toronto, the farmers until recently practised a type of farming which the Ontario Cost of Milk Production Committee of 1921 described as "horse and hay" farming. The declining price of horses and the increasing demand for dairy products from the city of Toronto induced many of these farmers to turn to dairying.

A second influence is competition with other milk products. Since butter is only one of several ways in which milk may reach the consumer, it is evident that any change in the demand for other milk products will have its effect on the butter industry. A great increase in the per capita consumption of whole milk and cream (from 240.1 pounds in 1921 to 470.8 pounds in 1929) has drawn supplies of milk from other branches of dairy production. The total milk supply consumed as fresh milk or cream has increased, particularly in districts adjacent to growing cities, such as Vancouver and Toronto.

In these two types of competition, the tariff is of minor importance. So far as it may change the price of butter relatively to that of other farm products or of other milk products, it is a factor operative in both instances. However, other factors obscure its influence. For example, changes in the price of grains are a more potent influence upon the type of prairie farming than are changes in the price of butter, whether influenced by the tariff or not. This is partly because a quick fortune may be made in grain production when conditions are good, and not from butter production, and partly because the prairie farmer has a natural preference for grain growing since it does not entail the steady routine of dairy farming. Returns from the whole milk trade are so much better than from the butter trade that it is inevitable that farmers should take advantage of the former: the return per pound fat received by the Fraser Valley Milk Producers' Association in 1930 was 74.7 cents for fluid sales and 34 cents for butter. A third influence affecting the course of butter production is the weather. Industries which depend essentially upon crop production, as does the butter industry, are very much at the mercy of weather conditions. An unusually hard winter, or a summer drought, causing a feed shortage, will raise prices through the shortening of supply as compared with demand, without the aid of tariff protection. Similarly, a mild winter or a good summer for the production of feed will tend to lower prices, whether a high tariff wall is in existence or not.

On the demand side, changes in the consuming habits of the people, together with population growth, will have an influence on prices, and therefore on production figures. The demand for butter has been increasing recently—due not only to the growth in population but also to an increase in per capita consumption. In 1921 the per capita consumption was 25.79 pounds; in 1925, 27.36 pounds; in 1929, 29.95 pounds; and in 1936, 31.42 pounds.

There is a wide difference between the effect of the tariff in Eastern Canada, where there are many outlets for the milk supply; in the Prairie Provinces, where farmers beyond the city milk sheds must use their surplus for butter, but where the influence of fluctuations in the grain crop is of paramount importance; in British Columbia, where the important dairying districts look upon butter production as a subsidiary to the city milk trade; and in the Maritimes, where cream production as an occupation is dove-tailed with other occupations, or is a side-line of the more specialized operations of fruit or fur farming or potato growing. Each geographical unit is subject to such different conditions, such varying influences are brought to play upon the butter market and butter production in each case, that each region must be considered as a different entity.

The influence of a tariff on production must be effected through prices. The action of the tariff is to restrict supply in relation to demand and, other things being equal, this results in a rise in price, which stimulates production within the tariff wall. Increased home production will alter the conditions of supply and demand and lead to a decrease in price. Again, the initial rise in price caused by the increased tariff may bring about a curtailment of consumption and this will tend to lower the price.

This process cannot take place while there is an export surplus, since the price cannot receive protection from the tariff and will be fixed on the world market. The only exception, where the commodity may benefit from tariff protection, is in the case of dumping, where the competing country finds it advantageous to sell the surplus at prices below the world prices in order not to flood its main market. With some commodities there is an export surplus at some seasons of the year and a shortage on the home market at others, and the tariff may protect home prices at certain seasons and be ineffective at other seasons. The price of the commodity receiving protection will rise each year during the season of low production and will tend to fall to world parity again when the export surplus reappears, as in the case of butter. Even when Canada's exports of butter were at their peak, winter production did not suffice for home demand, and it was necessary to store butter from the season of flush production to tide over the winter months.

In the first two decades after Confederation, the existence of a duty on butter can have had little influence upon butter prices. At that time Canada had a large export surplus, so that the price would be kept down to export parity during the flush season of production. This export surplus was available only during the summer and production in the winter fell short of demand. However, at that time it was not possible to import butter from the Southern Hemisphere owing to poor conditions of transport. The low season of production in the United States coincided with the low season in Canada, so that importation from that source could not have been much greater even if there had been no tariff protection. As conditions of transport improved and methods of refrigeration developed, the influence of the tariff upon winter prices probably increased. Small quantities of butter were imported from Australia and New Zealand for a few years before 1900, and as the century advanced these importations increased. Until 1910 the imports were so small in amount that their effect on winter prices cannot have been great, but from 1910 until the war they increased so greatly that Canada's export surplus of butter disappeared. The influence of the tariff on winter prices must have been important, particularly in Vancouver where the imports were mainly consumed.

During the war tariffs had little effect upon any trade. Shipping was disorganized and transport became extremely difficult. These conditions were far more protective to the butter industry, and to other home industries, than any tariff. The shipping problem interfered seriously with the New Zealand and Australian dairy industries. A year or two after the end of the war, before the shortage of shipping space came to an end but when adequate shipping was once more available, New Zealand and Australia, particularly New Zealand, found themselves in a very favourable position on the British butter market. European butter producers, such as the Danish, were still disorganized, and competition was not so keen as it has become since. New Zealand was able to dispose of over 90 per cent of her exports of butter on the British market and was not much interested in developing other outlets, such as Canada. Moreover, Canadian butter production was increasing at an amazing rate, largely owing to low grain prices, and there was little need for importation even in winter.

New Zealand would probably have taken a growing interest in the Canadian market after 1925, even if she had not benefited by the reduction in duty to 1 cent per pound. Her butter production was increasing rapidly, European butter producers had regained their positions, competition on the British market was becoming more and more severe, and the percentage of her butter exports which could be disposed of on the British market was declining. In Australia, the rate of increase in production was not so great and the results were less obvious.

In Canada, butter consumption was increasing steadily as a result of increasing population and per capita consumption. Canada's total consumption of butter increased from 226,654,977 pounds in 1921 to 256,248,609 pounds in 1925 and to 293,434,036 pounds in 1929. From 1921 to 1925 the increase in total production of creamery and dairy butter was 17.8 per cent, while from 1926 to 1930 there was an increase of only 6 per cent. A greater percentage increase in production of butter from 1921 to 1925 took place in the Prairie Provinces than in any other part of Canada. It increased by 46.4 per cent between 1920 and 1925, but from then until 1930 there was a tendency to decrease with some fluctuations. Low grain prices in 1922 and 1923 stimulated production in the early part of the decade, but after 1924 grain prices improved and interest in dairy production declined. The winter of 1926-7 was very severe and seriously interfered with dairying. The dairy commissioner wrote regarding the decline in dairy production:

> This comes almost wholly as a result of climatic or weather conditions, not merely during the period covered by this report but extending back nearly ten months previously. A feed shortage commenced over considerable areas in July, 1926, and reached serious proportions during the following winter.

The milk flow was consequently much reduced where the cows were in milk, but there is a further feature of the situation seriously affecting the dairy industry and from which it will require much longer to recover. Returns from the grain crop in the fall of 1926, owing to rust damage, were disappointing. Cash was scarce in many places, and beef prices were comparatively high. Consequently there was an extensive movement to the abattoirs of cows which under normal conditions would have been supplying the creameries, if not during the winter months, at least during the summer of 1927.[2]

In all the provinces, the most potent factor in slowing up the rate of increase in butter production was the growing demand for milk for other uses. The growing industrialization of the country during the boom period, and the rapid development of the cities, necessitated the absorption of a greater share of the total milk production for the fresh milk and cream trade, especially in Ontario and Quebec and in British Columbia. An increase took place also in the use of milk for manufactured products, such as condensed and evaporated milk and ice cream.

In Ontario and Quebec dairymen shipped milk and cream to the United States.[3] This trade developed very rapidly after 1923, and in the year ending March 31, 1927, 21,543,597 pounds of butter-fat were exported, the equivalent of over 26,000,000 pounds of butter. It was to Canada's advantage to continue this trade, even if it meant buying more butter from New Zealand. Increases in the United States duty rates, culminating in a rate of 6½ cents per gallon on whole milk and 56 6/10 cents per gallon on cream, imposed under the Hawley-Smoot tariff in June, 1930, stifled the trade.

These markets, the city milk and cream market, the condensed or evaporated milk market, the ice-cream market, and the market for milk and cream in the United States, were much more remunerative outlets for milk than the butter market. Consequently, their expansion in the years following 1925 would have detracted supplies of milk from the creameries even if the Australian Treaty had been non-existent and the price of butter had been slightly higher. On the other hand, such large quantities of butter from New Zealand were not without effect on prices. There would have been considerable importation even without the tariff reduction but this would undoubtedly have been smaller in amount. The margin of pro-

[2]*Annual Report of Dairy Commissioner for Saskatchewan, 1928.*
[3]See J. A. Ruddick *et al., The Dairy Industry in Canada* (Toronto, 1937), pp. 278 *ff.*

5

duction would have been shifted so that it would have been profitable to produce butter in Canada at slightly higher cost. Though there was no reduction in butter prices for some time after the tariff change, the price would no doubt have been higher than it actually was if the tariff had remained at 3 cents a pound against New Zealand. A shortage was bound to occur in Canada and this shortage would have been reflected in higher prices if importation from New Zealand had been more expensive.

The opposition to the Australian Treaty on the part of those most qualified to judge was based mainly on its effect upon winter dairying in Canada. It was contended by the National Dairy Council and others that butter from the Southern Hemisphere gave unfair competition to Canadian butter producers during the winter months, since it was produced under summer conditions. The lowering of the tariff in favour of Australia and New Zealand decreased the spread between summer and winter prices, and discouraged winter production. Winter dairying was not regarded as so important for its own sake as for its necessity to profitable operations the year around. It was felt that if winter cream production was rendered unprofitable, cream production as a whole would be discouraged. Thus butter production as a whole would be lessened, which in turn would lead to an increase in the cost of manufacture, since the volume handled by the creameries would diminish. Opponents of the treaty held that all such difficulties would be removed by increased protection against New Zealand and Australia. The spread between summer and winter cream prices would increase, making cream production in winter more profitable. This would simplify the dairy farmer's problem by putting his operations on an all-year basis, and would thus make cream production generally more profitable. Higher winter prices would lead to increased production of cream, not only in the winter, but throughout the year, owing to improvement of methods as a result of the greater profitableness of the industry. The increased volume of cream, in turn, would be beneficial to the creameries, for each creamery would be handling a larger volume and hence the manufacturing cost per pound would be lower. Moreover, the production of a greater percentage of cream during the winter would be a distinct advantage to the creameries. The more even their output from month to month, the easier it was to adjust the overhead charges.

The effects of the treaty upon the price of butter in Canada were clearest in decreasing the fluctuations between summer and winter prices. Before the treaty a variation of 10 cents per pound between the price in January and in June was usual. Following the treaty, as imports from New Zealand and Australia increased, the spread between summer and winter prices lessened. If the duty had not been lowered, it is very probable that the spread would have been wider in these years. It might not have been as much wider as the change in duty, since it might conceivably have paid New Zealand to export even at slightly lower prices. The spread between summer and winter prices was perhaps the most important aspect of the tariff on butter, for while some measure of all-year-round production was essential to the efficiency of the industry, winter production was bound to be more expensive than summer production, both from the farming and from the manufacturing points of view, and a price premium was essential. This was the main justification for a certain amount of protection for Canadian producers against those who were enjoying the advantages of summer conditions while they had to cope with the difficulties of winter.

The effect of the tariff reduction was also noticeable in the lessening of spread between importing sections and the rest of Canada. Owing to the accessibility of the Vancouver market to New Zealand, a decrease took place, following the treaty, in the premium at Vancouver over the price in Ontario and in the Prairie Provinces. However, though the influence of the tariff change may be traced in the lessening of the spread between summer and winter prices and between importing sections and the rest of Canada, there is no evidence that the Australian Treaty led to any marked depression of butter prices as compared with other prices in Canada. Following the tariff change of 1925, butter prices tended to rise as compared with the general level of prices, and with the prices of animal products among which butter would be classified. From 1927 to 1928, the price of butter fell while the index number for prices of animal products rose, but this could not be ascribed to the effect of imports from the Southern Hemisphere. At any rate, no drastic effect upon the general level of butter prices occurred as a result of the reduced tariff.

Coincident with the raising of the tariff in September, 1930, and the termination of the New Zealand agreement in October of the same year, there was a large increase in butter production in Canada. The total production of creamery butter increased by 8.7 per cent from 1929 to 1930, and by 21.6 per cent from 1930 to 1931. The apostles of protection were able to point to a glorious vindication of the benefits derived from tariffs. On the other hand, the winter of 1930-1 was extremely mild, especially on the prairies, and this made for increased dairy production. Poor returns from the grain crop forced the prairie farmers to take more interest in dairying as a means of securing an income, and low feed prices lowered the cost of production of milk. Dairying on the prairies again increased during a depression. It was more profitable in many cases to feed grain to the cattle than to try and sell it. Ontario and Quebec farmers who had been exporting milk and cream to the United States, and who were deprived of their market owing to the Hawley-Smoot tariff, turned to the creameries. All these factors were making for increased butter production apart from the tariff.

The home market was unable to absorb such a large quantity, an export surplus appeared once more, and during the summer of 1931 the Canadian price fell to export level for the first time in some years. As soon as the surplus was removed, the price rose above world parity, but during the summers of 1932 and 1933 it dropped to export level for short periods. While there were forces making for the increase in production which resulted in export surpluses, the raising of the tariff had considerable influence upon the supply situation in Canada in 1930-1. Anticipation of the tariff change in the fall of 1930 and of a consequent increase in prices induced dairy producers to divert the milk supply to butter production, and New Zealand sent all the butter possible into Canada before the imposition of the barrier. The exportable surplus was not nearly so great during the summers of 1932 and 1933. Canadian production fell off slightly—partly because producers realized that the higher tariff wall had not been effective in raising prices as much as expected—, the stocks of New Zealand butter which had entered before the increase in duty had been exhausted, and subsequent imports from that source were on a much smaller scale.

Conditions during these three years, however, made it obvious to all concerned that the tariff could be effective as a price-raising measure only when the butter industry was not on an export basis. As soon as Canadian production exceeded what could be absorbed on the home market, whether the tariff rate was 1 cent or 8 cents per pound, the Canadian price approximated world parity. Increasing consumption led to the disappearance of its exportable surplus in 1934 and prices remained above the world level, but production outstripped consumption in 1935 and the export surplus reappeared with the resulting tendency for prices to drop to world parity during the summers of 1935 and 1936. The tariff has been successful in maintaining the winter price in Canada well above the world level. The London market price tends to be lower in winter, the flush season of production in New Zealand and Australia, than in summer. Thus, if butter from these countries could be imported into Canada under the 1 cent per pound duty of the later twenties, there is no doubt that large quantities would continue to enter the Canadian market, bringing the winter price much nearer to the summer level than it has been. There has not been as great a spread between winter and summer prices as proponents of tariff protection had hoped after the raising of the tariff against New Zealand. Since 1930 the spread between the price in June and December (F. A. S. Montreal—No. 1. Solids) has never been more than 6 cents per pound and in several years has been considerably less. Thus the effects of tariff protection have not perhaps been as encouraging to winter dairying as had been hoped, but there is no doubt that it has been made more profitable than it would have been if imports of New Zealand butter had been forcing down the price during the winter months. There is evidence that the percentage of the total output of butter produced during the winter had tended to increase since 1930, especially in the Prairie Provinces. In Saskatchewan the average percentage of the total output of butter produced during the winter months for the years from 1925 to 1930 inclusive was 24.0 per cent, while the average for the years from 1930 to 1936 was 28 per cent.[4] This should not be given too much significance as showing the influence of tariff protection, since before 1925, when the duty on butter was still 3 cents a pound against Australia and New Zealand, the percentage produced during the winter tended to average the same as in the years following 1925. Nevertheless it is highly probable that the added protection to winter prices since 1930 has contributed to the tendency for butter production to be put on a slightly more even basis the year around.

[4] *Annual Reports of Dairy Commissioner for Saskatchewan.*

The inefficacy of tariff measures in protecting the price of butter at all seasons of the year led to the proposal of other means of increasing the income of Canadian butter producers. Even though the tariff might be of assistance to the industry in making year-round dairying more profitable, it was felt to be a great disadvantage that a comparatively small surplus in the summer months should have a depressing effect on prices. A bounty was proposed on butter exported, so that the butter sold on the home market at the same time would not be forced down to the export price. It was arranged in September, 1935, that the federal government would guarantee a minimum price of 23 cents per pound F.O.B. Montreal for first grade butter to be exported from the Dominion. This price represented as good a return or slightly better than could be obtained at that date on the domestic market. In October, when the domestic price stiffened, the guaranteed minimum for export was advanced to 24 cents. At the end of the season it worked out that the deficit paid to exporters amounted to approximately 1 cent per pound. It was generally agreed among those interested in butter production that "a serious decline in market prices of butter and cream was averted"[5] by this plan.

Another proposal was to encourage the production of cheese in order to divert the milk supply from the production of butter and thus remove the exportable surplus of the latter. While it is impossible to increase the return from one milk product unduly without detracting supplies of milk from some other product or products, thus creating a tendency for prices to fall into their original relationships again, it was felt that Canada would do well to dispose of any exportable surplus of milk in the form of cheese rather than in the form of butter. Canadian cheese has always held a preferred position on the British market, while Canadian butter does not suit the British taste as well as Danish or New Zealand butter, and usually sells at a discount. For this reason, it was lamentable that cheese exports were declining while there was still an exportable surplus of butter. During the summer of 1935 the Dominion government allotted the sum of one million dollars to be used under the Dairy Products Marketing Equalization Scheme for encouragement of the cheese industry. This subsidy was used to distribute to patrons of cheese

[5] *Annual Report of Dairy Commissioner for Saskatchewan, twelve months ended April 30, 1936,* p. 59.

factories 1½ cents per pound for cheese manufactured from July 1 to the end of the season. In spite of this bonus, the production of cheese increased by only 1 per cent over the previous year, while in 1936, although the bonus system was not repeated, production increased by 16.6 per cent over 1935. Diversion of the milk supply from butter to cheese production can become an important factor in the situation only in Ontario and Quebec. In the other provinces cheese is not produced in sufficient quantities to be of any great importance as an outlet for the milk supply, mainly because the cow population is too scattered to permit of the economic operation of cheese factories.

A third suggestion for improving the situation as regards the butter market has been to raise the tariff on other animal and vegetable fats and oils. It has been suggested that this might increase the consumption of butter and enable the home market to absorb the total production. This plan has not so far been carried out, but it is very doubtful if it would have the desired effect in regard to butter. Canada's per capita consumption of butter is already one of the highest in the world and it is therefore probable that the demand has reached a point where it has become extremely inelastic, and it is a question whether an increase in the price of the cheaper fats could be expected to lead to an increase in demand for the most expensive, *i.e.* butter.

The foregoing review of the effects of the tariff on the butter industry has shown that at various times undue influence has been ascribed to tariff changes in popular discussion. An attempt has been made to show the other influences at work upon the industry and to emphasize that, whether stipulated as such or not, the tariff on butter is bound to operate as a seasonal tariff and therefore can influence prices only at certain times of the year. Even if Canada were not on an export basis in regard to butter, she is bound to have a large export surplus of cheese for many years to come. While this is the case, there will always be the tendency for a certain amount of the milk supply to be detracted from cheese production to butter production—at least in Ontario and Quebec—if the price of butter is kept above the world price by any considerable amount during the summer, and this process will, of course, tend to bring the price of butter nearer to world levels.

The justification for seasonal protection to butter lies in the fact that, while the cost of production is higher in winter than in summer, the cost of production per pound of butter is higher the year around if operations cease in the winter. It has been suggested that Canada might concentrate on summer production of butter and rely on imports for her winter supply, allowing only the producers who could compete with those benefiting from the advantages of the summer of the Southern Hemisphere to carry on during the winter. This would make profitable dairying very difficult for the average cream producer. The summer season is hardly long enough to ensure a sufficiently high annual production per cow for reasonable returns on the investment. The cost of production of butter-fat on the farm was estimated by the president of the National Dairy Council as being about 10 cents per pound higher in winter than in summer.[6] The difference in cost of manufacture depends on the variation in volume. In thirty Alberta creameries during 1927, the average difference in cost of manufacture per pound between June and December was about 15 cents.[7] It cannot be expected and would not be desirable that the winter price of butter should be high enough above the summer price to cover such great differences in cost. Butter can be stored for six months for considerably less and this tends to lessen the spread aside from importation. However, a difference of a few cents is sufficient to give some incentive towards winter dairying. The farmer owns his stock and equipment in any case, and many of his costs continue through the winter whether he is producing milk or not. Similarly, the manufacturer's interest charges on machinery and buildings are invariable whether the machinery is idle or not. There may be no alternative occupation for the farmer or manufacturer, and in this case it is better for him to take a small remuneration for his labour than to be earning nothing at all.

The importance of dairying as part of a programme of mixed farming is a point which deserves consideration. Since the farmers producing cream for butter factories in Canada are rarely specialists, they have difficulty in competing with New Zealand farmers who specialize in the production of cream. In many parts of this country, mixed farming appears a necessity as a basis for the development of a sound agricultural community. It is only in occasional districts,

[6]*Hearing before Advisory Board on Tariff and Taxation, Butter and Cheese.*
[7]*Cow Bell*, Dec., 1929.

such as the Fraser Valley, that it would be wise to advocate specialization in dairying, and these districts are usually occupied mainly
with the city milk trade. The importance of dairying as a side line
to grain growing contributes to the sub-marginal production of cream.
It would not be wise, if it were possible, to raise the tariff so that all
such producers could cover the cost of production of cream, but some
degree of protection is probably advisable on their account. The
advantages to the country as a whole from the existence of a stable
and prosperous agriculture might well counterbalance any cost which
the consumers might have to bear through a higher price for butter
in certain months of the year.

When cream production is only a side-line or one of several
enterprises, the methods are not apt to be so efficient as when cream
production is a specialized operation. A certain amount of foreign
competition may be regarded as a necessary spur to efficiency. It
seems highly probable that the entrance of large quantities of New
Zealand butter in the late twenties proved a stimulus to Canadian
producers as far as both quality and cost were concerned. There is
need for improvement in Canadian butter production from the agricultural and from the industrial points of view, increased production
per cow and consolidation in manufacture being very important.
Steady progress is being made in both directions but it is likely that
a certain amount of external competition may still be beneficial, and
that if too high a tariff wall were maintained Canadian producers
might continue their inefficiencies, serene in the faith that they have
the home market securely in their control.

A moderate duty is probably of advantage to the butter industry
from the point of view of stable and efficient production; it can affect
the consumer only at certain periods of the year, and he will share
in its general benefit to the country as a whole. An export bounty
on butter, if continued for any length of time, would probably have
to be collected from butter producers or from all dairy producers.
The greater the amount to be exported, therefore, the greater the
deductions would have to be from income on account of the bounty,
and if butter production were stimulated to any great extent by the
artificial support to prices, the whole problem of adjustment between
the various products in the dairy industry might be rendered more
acute. The system of subsidizing the cheese industry presents a
similar difficulty in that, while it might conceivably effect an increase

in the price of butter at certain times through shortening the supply, the cost of the subsidy would eventually have to be levied on dairy producers and thus the industry as a whole might not be any better off. It does, however, have this advantage, that any encouragement it might give would be to that form of dairy product in which Canada is best able to meet competition on world markets.

THE CANADIAN MANUFACTURERS' ASSOCIATION—ITS ECONOMIC AND SOCIAL IMPLICATIONS

S. D. CLARK

THE Canadian Manufacturers' Association arose in response to very definite demands within the Canadian economy. It was, like similar organizations in Britain and the United States, a product of industrialization, emerging to take care of the needs of manufacturing enterprises resulting from the economic changes brought about by the railway and the use of iron and steel. As such it shared in the expression, for Canada, of a new method of economic activity and a new social philosophy. It was an instrument of market control and a social movement.

As an instrument of market control there was a difference only in degree between the Canadian Manufacturers' Association and other trade and professional associations, business combinations, labour unions, and, if "market" is taken to apply to all forms of competitive exchange, political parties, service clubs, or patriotic associations. Free bargaining implies a range of choice on the part of the individual consumer, but the pressure of time and means limits the number of choices which can be exercised. The object of any organization is to control some or all of the conditions of competition in a way which will provide it with the largest possible share of such a limited market.

Recent tendencies in the capitalist organization of society have made more strenuous the conditions of competition. The multiplication of consumers' choices owing to technological changes in production and distribution, and the development of new techniques of salesmanship, such as mass-advertising and mail-order and instalment selling, have resulted in an intensification of pressure upon the market, and have led to a greater elaboration of instruments of control. The results were apparent in the greatly increased number of interests serving the market, and in the more elaborate techniques of organization and salesmanship of such competitive producers as cigarette and confectionery manufacturers, newspapers and the film industry, railway and highway carriers, patriotic and young peoples' organizations, and political parties and service clubs. Combination was possible when the interest of certain producers was threatened by competition of others providing a substitute commodity or service. Thus railway companies, though competing among themselves, have adopted concerted methods of action, such as joint advertising and the attainment of government regulations, in meeting the competition of highway carriers. In a similar manner, cigarette manufacturers have co-operated in protecting or enlarging their market in competition with confectionery manufacturers. In brief, whatever the means employed, the end sought by any organization, whether of economic, political, cultural, religious, or recreational interests, was that of diverting the demands of consumers into channels of advantage to themselves.

The methods of market control employed by the various associations of manufacturers were determined by their respective constituencies. Whereas the Canadian Manufacturers' Association, serving all Canadian manufacturers, could apply only those controls which were intended to benefit the whole manufacturing group, generally at the expense of other interests, the trade association or combination, representing special trades or firms, could adopt techniques more limited in application. In both cases, however, the governing factor was the competitive relationship of Canadian manufacturers with one another and with other interests. New forms and areas of manufacturing introduced new conditions of competition which gave rise to new interests, and, to the extent that adjustment to the changed situation could not be brought about by existing instruments of control, new organizations resulted. The task of the Canadian Manufacturers' Association was that of taking cognizance of such interests emerging within the manufacturing community. Where they were complementary to those about which the Association had been organized, accommodation was secured by extension of machinery and activities; but where they were antagonistic, differentiation of functions between separate associations was necessary. The success of the Canadian Manufacturers' Association as an organ of the manufacturing group depended upon its ability in distinguishing its peculiar functions from those of other organizations which grew up about it.

Manufacturers' associations emerged in Canada in the mid-nineteenth century to express the needs of local industries which sought to control the domestic market, then largely dominated by British and American producers. The construction, in the fifties, of the Grand Trunk Railway, in providing British manufacturers with a readier access to the Canadian hinterland, led to the organization of the Association for the Promotion of Canadian Industry to secure higher tariffs.[1] Likewise, the industrial expansion of the United States after the Civil War, combined with the improvements in transportation, and the depression of the seventies, resulting in an increasing inflow of American commodities, gave rise to the Manufacturers' Association of Ontario which directed its attention primarily to the restriction of competition from that country.[2] The relative rigidity of consumers' demands at this time meant that price was the dominant factor in market control, and the object of these associations was that of establishing through higher tariffs a state-combination which limited competition and maintained prices to the advantage of local producers.

After 1879, however, the industrial frontier gradually filled in and, by the end of the century, began pushing back upon the metropolitan organization of trade and transportation. Such an advance, fortified within tariff walls, gave rise to new competitive conditions and created new problems of control. Emphasis shifted from controlling an expanding market, wherein competition with American and British manufacturers had been the crucial factor, to controlling a closed market which introduced in a striking fashion competition

[1]Cf. Horace Greeley, Labour's Political Economy; or The Tariff Question Considered, to which is added the Report of the Public Meeting of Delegates held in Toronto on April 14, 1858; Isaac Buchanan, The Relations of the Industry of Canada with the Mother Country and the United States (Montreal, 1864), pp. 490-5 and p. 130; Wm. Weir, Sixty Years in Canada (Montreal, 1903), pp. 105-18; Association for the Promotion of Canadian Industry, Its Formation, By-Laws, etc. (pamphlet, Toronto, 1866) ; Toronto Globe, April 15, 1858.

[2]H. A. Innis and A. R. M. Lower, Select Documents in Canadian Economic History, 1783-1885 (Toronto, 1933), pp. 816-9; Meeting of the Manufacturers' Association of Ontario held in St. Lawrence Hall, Toronto, November 25, 26, 1875 (pamphlet) ; Proceedings of the Annual Meetings of the Dominion Board of Trade, 1871-9; History of the Toronto Board of Trade, Annual Report, 1904; Industrial Canada, official organ of the Canadian Manufacturers' Association, Nov., 1901, pp. 81-2.

between domestic producers. The organization of a number of trade associations—iron and steel, furniture, milling, lumber, packing, shirt and collar,, piano and organ, brick, and canning—and the development of such techniques of control as fixing prices, limiting output, and export dumping were indications of the shift.[3] Primarily the objective of associations in this period was that of capitalizing upon advantages of tariff protection which were being dissipated by uncontrolled expansion and marketing.

With the possible exception of the iron and steel industries, the interests of manufacturing remained relatively unimportant before 1900. Industrial development was incidental to the major developments in transportation, finance, and commerce, and, although railway expansion and the tariff of 1879 had stimulated the establishment of manufacturing enterprises, the market was too limited in scope to permit any measure of large-scale production. The rapid expansion of manufacturing awaited the turn of the century.

The first decade of the twentieth century marked the creation by Canadian manufacturers of a nation-wide distributing organization, a development made possible and conditioned by the opening of the West. Emphasis once more shifted to securing control in new markets in competition with American producers. The rapid improvements in techniques and products of manufacturing, the exploitation of new power resources such as hydro-electricity, the increase in facilities of transportation, and the growing capitalization of industrial enterprises, meant mounting overhead charges and an increasing pressure upon the market, and led to renewed demands for such instruments of control as tariffs in order to restrict consumers' choices to the products of Canadian manufacturers. The organization of manufacturing interests conformed to the secular trends in industrial development. The Manufacturers' Association was re-organized in 1900 as a means of centralizing the various trade associations and regional manufacturing groups within a single national body.[4] Industrialism, developing along metropolitan lines, secured through a national association a metropolitan organization.

A growing membership, however, imposed strains on the Asso-

[3]*Cf.* W. J. A. Donald, *History of the Canadian Iron and Steel Industry* (Boston, 1915), pp. 245-9.

[4]Statements respecting the Canadian Manufacturers' Association in succeeding pages are based largely upon material gathered from *Industrial Canada*.

ciation in the way of representing the various interests seeking expression. While immediate and continuous attention was given to the tariff, the emergence of new factors affecting competitive conditions compelled a widening of the range of the Association's activities. The increasing importance of transportation with the extension of the western market, the rise in fire insurance rates after the Toronto conflagration of 1903, the intensification of problems of industrial relations with the development of labour unions, the growing complexity of provincial company laws, and the rapid expansion of export trade at the outbreak of the Great War, led to the creation of specialized departments, the appointment of a representative in Ottawa to carry on in respect to tariffs, labour, and other legislation, the establishment of an office in England for recruiting workers abroad, and the organization of manufacturers' mutual fire insurance companies and of an export association of Canada. With the outbreak of the Great War, although domestic and foreign markets expanded, the underlying factors governing competition were disturbed by the emergence of new instruments of control in the shape of mass-advertising and mail order and departmental store retailing. The continent-wide advertising of such magazines as the *Saturday Evening Post* created many customer preferences which cut across the lines of market control established by tariff regulations. Similarly, departmental stores and mail order houses, by means of full-page advertising in daily newspapers and highly-coloured catalogues of general circulation, canalized purchasing demands in directions often detrimental to local producers. Manufacturers, as a result, were compelled to place a greater reliance upon salesmanship as a method of market control. The increasing emphasis upon private advertising and the organization by the Canadian Manufacturers' Association of Made-in-Canada campaigns were indications of the shift. They suggested that new techniques of salesmanship made for a much greater flexibility in the demands of consumers and that the creation of effective desire was of as much importance as the tariff in determining the direction of demands.

The extension of the organization and activities of the Canadian Manufacturers' Association was indicative of the new demands placed upon it as a result of changing developments within the Canadian economy. While certain interests, such as those of iron and steel, paint, woollens, and liquor, insisted that the Association should concern itself with the single activity of obtaining a higher tariff,[5] the multiplicity of interests meant that by such singleness of purpose it could not continue to command the support of the whole manufacturing group. It had to diversify its activities with the diversification of the interests of industrialists.[6]

In spite of the steady widening of its functions, however, the Association failed to further the interests of all the manufacturers who were represented within it.[7] The development of manufacturing in outlying areas, especially in Manitoba and British Columbia, and the specialization of industrial processes, resulted in a growing complexity in the needs of manufacturing, and imposed severe strains upon the organization of the Association. In the early years, the favourably-situated Toronto members dominated the meetings of the Council and Committees, and, while the policy adopted in 1907 of holding some of the council meetings in Montreal gave the members of that city a greater opportunity to participate in the activities of the Association, the great body of members throughout the country remained without real representation.[8] The failure to maintain the support of distant members was made evident by the formation of the British Columbia Manufacturers' Association in 1913 and by the fall in membership in the Prairie Provinces, developments which threatened to destroy the claim of the Canadian Manufacturers' Association to represent the whole manufacturing group. Disorganization

[5]"If this Association", said a representative of the woollen interests, Mr. Kendry, at the annual meeting of 1907, "is to branch out in all the different lines we have before us to-day, I think its usefulness will be gone. The idea when this Association was formed was to have a tariff association" (*Industrial Canada,* Oct., 1907, p. 244). Kendry found considerable support among the members. *Cf.* also *Industrial Canada,* Oct., 1909, p. 292; Oct., 1910, p. 314.

[6]"We are", said Mr. T. A. Russell, in 1907, in defending the extension of functions, "such a large organization, and our interests are so varied, that we have to hold our membership and gain our strength by not assisting one man simply because the tariff is his whole business, but by assisting our members wherever they need assistance, so long as it is consistent with the proper management of the Association" (*Industrial Canada,* Oct., 1907, p. 244).

[7]Part of the problem was a result of lax membership rules which permitted the presence within the Association of groups which were not in complete sympathy with its objectives. *Cf. Industrial Canada,* Oct., 1905, p. 181; Oct., 1906, pp. 222-3, 240-1.

[8]"We call a general executive here in Toronto or Montreal", admitted R. D. Fairbairn, in 1911, "and it is practically a group of Toronto or Montreal men" (*Industrial Canada.* Oct., 1912, p. 363).

in the branches reacted upon the head office, and led to a growing feeling of dissatisfaction with the leadership of the Association.[9] The result was a complete re-organization in 1919. The office of general manager was created to concentrate effective leadership in the hands of one permanent official, four new departments were established, and five divisions set up to deal with regional or provincial questions. By strengthening the departmental organization and by providing machinery to give expression to the needs of members in outlying areas, the problems of the Association to some extent were solved.

The tendency towards the employment of professional functionaries and the development of organization along trade and regional lines were determined by the nature of manufacturing industries and by the peculiar economic and geographic character of the country. An increasing membership, combined with the growing complexity of manufacturing, imposed strains upon the Association which were met partly by the extension of its activities and by the delegation of certain functions to trade and regional bodies. Such adjustments, however, were indications but not solutions of the problem of collective action on the part of a group which was becoming in character steadily less homogeneous or distinctive. The increasing diversity of the needs of manufacturers was accompanied by a growing fusion of their interests with those of other groups in the community. The result was that the Association found fewer occasions on which it could organize its members in opposition to labour organizations, transportation or fire insurance companies, the chartered banks, or trading houses. Leadership, consequently, has tended to pass to trade or regional associations expressing the needs of special industrial groups or to financial organizations representing interests identified with manufacturing, banking, trade, transportation, and insurance. The Canadian Manufacturers' Association concentrated more upon advisory functions which presented no problem of conflicting interests (a tendency encouraged by the permanent officials who had a vested interest in such services and disliked activities of a more adventurous sort), or attempted, on general questions such as the tariff, labour, and transportation, to command the attention of its

[9]Colonel J. B. Maclean of the *Financial Post,* a member of the Association, carried on a bitter fight against the leadership in the years 1918-20. *Cf. Financial Post,* Toronto.

6

members by resorting to vague policies, supported by widely-accepted and stereotyped symbols and beliefs.

By bringing the issues which affected manufacturing industries as a whole before the members, the Association mobilized attention respecting them. While specific tariff schedules or transportation rates had a special application and were left accordingly to the particular interests affected, tariffs or transportation rates in general could be erected into broad issues which would secure a common response from all Canadian manufacturers. Thus through the Association the perennial, extensive, and common desires of manufacturers were caught up and embodied in concrete formulas, symbols, and beliefs which became guide-posts to action in the wider community. There was created, notwithstanding differences in interests between particular groups, a public of manufacturers with a distinctive set of values, a distinctive way of looking at things. The representation of this public was the unique function of the Canadian Manufacturers' Association.

To a considerable extent such values were carried over and embodied in master symbols accepted by the general public. The ideological incorporation of other groups into the policy of the Manufacturers' Association was rendered necessary by the numerical weakness of industrialists in comparison with the large voting classes in the community. *Industrial Canada* could not wield equal influence with the official organs of agriculture or labour because it reached far fewer voters. Accordingly, while agricultural or labour organizations could rely on membership campaigns which involved appealing to a common interest within the group, the Canadian Manufacturers' Association had to institute educational campaigns which involved appealing to the interests and sentiments of people outside the group. It meant the development of techniques of propaganda as distinguished from organs of expression, and the elaboration of master symbols making a general appeal.

The spread of literacy, the growing importance of the newspaper, and the development of large corporations, have conspired to render more effective the assumption of leadership by such prestige groups as manufacturers situated in the large metropolitan centres. The diffusion of cultural traits and beliefs expressive of industrial interests has taken place over an increasingly wide area as the market expanded. Industrial production and marketing depended upon operation on a national scale, and made obsolete the social patterns based upon a frontier-colonial organization.   Thus elaborated symbols of nationalism, developed by orators, journalists, poets, and essayists, were employed to justify the extension of market control into the outlying regions of the Dominion.[10]   The configuration of symbols, points of confidence in the minds of the general populace, tended to pattern themselves upon the definition of the needs of such expressive groups within the community.   Such is the role of a highly-organized economic group in the cultural life of the community.   By means of direct propaganda, advertising, and informal contacts, values, notions, and doctrines formulated within such organizations as the Manufacturers' Association tended to become a part of the cultural sediment of the great mass of Canadian people.   To some extent at least, the Association has placed its stamp upon the national life of the country.

On the other hand, the Manufacturers' Association was a product of its community.   The interests of the population, organized through innumerable associations, societies, and clubs, intertwined with one another in a baffling complexity.   The particular issue determined the alignment of groups and the nature of the symbols upon which attention became focussed.   Thus members of the Canadian Manufacturers' Association have found themselves within various organizations, supporting or opposing community objectives, prohibition for instance, upon which there was no united opinion of manufacturers.   Even as members of the Association, they aligned themselves with different groups depending upon the particular issue.   On questions of tariff protection they secured the support of industrial workers in resisting the demands of farmers and mining promoters.   On questions of labour legislation, on the other hand, they co-operated with farmers and mining promoters in opposing the demands of labour organizations.   The Canadian Manufacturers' Association has fought in turn the railway companies, the Canadian Fire Underwriters' Association, the agricultural and mining organizations, and the labour unions, depending upon whether the issue was one of transportation, fire insurance, the tariff, or industrial relations.

In this sense the affiliations of the Association were opportunistic. They could be predicted only in terms of the particular issue.   Groups

[10]Cf. F. H. Underhill, "The Conception of a National Interest" (*Canadian Journal of Economics and Political Science*, vol. I, Aug., 1935).

united when certain interests were threatened, but inter-group align-
ments, when not concerned with the objectives which brought them
together, displayed little consistency in policy or action. While the
nature of the issues generally may have favoured the affiliation of
manufacturers with other business groups in the community, conclusions respecting the permanency of such unions must necessarily
be hazardous. The study of an organization such as the Canadian
Manufacturers' Association reveals the danger of a too simple view
of class conflict as a phenomenon of the modern state. On the other
hand, it serves to emphasize the fact that citizens act as members of
groups, rather than as individuals, when participating in politics. The
residuum of political power in the state is not readily discernible,
and the tendency to locate it in numerical majorities involves dangers
as great as the contrary tendency to locate it in a single dominant
class or group.

MONETARY THEORY AND POLITICS

V. F. COE

THE purpose of this essay is to notice briefly the close connection between monetary theory and politics. The first part deals with the political uses of monetary reform proposals and suggests that the monetary economist be responsible for a more serious analysis of the political process. In the second part it is pointed out that certain maxims purporting to define the economist's function are of little value because of the essential character of contemporary monetary theory.[1]

I

If monetary reform is defined broadly so as to include both modest proposals and comprehensive schemes, it is clear that a great deal of energy is going into efforts to improve economic conditions by monetary devices, and that the subject is of practical political importance. The literature is endless, but one may mention at random a number of the recent proposals: devaluation, the 100 per cent reserve system, the compensated dollar, social credit, dated stamp money, wider gold points, stabilization funds, the abolition of bonds, control of investment in order to get a zero rate of interest, flexible reserve requirements, deficit spending by governments, and policies of great variety designed to make the actions of central banks more "intelligent".

The growing intrusion of these subjects into politics since the war, and particularly during the last depression, is a matter of common knowledge, but a few recent examples may be noticed. At the present time a Social Credit government is in power in Alberta and is committed to the installation of a new financial and monetary system which will reduce the cost of living and make possible the payment to every adult in the province of a monthly dividend of at least $25.

[1]Although many events and numerous writings on monetary matters have played a part in forming the attitude expressed in this paper, it should be said that the ideas were precipitated by a visit to Alberta in the summer of 1937. *Cf.* an article by the writer on "Dated Stamp Money in Alberta" in the *Canadian Journal of Economics and Political Science*, vol. IV, March, 1938.

In the 1936 presidential campaign in the United States, the party
assembled by Coughlin, Townsend, and Lemke put forward a medley
of monetary proposals, including nationalization of the Federal Reserve System, a free gold market and a higher price of gold, the issue
of more money, and the institution of a revolving fund financed by a
transactions tax so that old-age pensions of $200 a month could be
paid.   In Germany, before Hitler took power, the Nazis' political
literature denounced "interest slavery" and drew a distinction between national, creative, Aryan capital and international, exploitive,
Jewish capital; Hitler promised to abolish the gold standard, repudiate public debts, abolish taxes, and finance public works by
"certificates".[2]   Similarly, the programme of Mussolini's Fascist
party in Italy included a promise to nationalize all banks.[3]

These are examples of monetary reform proposals used for
political demagogy.   They are extreme, but they illustrate the possibilities of the subject.   They raise the question, What are the
advantages of monetary reform proposals as political issues?   In a
particular form this same question is, Why do demagogues seem to
find this subject so useful?   A thorough study would have to go far
afield into contemporary politics and social problems, but there are
some points which seem fairly clear.

Political movements based upon monetary reforms can flourish
because there is a fairly large part of the public, a well-educated and
vocal part, which believes that planned changes in the monetary system will lead to higher incomes.   The existence of this public makes
it profitable for political parties which are not dominantly interested
in economic reform to incorporate monetary issues in their programmes.   Of this public the economists who agree are an important
part.   They do a great deal of the required writing and talking and
they inspire others to write and talk along the same lines.   Both
simple and subtle thinking is necessary to form the culture out of
which monetary politics arises.   It would be unfair to single out

    [2]Cf. F. L. Schuman, *Hitler and the Nazi Dictatorship* (ed. 3, London,
1936), pp. 117-8.
    [3]An example of the reverse sort, where political use was made of estab-
lished financial institutions, was the campaign of the English Conservative
party for the National government and against the Labour party in 1931, when
the threat was made that the policies of the Labour party would bring England
to disaster by driving her off the gold standard.   This is the typical use of the
monetary *status quo*.

particular economists and point to their appearances on political platforms or before trade bodies on behalf of monetary schemes, or to point to the ill-considered conclusions and the isolated exaggerated passages which are always being sought and found for political use. It would be unfair because, though some economists have courted notoriety on this subject, the typical and much more important participation of economists in monetary politics has been in the course of ordinary university work, through teaching, personal discussion, and writing.

In many countries it was the recent depression which converted monetary reform from a hobby of small groups into practical politics. Socially it was impossible for anyone, even for the sternest advocate of laissez-faire, to say that the depression was good. Those who believed that the trade cycle was a necessary characteristic of capitalism became *ipso facto* "subversive elements". In a deep depression many persons ordinarily comfortably off are affected and of these the ones who already believe that "the fault lies on the side of money" become centres of education and political activity for many others. Besides the complex reasons supplied by the economists for the belief that one or another monetary measure will bring about the elimination of slumps, there are, of course, numerous other layers of ideas which play a part in monetary politics. Thus many persons are disposed to accept the statement that the elementary problems of production have been solved or soon will be. When they are told: "If the fault is not on the side of production, it must be in the money system", the conclusion seems plausible to them. But such conclusions are plausible only because the ground has already been prepared by a good deal of discussion: they possess no logical coherence whatsoever. These popular monetary ideas are significant not because they indicate how persons become convinced of the need for monetary reform but rather because they indicate the presence of a considerable number of people prepared to follow political leaders who advocate it.

On the lowest intellectual level monetary politics can be effective because of widespread beliefs akin to those in magic. Ignorance is so general and for many the working of money is so mysterious that the most absurd theories are believed in. Among the causes of this ignorance there is, first, the low standard of popular education in even the most advanced countries. Secondly, though ordinary experience makes many people familiar with the general nature of production and distribution, relatively few have sufficient dealings with banks to enable them to know what a bank does. Furthermore, the bankers, privy to many men's plans, wrap the details of the banking business in shrouds of secrecy, and this traditional secrecy earns not only the customer's confidence but also the public's suspicion. Central banks and government treasuries usually act in the same secretive way. Since they find it difficult to lay down hard and fast rules of conduct for themselves, they often hesitate to state their policies or even to give information for fear that political opponents may derive an advantage.[4]

The general ignorance of monetary matters, which poor education, lack of experience, and the policy of the authorities combine to create, is as helpful to the political demagogue as is the enthusiasm about the schemes in certain smaller circles which furnish the active propagandists and workers necessary in politics. General ignorance makes possible belief in money magic among wider circles and leaves still wider circles defenceless before the demagogues.

The foregoing statements are merely the beginning of an explanation of the advantages of monetary reforms. The basic political advantage is that a change in the monetary system seems to most people something relatively easy to effect. If the ideas of the monetary reformer are accepted, the worst of the world's misery is to be attributed to one part of the economic mechanism, and this part can be repaired without damage to any other part. In particular, property rights will not be touched; therefore big business and small business will be left undisturbed, except that they will have larger profits. Interest, wages, and rent continue as before, but everyone will have a larger income. The fact that so much of the economic system can be left as it is, at any rate in the mind's eye, means that no large class of people need be alienated by the prospect of the reform. The politician armed with monetary proposals can denounce inadequate relief and exorbitant taxation in the same speech; he can sympathize with low wages and depression profits; he can appeal to those "who want a change" and to those who don't want a change.

[4]Partisan disputes, however much they may hurt the government at the time, are ways of educating people about money—and perhaps the only effective ways. The political disputes involve wide discussion, and though the absence of such debate may raise the level and tone of the discussion in some groups, this improvement in the highest circles may be at the expense of greater ignorance generally.

Furthermore the promised reform appears easy to accomplish because the part of the economic system to be changed is already the province of the government. Monetary reforms would not in most countries require any constitutional changes. Other types of intervention are likely to cause wrangles about the proper functions of government, but about government control of money there is almost no dispute, and this is a definite political advantage.

The simplicity of monetary reforms can be illustrated by appropriate pictures. One, which applies to most central banking proposals, is that of the government pulling levers. The reform consists in merely pulling a few levers now, and hereafter having the experts pull the right levers at the right time. A second picture is that of a quick surgical operation, performed by the government. The 100 per cent reserve scheme is an example. The reform consists in taking out the diseased organ, the fractional reserve system, and substituting a healthy organ, the 100 per cent reserve system. These analogies, of course, overlook the political problems entirely, and they also facilitate the overlooking of relevant economic problems.

It is, of course, in depressions that monetary proposals increase in political value. The hardships of the severe depression shake the economic and political system. The demand is for "a way out", a "plan", a change in the system. Political parties asking for drastic changes grow. Among them may be new parties with "queer" monetary ideas. These monetary parties need not always make their way on their own strength: they may receive the backing of a conservative party anxious to split the "protest" vote. But the more conservative parties may also be driven in the depression or the period following to adopt drastic monetary planks and campaign against poverty and the "financial system". In general, the more hopeful is the political outlook for the old-line party, the more vague will the official monetary plank be. A party financed by bankers and industrialists can seldom afford, even for vote-catching purposes, to promise to install heterodox financial systems.

However the examples of the Fascist parties in Germany and Italy show that proposals for drastic monetary changes can be used in a campaign of promises to every group, and can be dropped once power is attained. When the economic system is near collapse, the conservative parties unpopular, and radical changes seem imminent, the Fascist parties tend to get conservative support. The Fascist party has a programme of drastic reforms which it does not intend to carry out.[5] For this party's purposes monetary proposals are admirably suited, for the reasons already cited. The programme of dictatorship which is carried out and the suppression of opposition parties prevent effective criticism of the failure to carry out promises.

In prosperous periods the advantages of financial proposals are more limited, but even in these periods the depressed area and the depressed class provide scope for the politician with monetary reforms. No special comment is needed about the former. As for the depressed class, everyone will think of the number of monetary movements which have flourished among farmers. The farmers and the small merchants are the two large classes which have direct experience with financial institutions. The farmers as a class are periodically in conflict with the banks and other financial institutions through inability to borrow as much as they want or inability to pay back principal or interest. It is well known that farmers as a debtor class are favourable to inflationary measures; and, more generally, all political movements based upon monetary changes and denunciations of the financial institutions find the farmers receptive.

In a period of monetary change and flexible policies, certain business groups can be enlisted to agitate for particular policies through political parties. Thus it is to be expected that owners of gold and silver mines will want a higher price for gold and silver and that export manufacturers will want the currency depreciated. But in such movements the opposition from within the ranks will be greater than with farmers, because of the network of controlling relations between export and domestic industries and between industry and finance.

The wage worker is not immune to political action for monetary innovations. If the scheme involves a direct payment to him, he is naturally interested. The Douglas Social Credit promise of a monthly "dividend" is calculated to attract all low income groups. That the handsome plans of social security which can be conjured from monetary ideas offer rich political possibilities was shown by the rapid growth of the Townsend movement in the United States to a membership of several millions.

The great weakness of those monetary reforms which promise

[5]Some of the frankest statements on this point are contained in the early German editions of Hitler's *Mein Kampf*.

much is that no successes—of the required magnitude—can be pointed to. People are sceptical as well as credulous, and politics is not simply a matter of making promises. So long as the demagogue cannot establish a dictatorship there is a chance in politics to expose the grosser monetary charlatans, and in the event of an election, the exposure, though costly, takes place.

The economist's role in this political process has already been noted. But if one can judge by the conduct of some of the most prominent monetary theorists, neither this role nor the aspects of politics just outlined have received much thought. Almost none of these men would maintain that monetary theory is a very certain or settled subject. Yet in recent years caution was thrown to the winds and monetary schemes poured from the economists' pens. A good many of these proposals *must* be faulty. But one could hardly say of the literature that the uncertainty of the matters had led to modest statements and claims. Overstatement is perhaps unavoidable; in so far as it is, the public is certain to be misled.

Economists in their writings on matters of policy reveal two attitudes towards politics. The first is that of one advising a states-man who needs only to have certain technical problems resolved in order to decide, on extra-economic grounds, what is the best policy. The second attitude is traditional, and is exemplified in Adam Smith's reference to "that insidious and crafty animal vulgarly called a states-man or politician". The modern counterpart of this mistrust is cyni-cism—a cynicism much less enlightening than Adam Smith's de-nunciation of interference, since he was showing how well an inde-pendent economic system could work, while his successor is usually unwilling to make this positive statement.

These two attitudes often come to the same thing: such ignoring of the process of politics that the economist's work is totally wasted. It may be granted that they often enable the economist to concentrate on the analysis which he can do best, and often enable him to escape the charge of partisanship and bias (even when he plays into the hands of one political party). But there are drawbacks, and to illus-trate them the problem of monopoly control may be cited. Despite the stream of books and articles on monopolies that has poured out year after year, despite popular agitation, legislative discussion, the passage of laws, and the working of regulatory bodies, it is fairly clear that nothing much has been done to control—let alone to eliminate—private monopolies. Prices remain high and rigid, even in severe depressions. Tariffs are high, profits are large. Everyone knows that certain firms are monopolies, the dominant intellectual opinions and ideas of social welfare have long been "against" monopolies, and yet nothing is done. In the face of the tremendous failure on this matter, it is a wonder that any interest is left in paper schemes of control, presented without any analysis of the relevant politics. Suppose the analysis of the nature of business and of the effects of monopolies to have yielded the conclusion that monopolies must be regulated or eliminated, what is needed is not just the draft of a law nor an explanation of what the administrative body should do. The questions of why the past success has been so small and whether the future is likely to be any different need to be met. In a democratic country an economic policy must be initiated, made known to the public, carried through the legislature, and administered, in a political system of parties, each one of which is controlled by certain groups of people and each one of which makes its chief appeal to certain groups. What chance has a particular measure that the economist proposes of getting through this process and functioning in the way he pictures it to function? Apparently in the case of measures to control monopolies there is very little chance. At this point, there is no use in dissolving into cynicism about the corruption or ignorance of the persons concerned. It is just as academic to do this as it is to ignore all the difficulties. The state carries out certain policies, some of them very complicated, and part of the problem is why it does carry out these policies and not the one in question. Suppose that the problem of monopoly control raises the question of monopolists' contributions to party funds, and monopolists' control of newspapers. Must these practices be abolished for monopoly control to work? Can they be abolished? A reasonably well-informed citizen must ask himself these questions, and, with much less information than the economist has available, must try to answer them. The only objection to the economist's supplying a more complete answer is that it draws him into very controversial and unsafe waters, but this is hardly a valid objection.

It will be said that so complete a political study cannot be made for every policy, that the economist has his own terrain, prices, output, and the like, and that the job here is difficult enough. True, but where the field is littered with failures, one who puts forward a new plan can hardly escape responsibility for a study of the failures.

Questions which raise doubts as to the possibility of a given type of control can at least be raised by the author for the reader. In a great many cases it ought to be expected that the economist himself should plainly say that his policy is academic, and state why it is so.

When the economist's reform is a matter of getting experts to pull the right levers, it is only sensible that the probability of the right experts being used and the right levers being pulled should be considered. In particular, if the reform to be brought about in this way promises substantial improvement in the standard of living, one wants to know of historical precedents for the optimism. When the reform is in the nature of a surgical operation, it is just as necessary for the economist to know what politics is like as it is to know how the economic system works, and again one wants from the economist who holds out prospects of great improvement through a piece of economic surgery some signs of worry as to whether the scheme can possibly be born. "What historical examples of such surgical operations on the economy has the theorist considered?" and "Did they result in marked improvements in the standard of living?" are questions the monetary reformers need to ask. Besides a political analysis, drastic reforms of the financial system require an institutional study. For instance, such a reform as the 100 per cent reserve system calls for a consideration of the advantages of the fractional reserve system to individual bankers and entrepreneurs, a consideration of the banks as instruments of business control and business strategy, and a study of the other avenues which would be open to individuals for the attainment of the ends now served by the fractional reserve banking system. The general point is obvious, but the writer does not know of one drastic monetary proposal of the lever type where the political difficulties have been analysed, nor does he know of one reform of the surgical operation type whose proponents have raised and answered the kind of question asked above.

The monetary economist takes a hand in the political process in so far as his writings are read and influence people and in so far as he talks in public, on the platform or in the expert's chair, and even in so far as he talks in private. Since he cannot escape the role of political adviser and since monetary reform is political, the wise course is to assume the responsibility explicitly and deal with the political process where it is important. Without a more complete analysis than has been customary, large claims for monetary proposals, even if put forward in theoretical writing, raise unjustifiable hopes, drain intellectual and political energy into useless channels, and help to lead people into the hands of demagogues and cranks.

II

It is a commonplace that the modern theory of exchange is a description rather than a justification, and accordingly a good portion of economic writing has striven to rid the subject of its ethical pre-suppositions. Some difficulty still exists in the statement of the fundamental assumption that in equilibrium each individual is doing the best possible for himself in the circumstances,[6] or that each is doing, in the given circumstances, the best he knows how to do; but as compared with fifty years ago there is to-day less emphasis on the word "best" and more on the phrase "in the given circumstances", where most of the matters controversial for social policy are really impounded. Corresponding to the effort to state a theory which is ethically and politically indifferent, there has occurred the change of name from "Political Economy" to "Economics", the creation of the separate subject of "Welfare Economics", and the decline of utility theory. In conformity with this scientific point of view it is now frequently said about the economist's role that *qua* economist he must concern himself with means rather than ends, that he can properly advise as to which measures will achieve a given end and not as to whether the policy is good, or that he can properly deal with certain of the effects of a proposed intervention but cannot as an expert say that the intervention should or should not be carried out.[7]

The extent of the change in the practice of the economists can, however, easily be over-estimated. The person whose judgments of good or bad have been known to influence his reasoning as to cause

[6]Of course it is even more prejudicial to say that in equilibrium the gains of each are maximized.

[7]*Cf.* O. Morgenstern, *The Limits of Economics* (London, 1937) where the argument put forward, though perhaps influenced as to form by the author's position in a Fascist state, is the prevalent one referred to above. Dr. Morgenstern wants an economics adaptable to any kind of political situation, but the efforts to adapt economics to the ends of liberalism and socialism he views with holy horror. It is odd that, in a book written to eliminate bias and ethical judgments, the author, when he wants to name a political dictator, can select only President Roosevelt (p. 145).

and effect has never been held up as a model in economics.[8]   On the other hand, despite the number who adhere on special occasions to the above maxims about means and ends, there are not many economists who, when pressed for advice, are able to confine themselves to cause and effect statements.   Though we have perhaps seen the last of the great attempts to extract from a system of differential equations not only an explanation of the determination of prices but also a proof that the competitive capitalistic system is the best, it is doubtful whether economists will entirely foreswear comparisons of different kinds of economic systems.[9]   The fact is that even while they are applauding their successful purification of the theory of exchange, economists are deserting that theory and spending their time with the most political part of the subject they can find, that is, with monetary theory.   The theory of money has now become the theory of employment and of the trade cycle, and these subjects, broadly viewed, constitute the largest problems of modern politics.

The rapidity of this switch to monetary theory is interesting.   It was natural in the period of monetary turmoil after the war that monetary theory should emerge and develop.   But it is not so natural that in time of depression the investigation into the trade cycle should be primarily monetary or that a theory of employment should be a monetary theory.[10]   One reason is the character of the equilibrium, or supply and demand, theory which emerged out of the value problem.   Equilibrium theory seems to promise a world distressed by unemployment absolutely nothing.   Before the war and even in the twenties, it was all very well to illustrate the working of the economic system in terms of a tendency towards an "equilibrium", to teach that things were not what they were because of accident, custom, or exploitation, but because everything determined everything else, and that no one factor or set of forces was dominant.   But the very high development of this theory of a smoothly functioning competitive economy was an obstacle to its use when unemployment became so large that it could no longer be happily looked upon as frictional.

[8]The worst offenders against science in this respect are found among the writers of elementary text-books on economic principles. This is unfortunately the place where the offence is most serious.

[9]Professor Pigou's *Socialism versus Capitalism* (New York, 1937) is an indication that they will not.

[10]Begging the question of what such a statement means—if it any longer has meaning.

Monetary theory, by contrast, was undeveloped; it lacked rigour and complexity; it was not fettered by exact statements of presuppositions and qualifications; and it was fortunately only loosely tied to equilibrium theory. Hence it could more easily be applied to the problem of unemployment, and could develop more freely and quickly.

Apparently no conflict is seen between this development and the maxims of conduct which are accepted; but the conflict exists. What does it mean for an economist in this field to deal with means rather than ends? Suppose that he, conscientiously, does not say whether a given policy is good or bad but only what the effects are. As soon as, in his statement of cause and effect, he comes to the conclusion, "And so it will increase unemployment", he has damned the policy. Since there is almost complete unanimity of opinion that unemployment and the depression are evils, there is no better way of saying that a policy is bad than to say that it increases unemployment. The newer monetary theories are so formulated, with employment (or investment) as one of the important variables, that when any policy or proposed change is considered theoretically, there follows almost automatically a conclusion about the volume of employment. The conclusion is inevitable that in this field our maxims for the conduct of economists are meaningless.

But it is monetary theory which is to-day of chief practical importance for all economic problems. General wage increases are no longer resisted on the ground that the lower wage is the natural or normal or fair one. Instead, the objection is made that an increase of wages will reduce investment and employment. The defenders of wage increases attempt to show that they result in *more* investment and employment. For some time a good many economists have neither praised nor condemned trade unions. They have simply said that when successful they lead to unemployment. The monetary analysis dominates taxation and public expenditure; and the older canons, the theory of shifting and incidence, and progressive taxation ideas, have all become of secondary importance as sources of satisfactory reasons for governmental activities. "The state of business confidence" has recently become an important variable in monetary theory, and thereby the subject is tied as closely as possible to current politics. For it is clear on this view that no governmental policy (nor indeed any happening anywhere) which unsettles business confidence can be approved. No government can succeed except one which is in close touch with the larger investors and which acts only after sounding them as to what measures will increase their profits. The economist's task is simplified to that of finding out how representative business men feel, have felt, and will feel.[11] It is clear, too, that when monetary theorists make statements about the importance of business confidence in relation to a particular policy, they are often saying something like: "Elect party A and not B" or "The government must drop its bad policies".

Modern monetary theory has been so fashioned that it yields conclusions about wages, trade unions and all labour questions, public works and all public expenditures, tariffs, international trade and international finance, speculation and all of domestic finance, social security schemes of all kinds, and indeed every economic matter of controversy. By relating all economic questions directly either to employment or investment, modern monetary theory furnishes a drastic political argument on every issue to which it is applied. The social importance of the business cycle ensures the political use of these arguments on every economic matter which is, or can be made, a matter of public policy.

In some matters such as tariffs and Fascism and Communism the maxim that economists deal with means and not ends is put forward to indicate that caution of statement is necessary because some of the grounds of choice are non-economic. It is, however, precisely on matters where the non-economic is important that it is easy for the public to know whether or not the economist speaks with reason. The place where the caution ought to be urged is in the realm of monetary theory, where it least exists, and where the layman cannot so easily tell when the economist is speaking with reason. Here the economist is dealing with an end that is universally accepted—employment. If employment should be considered a "means" rather than an "end", the argument is not affected, for so many ends, so many non-economic values, common to nearly everyone, depend upon employment that the question of whether or not a given policy increases employment is often the all-important question. If the economist convinces the public that a given policy will reduce unemploy-

---

[11]However it is certain that monetary theory will not be vulgarized until it consists of one or two propositions about business confidence. In the statements of business leaders on public affairs, it is noticeable that reference is made to business confidence only when no better argument is at hand, and that iact alone will doubtless lead to a more careful use of the term by economists.

ment, he has gone a long way towards convincing the public that the policy is good. By contrast the equilibrium theorist has almost nothing to say which is of similar social consequence.

Monetary theory is political because it deals with one of the most important social evils: it has, so to speak, taken that evil and made it one of the chief variables in its abstract system. No one would maintain that the subject should be made non-political by eliminating the subject-matter of chief interest. Restrictions as to what the economist should and should not analyse will not help in this situation. For the economist who is involved in politics to disclaim the role because he does not campaign for a particular party is hypocritical. In dealing with the explosive subjects of politics, the economist can hardly expect to escape some explosions. If he is charged with bias, the only recourse he has is to refer to the statements of cause and effect he has made and ask for a discussion of them. Indeed, there are reasons why the public should be suspicious. The increasing hiring of economists by private firms and governments makes it the part of prudence for the public not to take the economist on his own say-so as an impartial expert. But in any case the economist writing on political matters is part of a political process— that is, in so far as he draws or helps others to draw any conclusions for public policy at all. Objectivity, in some vague sense of being outside this process, is nonsense. Sometimes the semblance of objectivity is achieved by weakness of conclusion; but in economics, as elsewhere, objectivity will in the long run be tested by truth of statement. If the economist by studying his subject cannot modify his preferences—cannot change particular values which he holds, or particular ends which he wants to see attained—then the whole study may as well be abandoned. There is seldom any need for any person, in studying economic policies to modify his most general ends or values, for in their general form these ends—truth, beauty, goodness—are so abstract as to be empty of meaning for particular courses of action. To put briefly a complicated point, those who would have the economist deal with means only rather than with ends, first, ask for the impossible when the problems are of social importance, secondly, think that ends are entirely separate from means, and thirdly, over-emphasize the privacy of values, forgetting that if they are talking about ultimate values, those which have to be stated generally are widely held.

SOCIAL EVOLUTION AND MODERN ANTHROPOLOGY

C. W. M. HART

IN a recent authoritative paper[1] upon "The Concept of Evolution in Sociology", Dr. Ginsberg has considered in detail, whether, as most anthropologists and sociologists of the present day maintain, "evolutionary notions have outlived their usefulness in sociology". His conclusion is that, valid as are most of the anthropologists' objections to the evolutionary treatment of society as practised in the late nineteenth century, nevertheless there is still room in sociology for the concept of evolution. The anthropologists, however, are not convinced by his argument, and if his essay was intended as an attempt to rehabilitate evolutionary concepts in sociology, there can be little doubt that it has so far failed to change that "hostility to evolutionary ideas and methods" which he deplores. The last authoritative pronouncement of American anthropology on the subject, Dr. Goldenweiser's article upon "Social Evolution" in the *Encyclopaedia of the Social Sciences,* indicates that the hostility is as strong as ever. The subject is important enough to warrant a little more discussion. With Dr. Ginsberg we consider that the last word upon the concept of evolution in sociology has not been said when we admit the validity of the arguments against Morgan, Spencer, and Tylor, that writers like Dr. Goldenweiser and Dr. Lowie put so forcibly. Their arguments are, however, not arguments against evolution as such, but rather against evolution as used by Morgan, Spencer, and Tylor. In most discussions of the subject, a layman might very easily get the impression that these three writers were responsible for the evolutionary concept and that because they are discredited nowadays therefore evolution is discredited. It is worth while pointing out that evolution was propounded also by Darwin and Huxley, and it is with Darwin and Huxley that evolutionary concepts stand or fall. Dr. Ginsberg's view is that Spencer, Tylor, and Morgan may have been wrong in detail, indeed certainly were wrong, but in principle they

[1]M. Ginsberg, *Studies in Sociology* (London, 1932), ch. iv.

were right, and therefore by altering their detail the use of evolutionary concepts in sociology can be made fruitful. The view expressed
in this paper is rather that these three writers were not only wrong in
detail but entirely unsound in principle; that they never fully understood what Huxley was driving at, and that any rehabilitation of
evolutionary concepts in sociology can be achieved only by going back
to Huxley and his view of man's place in nature. If we can substantiate this view, anthropologists may be more willing to reconsider
the possibility of using evolutionary concepts, since among them the
prestige and influence of Huxley are as high as ever. The problem
may be clarified by a brief consideration of anthropological theory
during the last half-century.

      A basic cause of confusion is the subdividing of anthropology
that has gone on in the seventy-five years since Darwin. The biological aspects of evolution were passed on to the biological sciences
by Thomas Huxley, and one department or subsection of anthropology
to-day is concerned with the application of biological evolution to
human beings. With these, the physical anthropologists, there is no
argument, and the shades of Darwin and Huxley look upon their
contemporary efforts, with, we imagine, complete approval. The evolution they are concerned with is genetic or biological. In the field of
social evolution, however, it is another story entirely. Those anthropologists whose interests and researches pertain to man as the in-
ventor and user of culture, or to man as a social being, had their
evolution mediated to them not from Huxley the scientist, but from
Herbert Spencer the philosopher, and in the history of "social evolution", Spencer occupies the same apostolic position that Huxley
occupies in the story of genetic evolution. The cleavage to-day between physical anthropology and social anthropology can be traced
back directly to the all-important fact that Huxley was a scientist and
Spencer a philosopher, allied as they may have been during their
lifetime.

      One anomalous result of this cleavage can be seen in current
anthropological theory. A prominent American anthropologist recently remarked that "No anthropologist in America nowadays believes in social evolution", and he could have included practically all
English anthropologists, except Dr. Marett, without invalidating his
statement. Yet anthropology is the subject which, in the English-

speaking world at any rate, grew directly out of Darwin's theory. It aims essentially at the application of scientific method to the study of man himself, and until, in the mid-nineteenth century, Darwin and Huxley propounded the theory and to all intents and purposes proved it, that man was an animal, subject to the same influences and governed by the same laws as the rest of the animal kingdom, the world, both of scholars and laymen, firmly rejected the idea that scientific method could be applied to the lord of creation. He was *sui generis,* unpredictable, unmechanical, unique.[2]

We have always been taught that Darwin and Huxley changed all that. They put man into his proper place in the natural order, eliminated the gap between man and the rest of the animal world, and gave to science a theory that saw in each successive stage of life "the explicit unfolding of potentialities implicit in an earlier stage". And yet anthropologists, people whose science grew out of Darwinism, do not believe in social evolution any more! Does that mean that, after all, the fundamentalists were right and Darwin wrong in the great nineteenth-century controversy? That the studies of modern anthropologists have led them to the view that evolution is an incorrect story? Not necessarily, it is not genetic evolution that is in question but social evolution, that strange concept that existed before Darwin was born, which received a big stimulus from Darwin's work, and which is still used so glibly and uncritically by contemporary social writers.[3]

[2]It is true that twenty-five years earlier Comte had coined a new word—sociology—for the scientific study of man, and had worked out in advance the methodology required for such a study, but in the English-speaking world at any rate, Comte had comparatively little influence except among a handful of intellectuals, certainly nothing like the influence of Darwin and Huxley. Perhaps this was because his abstract and somewhat rhetorical arguments were not as convincing as the concrete here's-the-evidence-and-you-can't-get-away-from-it style of presentation of the latter pair. Forty years later when Durkheim began to substantiate Comte's abstractions with concrete material, Englishmen were too engrossed with Herbert Spencer and Americans with Lewis Morgan to pay any attention to him. Also Comte's extreme mechanism did not commend itself to the English scholarship of the day. Huxley, it is true, was just as mechanistic, if not more so, but mechanism in a scientist was excusable, and indeed to be expected; mechanism in a philosopher, as Comte purported to be, was unforgivable, if not a contradiction in terms.

[3]A hint of how uncritically it is used can be obtained by consulting the index to Dr. Sorokin's *Contemporary Sociological Theories.* There one is told,

The word evolution was used in English before the publication of the *Origin of Species* in 1859, but the free use of the word and the idea has only become popular since that date.   Now Darwin and Huxley were primarily biologists and it was with biological material that they were chiefly concerned.   The links they forged between man and the animals were biological links, the resemblances they pointed out were biological resemblances.   Huxley and his successors showed that "the bodily structures of man and the higher apes are, bone for bone, muscle for muscle, nerve for nerve, and organ for organ, extraordinarily homologous or similar in arrangement".[4]   All recent work has justified the truth of Huxley's well-known dictum, that "whatever system of organs be studied, the comparison of their modifications in the ape series leads to one and the same result— that the structural differences which separate Man from the Gorilla and the Chimpanzee are not so great as those which separate the Gorilla from the lower apes".[5]   And he goes on in a most significant passage: "It would be no less wrong than absurd to deny the exist- ence of this chasm [between man and the higher apes] ; but it is at least equally wrong and absurd to exaggerate its magnitude, and rest- ing on the admitted fact of its existence, to refuse to inquire whether it is wide or narrow."[6]

We shall return in a moment to the relevance of this passage for those dealing with social evolution.   We are concerned at the moment with pointing out that it was with biological resemblances Huxley was dealing and there can be no doubt that he saw clearly what the problem really was.   The job immediate and urgent of biological science was to break down the unreal and unjustified barrier which man in his egotism had erected between himself and the animal world.

on looking up "Evolution", to "see change", as if change and evolution were synonymous.   If evolution means change and nothing more, it is difficult to see why the nineteenth century became so agitated by Darwinism; to say that nature changes is hardly a new or a provocative statement.   It is just this habit of calling any historical change evolution which exasperates workers in the biological sciences with their sociological colleagues.   *Cf.* on this point the article on "Evolution" by Dr. Needham, in the *Encyclopaedia of the Social Sciences.*

[4]F. H. Hankins, *Introduction to the Study of Society* (New York, 1928), p. 45.

[5]T. H. Huxley, *Man's Place in Nature* (Everyman edition), p. 96.

[6]*Ibid.*, p. 97.

"I have endeavoured to show that no absolute structural line of demarcation, wider than that between the animals which immediately succeed us in the scale can be drawn between the animal world and ourselves; and I may add the expression of my belief that the attempt to draw a psychical distinction is equally futile, and that even the highest faculties of feeling and intellect begin to germinate in lower forms of life."[7] This statement, which concludes his essay on "Man's Relation to the Lower Animals", might almost be used as a summary of the task on which Huxley spent his whole life. He was aware of the current belief in the gap, he thought it unjustified and scientifically untenable, and he endeavoured to close it. Those who believed in the reality of the gap, who believed that man was fundamentally and absolutely different from the animals, rallied to defend their thesis. Man is not an animal because he has a soul or because he has reason or has civilization or speech or writing or religion or art or an economic system; these were only some of the answers. The argument became so bitter that the gentle Darwin was intimidated and reduced to a charitable silence, but the pugnacious Huxley was stimulated to ever harder hitting. And viewed in perspective Huxley seems to have won that battle. He at least won it genetically, and it was with the genetic fight that he was primarily concerned. The fact that man is structurally descended from the lower animals is now accepted without question by all educated people, though the evidence for that view and the study of the evidence do not occupy as prominent a place in education as they deserve.

While Huxley was fighting and winning his own biological battle, a peculiar thing was happening to the social philosophers. The most important social philosopher of Huxley's day was Herbert Spencer and Spencer was one of the ablest of Huxley's allies. Spencer readily left genetic evolution to Huxley—fortunately for the future of biology perhaps—and devoted his time to social evolution. If evolution was a valid hypothesis, then everything in the world had an evolution; to deny it was to stamp oneself a reactionary. Therefore society had evolved too. Spencer's *Principles of Sociology* are voluminous and meticulous, yet on the all-important subject of the gap between animals and men in social life, and the question raised by Huxley as to whether the "highest faculties of feeling and intellect begin to germinate in lower forms of life", he is most unsatisfactory, and if it be

[7]*Ibid.*, p. 102.

not presumptuous to apply such an adjective to such an encyclo-
paedic writer, sketchy. The vitally significant passage in Spencer
is the following:

> While recognizing the fact that the joint actions of parents [among lower
> animals] in fostering their young, foreshadow processes of a class beyond the
> simply organic; and while recognizing the fact that some of the products of
> these joint actions, such as nests, must be taken as foreshadowing products of
> the super-organic class, we may fitly regard Super-Organic Evolution as com-
> mencing only when there arises something more than the combined efforts of
> parents. There can of course be no absolute separation. If there has been
> evolution, that form of it ·here distinguished as super-organic must have arisen
> by insensible steps out of the organic. But we may conveniently mark it off
> as including all those processes and products which imply the co-ordinated
> action of many individuals—co-ordinated actions which achieve results exceed-
> ing in extent and complexity those achievable by individual actions.[8]

Spencer here is trying to perform a feat that taxes the ingenuity
of all writers upon social evolution. He is aware that "there can be
no absolute separation" of the organic and super-organic, that one
has "arisen by insensible steps" out of the other. His conscience
will not permit him to ignore the evidence. But having mentioned the
bees and the sentinels of buffalo herds, the exchange of services, some
idea of property and adoption of orphans among the Primates, it
is with a sigh of relief that he dismisses them all a few pages later
with the remark: "Having observed thus much, we may henceforth
restrict ourselves to that form of Super-Organic Evolution which so
immensely transcends all others in extent, in complication, in importance as to make them relatively insignificant,—almost too insignificant to be named at the same time. I refer of course . . . to . . .
human societies."[9] Super-organic behaviour is new with man, and
yet to the true evolutionist nothing is new but must have a germinal
or potential form lower down; how adequately to express that double-
sided proposition worried even Spencer.

We are not, we hope, reading into the context a meaning that is
not there when we suggest that in these two quotations there is
apparent the beginning of that trend which becomes so much more
noticeable in Tylor and Morgan, to pay merely lip-service to the possibilities of super-organic behaviour at lower levels than man, and
to equate the super-organic level with the human level. Spencer's

[8]*Principles of Sociology* (ed. 3, New York, 1890), vol. I, p. 4.
[9]*Ibid.*, vol. I, p. 7.

"we may henceforth restrict ourselves" to human societies, may have been merely a rhetorical phrase, but it was taken rather literally by his followers, and we search the pages of most of the writers on social or super-organic evolution after him for any adequate recognition of the fact that there can be "no absolute separation" of the organic and super-organic worlds, and we search in vain.

The details of Spencer's evolutionary theories need not concern us. They have been described, criticized, and defended often enough, and it is not the details that are of interest in the present discussion. The important point is the amount of emphasis that was put upon the gap between the organic and the super-organic. Huxley's inclination was to minimize the size of the gap as much as possible; man's deeply seated belief that he is the lord of creation stresses it too much already. Spencer is, at the least, inclined to view it as much wider and much more significant than Huxley was. Stemming from Spencer, a large number of books appeared during the following thirty years in which the gap between organic and super-organic evolution became wider and wider. The best known and most influential of these writers were Tylor and Lewis Morgan, the details of whose work need not detain us here.

Huxley, as generalissimo of the evolutionary forces, seems to have left the Spencerian flank pretty much alone, and while regarding it as an ally, paid little attention to what it was really doing. The result was that the two flanks, the social and biological, developed each along its own line and got further and further out of touch with each other. How far out of touch they were does not appear to have been really appreciated by any social writer before 1891 when Dr. Westermarck in his *History of Human Marriage* took the social evolutionists sharply to task for the distance they had gone from sound Huxley-ian method. Westermarck being a Finn and therefore an external observer, saw more clearly than his English colleagues what had happened to English social-evolutionary studies, and though politeness prevented him labouring it overmuch, his Introduction makes very clear his basic criticism. In his view the primary cause of the cleavage between social-evolutionary studies and Huxley's point of view was that much used and very dangerous word "origin". The biological evolutionists dealing as they were with living matter had certain difficulties in explaining the origin of life—and indeed still have. But they knew what the simplest form of life was, the amoeba; and the most complex was, of course, man. Thus for their evolutionary series they had a starting point and a finishing point and their efforts could be concentrated upon filling in the intermediate steps. But even if we grant the extremely dubious premise of Spencer and his followers that the finishing point of social evolution is nineteenth-century England, where is the starting point? There seems to have been little attention paid to this question; the answer was taken almost for granted by every writer on social evolution. The starting point for all social evolution was "obviously" to be found in the so-called primitive societies which were scattered over the more outlandish parts of the world. Tylor, it is true, was rather meticulous in trying to give fixed meanings to the loosely used words "primitive" and "civilized", and brought forth his well-known division of cultural stages into savagery, barbarism, and civilization, each with its own stigmata. But even Tylor assumed that the starting-point of his social evolution was to be found somewhere in the "savage" stage of culture, among the most "savage" of the "savage" people of the contemporary world.

It was just this assumption that the origin and earliest forms of our modern institutions were necessarily to be found among the "lowest savages" that Westermarck refused to accept without scrutiny. He confined himself to one institution, namely marriage, and he asked himself where he was likely to find the origin of marriage. It was true in his time, and it still is true, that every people in the world, whether savage or civilized, have some sort of public recognition of the fact that a man and a woman have entered into a mutual arrangement which will legitimitize for social purposes any children born to the female partner. Marriage in this sense is universal among human beings. Any differences in marriage between different cultural groups are always in the accidental or non-essential things, like whether the man or the woman takes the initiative in courtship, details of the wedding feast, ceremonial details, or the number of extra spouses allowed to one of the partners. And even these trivial differences of detail do not correlate with any other differences of culture from people to people, as Hobhouse, Ginsberg, and Wheeler were conclusively to demonstrate a little later.[10]

Is there any reason, then, for thinking that the kind of marriage

[10]Hobhouse, Ginsberg, and Wheeler, *Material Culture and Social Institutions of the Simpler Peoples* (London, 1915).

practised by Western Europeans (particularly Englishmen) in 1891
is any more evolved or higher or more complex or less primitive or
chronologically later than the kind of marriage practised, also in
1891, by for example the Eskimo, or the African Bushmen? Westermarck, not being an Englishman, could not see that there was; to
him they were all different types of marriage and why one should
be put higher in an evolutionary scale than another he did not understand.   Still less did he see how he could logically select any one of
these types as the "origin" of all the others.   To him "origin" if it
meant anything meant earliest type.   How one could find an earliest
type among the various forms of marriage in the contemporary world,
seeing that they were all similar in essentials and differed only in
superstructural detail, he did not profess to know, and no writer from
Herbert Spencer to Robert Briffault has been able to enlighten him.
His line of argument was *mutatis mutandis* the same as that used
nowadays by all anthropologists against the protagonists of the Aryan
myth.   Just as there is no evidence to justify a belief in higher and
lower races, since nobody has any idea which races preceded others
on the earth (if indeed there was any precedence at all), so there is
no justification for believing in superior and inferior institutions
unless an ethical evaluation is brought in, and to Westermarck who
was a scientist, ethical evaluations were irrelevant.

But that does not solve the problem of origins.   If all forms of
marriage are to be regarded as different cultural groups' responses
to their different environments and different histories, and if we
postulate, as the anthropologist must, a line of evolution just as long
and elaborate, though not as well documented, for the evolution of
Eskimo or Bushmen marriage as for English marriage, how are we
to find a starting point or an "origin of marriage" among them?
Westermarck's reply is quite clear and specific.   "If we want to find
the origin of marriage, we have to strike into another path . . .
which is open to him alone who regards organic nature as one continued chain, the last link of which is man.   For we can no more
stop within the limits of our own species, when trying to find the root
of our psychical and social life, than we can understand the condition
of the human race without taking into consideration that of the lower
animals."[11]   So to find a starting point for his evolutionary history

[11]*History of Human Marriage* (ed. 3, London, 1901), p. 9.

of marriage, he proceeds to investigate the sexual and mating habits of the lower animals.

It is a measure of the gap that had opened up by this time between the genetic evolutionists on the one hand and the social evolutionists on the other—of the gap between the successors of Huxley and the successors of Herbert Spencer—that this statement of Westermarck, obvious and Huxley-ian as it is, should have had to be made and that when it was made it should have been regarded as mildly revolutionary. What is revolutionary about it? To students of Darwin and Huxley, nothing at all; it is a truism. To students of Spencer, Morgan, McLennan, *et al.*, it appeared revolutionary because it amounted to saying on the social level what Huxley had established on the structural level, that there is no gap between man and the animals, that a unitary view of organic nature must be taken by twentieth-century thinking, and that evolutionary schemes even when dealing with such a human product as marriage must not forget, must indeed emphasize strongly, that man has grown out of another order of life and presumably many of his institutions have grown with him.

In a nutshell, what had really happened to evolutionary theory between 1859 and 1891 was that, while Huxley had spent his life labouring on the genetic front to get his contemporaries to accept "the unitary view of organic nature", and to reject the old dualistic view which saw man on one level, the rest of the animal world on another with an impassable gap eternally fixed between, the pass had been betrayed by Spencer and his followers, who, by assuming that society was one thing and biology another, had merely substituted a new dualism for the older one, and had opened up as big a gap between man and the rest of nature as had been there in pre-Darwinian days. The extraordinary thing is not that this should have happened, but that nobody seems to have been aware of what was happening until Westermarck pointed it out.

The theoretical importance, then, of Westermarck lies in the fact that he drew attention to the gap that appeared in all current writing upon social evolution between man and the rest of nature, that he regarded it as that same old gap that the fundamentalists had insisted upon in their argument with Huxley, and that he set about closing it in the only possible way, by tracing such a characteristically human institution as marriage from its human forms back into the forms used by some of the animals. How successful he was in doing this is problematic; it is his method, not his results, that we are interested in, and indeed it was the method rather than the results that Westermarck himself was interested in. His interest in animal behaviour as such was not very great; his subsequent career indicates clearly that his fieldwork interests are very much greater in sophisticated societies such as Morocco than they are in the group-life of monkeys or apes. His sole reason for considering the mating habits of animals in the history of human marriage was his strong belief that a failure to consider that material necessarily involved a failure to regard "organic nature as one continued chain", and any such failure was unsound method.

For this reason, then, Westermarck must be included in the very small company of those writers upon social evolution who can truly be counted as followers of Huxley. Indeed the company is so small that among English and American writers there seems to be only one other member of it, namely Hobhouse. Hobhouse, who was contemporary with Westermarck at the London School of Economics but who approached the problem with a different background and a different method, made an even more ambitious and elaborate attempt to close the gap. Like Westermarck, he was sufficiently imbued with the spirit of Huxley to be determined to regard organic nature as one continued chain, and to avoid the dualism which was so noticeable in most of his contemporaries. But he carried out his scheme more systematically than Westermarck and his philosophic training led him to search for one all-pervading trait or character which would synthesize the whole field of evolution both genetic and social. Westermarck's effort had been confined to one institution; Hobhouse took the whole field of human behaviour for his province and eventually concluded that a monistic view of the whole of life, from the amoeba to contemporary English Georgian democracy, could be achieved by regarding it all as the evolution of what he called mind. "His method", says Ginsberg, "broadly was to establish what may be called a morphology of mind, that is, to examine and classify the various forms of mental activity and social groupings, and to trace the stages whereby they have successively evolved."[12] The final concept of mind to which his studies led him was that of an entity

[12]J. A. Hobson and M. Ginsberg, *Hobhouse, His Life and Work* (London, 1931), p. 110.

which pertained to all life, since the essence of mind was conation, and conation was "co-extensive with life".[13]

This may, we think, be legitimately queried as a question of fact. It involves accepting that those activities of organisms which are usually called instinctive and those activities of some organisms which are usually called reasoned, are in substance the same thing; that reason is a more highly evolved or better organized form of instinct. Whether we can accept this or not is as irrelevant to the present discussion as whether we can accept Westermarck's demonstration of marriage among the lower animals. The point we are engaged in stressing is that both these writers in their different ways were engaged in trying to bridge the gap between biological evolution and social evolution so that the study of man's social behaviour and biological studies could be pursued along similar and not diametrically opposed paths.

Westermarck's book represents an enormous amount of sustained research and sifting of evidence. Hobhouse devoted a lifetime of hard work to the study of his material and the elaboration of his thesis. Yet it is astounding how little impression either of them made upon their contemporaries or upon present-day anthropology and sociology. Westermarck's work is dismissed as a classic and never read; Hobhouse is dubbed a philosopher, and therefore presumably unworthy of attention by practical scientists. Outside of anthropological-sociological writing, in such fields as philosophy or psychology or political theory, both of them are ignored. This latter fact would be less serious were it not for the correlated fact that Tylor's three stages of barbarism, savagery, and civilization, and the Morgan-McLennan thesis of "matriarchy" preceding "patriarchy" are still widely accepted as sound science by the disciplines mentioned though they are universally rejected by current anthropology.

At first sight it might seem surprising that a trend, apparent as long ago as 1891 and vigorously resisted by such capable writers as Hobhouse and Westermarck, should nevertheless have become so accentuated that in 1937 anthropologists are giving up the effort to oppose it and are saying in effect: "Social evolution as commonly used nowadays is an absolutely useless concept; let us try and forget the whole thing or at least leave it to the philosophers and political

[13]*Ibid.*, p. 121.

theorists and concern ourselves with something else." But it ceases
to be surprising when we remember the deeply rooted conceit of man
who is determined, whatever science may say, to find some excuse
or some bad logic to justify his cherished belief that he is not an
animal. The qualities upon which he based his argument used to be
physical ones—upright posture, hairlessness of face, high forehead,
and so on—but Huxley, bone by bone, muscle by muscle, demolished
that argument. Now, the qualities upon which man prides himself
and which justify his complacency are social. We are different
because we have society, or culture, or institutions, and the animals
have not.

This belief of man that he is different may be true; scientifically
the question is still open. Westermarck's study of marriage shows
clearly that at present it is a matter of definition whether we conclude
that the animals have marriage or not. On his definition of marriage
many of the mammals do have marriage of a sort. On certain other
definitions they have not. Apart from marriage there is no evidence
either way since nobody has investigated any other institution along
similar lines. Yet the whole field is bristling with similar problems
requiring investigation. To select one at random, Professor Radcliffe-Brown has constructed an elaborate theory of religion in which
his concepts of social euphoria and social dysphoria are basic. Social
dysphoria refers to the unsettled and disturbed condition of society
brought about by unusual and unexpected changes in the environment. We know in addition that Pavlov was able to produce what he
called a "neurosis" in a dog by experimentally causing the dog's
environment to behave in an unprecedented and unreliable manner.
This seems to open up a problem in social evolution, the possibility
of a genetic relationship between the dog's and the human being's
reliance upon the environment as a stable and known entity. Yet
Radcliffe-Brown, instead of seeing the problem and its relevance for
his theory of social evolution, is false to Huxley and weakly follows
Spencer by basing his social evolution upon the quite unproven assumption that biology is one thing and culture another. So did the
fundamentalists of the eighteen-sixties say to Darwin and Huxley,
man is one thing and animals are another.

This is not, of course, to argue that animals must have a culture
as the term is usually used in anthropology. There are two statements about any evolutionary process which can be made and which

are both true, though they look at first sight to have an appearance of contradiction. One is the well-known statement that there is something new at every stage of evolution, as the upright stature of man is new and not present in the higher apes; as wings are new in birds and not present in reptiles, and so on. The statement that culture is new with man and not found at lower levels of organic life is an example of this type of evolutionary proposition, and it is probably as true as those just quoted. But the other proposition is just as true, namely that there is nothing new in evolution, that at each level or stage we find traits or qualities which while appearing new are really realizations or actualizations of potentialities present in the lower stages. A lizard's foreleg is not a bird's wing yet the former is the potential form of the latter. Many writers tend to overstress the truth of the first proposition at the expense of the second, to emphasize the newness (which is apt to become synonymous with uniqueness) of each new trait in the evolutionary story, especially the newness (and hence uniqueness) of the human level, and as a necessary result they tend to forget the great discovery of the nineteenth century, that organic nature is one continuous chain. It is true that in Tylor's classic definition culture is defined in terms of man alone, "capabilities and habits acquired by man as a member of society", but it is a central thesis of this essay that Tylor, *inter alia*, led most anthropologists astray, and perhaps it is that definition more than any other single sentence that is responsible for the present gap between biological and social studies. Is there any real evidence that man is the only species which can possibly profit by living in a society and thus acquiring capabilities and habits which aid his survival as a species? That methods of behaviour learned after birth from the fellow members of the same species do not exist at all at any other level of culture, except the human level? If such evidence did exist, it would destroy entirely the view of nature as one continuous chain; the gap between organic and super-organic evolution would be as great as that between inorganic and organic, and astronomy would be as relevant to anthropological studies as biology. The evidence, as most anthropologists are aware, is at present hopelessly confused and anecdotal. We suspect that a gorilla on a desert island, though he might manage to survive a little longer than a human, would be in almost as artificial and unnatural a position as the well-known man on a desert island. The best recent work on the social life of monkeys and apes, that of Dr. Zuckerman, is strongly indicative of the fact that in social life, as in morphology, the gap between the higher apes and man is as small if not smaller than Huxley suspected and as few writers since Huxley have been willing to admit.[14]

Perhaps this conclusion will be disputed, and it can be disputed until further research has been done and further evidence available. But where evidence is scarce and contradictory the duty of scientific anthropology is clear. The problem will not be clarified by dogmatic assertions that biology is one thing and culture another, some physiologists assert the contrary just as dogmatically and with just as little evidence. Nor are we helped by increasing emphasis upon the emergence of something new at each level of evolution, since such an emphasis tends to destroy the continuous chain view of nature. Still less justifiable on any ground of scientific morality is the current American attitude to stand aside and allow the field of social evolution to become the happy hunting ground of philosophers, Marxians, and moralists, a field already so filled with subjectivity and unscientific dogmatism that no respectable anthropologist will have anything to do with it.[15] It should be remembered that it was the earlier anthropologists, especially Tylor and Morgan, who first put the study of social evolution on its present erroneous path and that, therefore, there is a clear duty upon anthropologists to take over that field again and restore some order and some scientific method to it. The work of Dr. Boas and his school has destroyed completely the social evolutionary schemes of Morgan and Tylor. But the task of rebuilding upon a sounder foundation a scientific theory of social evolution has

[14]We have deliberately abstained from arguing a pre-human origin for culture from the well-known fact that many insects, notably the ants and the bees, have some sort of social life. Such an argument, attractive as it is, is not really valid. There is an enormous biological gap between the ants and man, so enormous that it is virtually certain that, whatever the origin of man's culture may have been, it was not inherited from his "ant-ancestors". We suspect a relationship between the social life of apes and of humans because they are biologically cousins; we suspect no relationship between the social life of ants and of humans (except a vague analogy), because of the biological remoteness of the two species.

[15]An honourable exception is Professor Lowie, who periodically tries to remove some of the more glaring errors in the field, as in his recent paper on "Lewis Morgan in Historical Perspective" (in *Essays Presented to A. L. Kroeber*, Berkeley, 1936), but even he regards social evolution as a lost cause, and its present exponents suitable for only destructive criticism.

sooner or later to be undertaken. And the way to do it has already been indicated by two writers whom anthropologists are apt to dismiss as armchair philosophers, Hobhouse and Westermarck. It is paradoxical that Hobhouse, perhaps the most abstract and philosophic writer on social evolution, should have spent years in the actual observation of animal behaviour, years of fieldwork upon animal activity, before he wrote a line upon social evolution. In so doing, he exemplified a method that modern anthropologists would do well to copy if they desire to make social evolution an observational branch of study. Only by following such a procedure can nature be seen as a continuous chain, and any procedure which fails to do that can be dismissed as pre-Darwinian.

In the last few years anthropologists have broken away to a certain extent from their former preoccupation with preliterate societies. The Harvard work in Ireland, and the recent studies of Newburyport and other modern American towns, indicate that anthropology is extending its observations into the more sophisticated or more "modern" layers of human society. Presumably the ultimate aim of all such studies, of indeed all anthropological fieldwork, is to gather material for the widest possible comparative study of culture. As long as such studies are confined, however, to human cultures, there will still exist that gap between biological and social studies, that dualism of nature that Huxley detested so much. In the last resort the only real difference between a comparative study and a genetic study is the absence of a time factor in the former. Professor Radcliffe-Brown, who is the foremost exponent of the anti-historical method in anthropology, dislikes the so-called historical studies of Professor Kroeber chiefly because he can find no way of arranging anthropological material in a temporal sequence.[16] That absence of any satisfactory temporal sequence is due to the generally accepted proposition that every culture in the world has had its own unique history and we cannot therefore say that any culture observable in the present-day world is an earlier form of any other. The idea of stages has gone. But there is one stage of culture which anthropology has forgotten, the animal stage.[17] It exists for observational purposes

[16]Cf. the controversy between Radcliffe-Brown and Kroeber in *American Anthropologist*, vols. XXXVII and XXXVIII, 1935-6, *passim*.

[17]Except by Professor Kroeber, who nine years ago (in *Quarterly Review of Biology*, vol. III, 1928), directed the attention of social anthropologists to

in the modern world and nobody disputes that it is an earlier type than the human stage. If, then, anthropology needs comparative material for its generalizations and if, in addition, some students would like material that carries with it the certainty of being chronologically early in history, there seems as much justification, if not more, for extending the anthropologist's field of interest from the Andamans to the anthropoids, as there is for extending it from the Murngin to Newburyport.

Dr. Zuckerman seems to dispute this view. Discussing the origins of human culture in a more realistic way than any previous writer on "origins", he asserts that, on account chiefly of the danger of arguing from the behaviour of one animal to another, "discussions about the social behaviour of man now extinct, and known only by their fossilized bones, would still remain on the level of speculation even if everything possible were known about apes and monkeys".[18] But this only amounts to saying that the social life of gorillas is not necessarily identical with that of chimpanzees or of Pithecanthropus. It does not contradict the position maintained in this paper. For, as the same writer hastens to point out, it is only the behaviour common to all sub-human primates that can be regarded as evidence of the origin of human culture. "The behaviour of the sub-human primate represents a pre-human social level, a level which, though without culture itself, seems to have contained the seeds that grew into the culture of primitive man."[19]

An evolutionary study must have some fixed point, either to start from or at which to finish. Otherwise there is truth in the remark that change cannot be studied at all since all one has is a heterogeneous collection of different forms of the same thing. But if either the latest form or the earliest form is known, then the heterogeneous collection falls into an orderly sequence. The cardinal mistake of the Tylor-Spencer-Morgan school was to think that the latest form

---

the importance of modern studies of ape behaviour; without appreciable results however. It is noteworthy that in this article Kroeber passes a most unexpectedly favourable judgment upon Durkheim, which might tend in some small degree to corroborate the view implied above, that a meeting place for the conflicting points of view of Kroeber and Radcliffe-Brown might be found in social evolutionary studies based upon common agreement as to the nature of culture origins at the sub-human level.

[18]S. Zuckerman, *Social Life of Monkeys and Apes* (London, 1932), p. 26.
[19]*Ibid.*, p. 26.

of social evolution was fixed "in contemporary civilized society". On that assumption sociological differences did fall into a certain sequence. That sequence has been completely demolished by modern anthropology. Modern anthropology, finding it so easy to demolish, concluded, not unnaturally, that the whole idea of social evolutionary sequence was invalid. This, of course, does not follow. Another fixed point is possible, not the latest form but the earliest. If anthropologists would consider the possibilities of arranging social facts into an evolutionary sequence taking the sub-human primate level as the starting point, it is possible that they would eventually come to agree with Dr. Ginsberg that evolutionary concepts can still be used fruitfully in sociology, provided, as we have laboured to point out above, they are evolutionary concepts that are in keeping with Huxley's methods and principles, and not the pseudo-evolutionary concepts that were engrafted on the social sciences by Herbert Spencer.

IMPERFECT COMPETITION AND INTERNATIONAL TRADE THEORY

O. J. McDIARMID

THE value theory[1] employed in rationalizing the localization of industry between regions and countries and in price determination with respect to internationally traded goods has been more primitive, and therefore less realistic, than that employed in explaining price relationships in a closed market. Domestic value theory has led, and international trade doctrine has often followed in the process of modification and improvement. The theory of comparative advantage handed down by the English classical school from Ricardo through John Stuart Mill, Senior, and Bastable to Professors Taussig and Viner, has been subjected to criticism in recent years, chiefly as a result of its reliance upon what many consider an outmoded real cost theory of value. Most recent writers in the field of foreign trade theory have either discarded the attempt to measure comparative advantage on any real cost basis, or have used comparative "opportunity cost", measured in terms other than some kind of human effort or sacrifice. Professor Ohlin's treatment is the outstanding example of the former, being an application of the Cassel system of interdependent factor and commodity prices to the international field.[2] Though Professor Haberler has retained the Ricardian terminology of "comparative advantage", his measure of costs is an entirely objective one, being the amount of alternative product which an economy is obliged to forgo to produce a unit of the commodity, the cost of which is being measured.[3]

During the last decade, the development of theories of imperfect

[1]J. H. Williams, "Theory of International Trade Reconsidered" (*Economic Journal*, vol. XXXVI, June, 1929) has criticized the immobility of factors postulate of the classical theory, and E. S. Mason, "The Doctrine of Comparative Costs" (*Quarterly Journal of Economics*, vol. XLI, Nov., 1926-7) objects to the use of a real or labour cost theory of value. See also Bertil Ohlin, *Interregional and International Trade* (Cambridge, Mass., 1933), appendix III.

[2]*Ibid.*, appendix I.

[3]Gottfried von Haberler, *Theory of International Trade* (New York, 1936).

competition has encouraged international trade theorists[4] to reconsider their doctrine in the light of new modifications of, and
corrections to, domestic value theory.[5] Since the major portion of
this paper attempts to point out the limitations in existing theory
when competition is "imperfect" or, if one prefers to follow the
Chamberlin analytical approach, "monopolistic", the argument
may appear to be rather negative in its implications. The introduction into international trade theory of situations where competition is not perfect seems to destroy some of the postulates
which distinguished that branch of economic science from domestic
value theory.

We may concede that the assumptions of perfect competition,
while not often descriptive of conditions on the domestic markets
of the world, are more valid in international economic relationships.
World markets for the basic raw materials are usually pervaded
by a larger element of atomistic competition than domestic markets
for secondary manufactured goods, and the price differentials
existing between them result from real differences in quality of
product or from varying transport costs, rather than from the discriminatory policies of sellers or buyers acting in favoured economic positions. However, a consideration of such internationally
marketed commodities as automobiles, farm machinery, luxury
goods such as those in the production of which the French are
specialists, and other products sold with much the same mer-
chandising technique on the world as on domestic markets, illustrates the need for extending the theory of limited competition into
the international field. Leading classical writers in this field have
been careful to consider in their theorizing distinctive commodity
groups, such as the leading raw materials or secondary products of
natural resources, and therefore have been charged with making
the facts to some extent fit the postulates of their theory. To
discard the assumptions of perfect competition as regards inter-

[4]See *Explorations in Economics*, prepared in honour of Professor Taussig
by a group of his students and colleagues (New York, 1937).
[5]The theory of *imperfect competition* (see Mrs. Robinson) regards the degree
of competition as being in inverse ratio to the elasticity of the individual firm's
demand curve, while the theory of *monopolistic competition* (see Professor
Chamberlin) emphasizes the interdependence of supply and demand curves where
there are selling costs, and also the factor of non-price competition in the
discussion of differentiation of the product. It would seem that these two
approaches to the problem are complementary.

nationally traded commodities, necessitates a substantial revision of the orthodox theory of international division of labour and neutral market exploitation.

International trade theorists have freely assumed that the economic mechanism of a country may be treated with the same homogeneity postulates as a single individual or firm. The acceptance of the simplifying assumptions involved in the use of collective demand and supply curves, the latter considered as positively inclined or horizontal and the former as negatively inclined throughout, and the limitation of the number of commodities to two for expositional purposes, have led to the use of the assumptions and results of free barter trade between individuals in international trade theory. Devices such as the exchange ratio curves employed by Marshall, or the opportunity cost-indifference curve apparatus of more recent writers, useful as they are for group analysis when the assumptions of free competition on which they were constructed are fulfilled, are not very appropriate tools for describing the approach to, and the results of, equilibrium under the complex situations with which modern value theory has to deal.   The problem of defining the relevant costs under limited competition when each firm does not produce up to the point of competitive equilibrium and where ambiguity creeps in because of the inequality of average and marginal costs (the latter being important for equilibrium determination) at the point of maximum entrepreneurial profits, makes the classical method, under which unequivocally measurable real unit costs are the only relevant factors, a very clumsy one for theoretical analysis in a monopolistic situation.

The opportunity cost-indifference curve apparatus, recently used by Mr. Lerner and Professor Leontief to describe an equilibrium situation in international trade between two countries each capable of producing two commodities, is not well adapted for this purpose if production of either or both the commodities has become monopolized in either of the countries in question.[6]   If the objective of the monopolist is attained, that is, if he maximizes his money profits, the maximum social product will not likely be arrived at.

[6]See W. Leontief, "The Use of Indifference Curves in the Analysis of Foreign Trade" (*Quarterly Journal of Economics*, vol. XLVII, May, 1933); and A. Lerner, "The Diagrammatical Representation of Cost Conditions in International Trade" (*Economica*, vol. XII, Aug., 1932).

The criterion for monopolistic equilibrium is no longer, as under perfect competition, that the exchange ratio curve (AB in figure 1) is pushed up to the point of tangency with the highest indifference

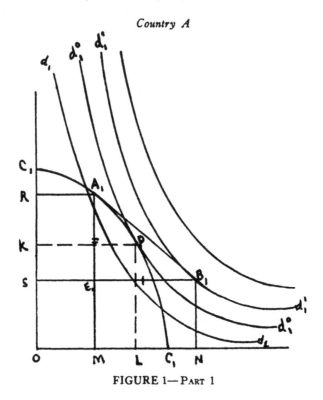

Country A

FIGURE 1—PART 1

curve compatible with each country's own opportunity cost situation and the conditions of production and demand abroad[7] in

[7]In figure 1, parts 1 and 2, the equilibrium situation for two countries (A and B) producing two commodities which we may designate commodity 1 and 2, is illustrated. Perfect competition prevails throughout both markets. If no trade is carried on, the point P in each diagram is the equilibrium position for the countries and the domestic exchange ratios could be indicated by the slopes of tangents drawn to the two substitution-ratio curves and the contiguous indifference curves at contact point. A higher indifference curve (real income level) is reached in both countries if they engage in international trade. C_1C_1, figure 1, part 1, is the substitution-ratio curve (see Haberler, *Theory of International Trade*, p. 176) for country A, and C_2C_2 for country B. The two groups of curves d_1d_1 and d_2d_2 are the indifference curves or, in international trade theory, the real

the international trade goods industries. Under monopolistic equilibrium, the cost ratio (slope of the alternative cost curve) is equal to the price ratio (slope of the indifference curve) only if the

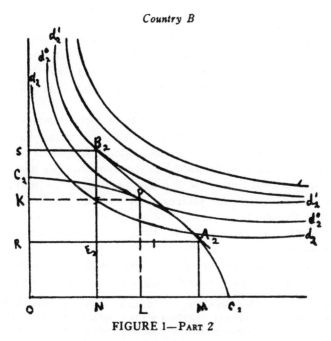

Country B

FIGURE 1—PART 2

Production and consumption of commodity 2 are indicated by OM and ON; that of commodity 1 by OR and OS.

$$A_1E_1 = B_2E_2$$
$$E_1B_1 = E_2A_2$$

former curve includes the element of monopolist's services evaluated at the amount of profit the latter is able to realize when producing

income levels of the two countries when consumers' choice is confined to commodities 1 and 2. When trade is opened, commodity 1 flows from A to B and commodity 2 from B to A. Under free trade and perfect competition, A produces RA of commodity 2 and AM of commodity 1. Its real income level moves up from indifference curve $d_1^{\circ}d_1^{\circ}$ to $d_1^{1}d_1^{1}$. The international and domestic exchange ratio between the commodities 1 and 2 is $\dfrac{AE}{EB}$. The real income in B has moved up from $d_2^{\circ}d_2^{\circ}$ to $d_2^{1}d_2^{1}$.

Professor Viner (*Studies in International Trade*, New York, 1937) makes an extended criticism of the use of indifference curves and opportunity cost or subat the point of monopolistic equilibrium.   In this case the problem is tautological, and the cost curve cannot be used as an independent variable in the pricing process.

Despite the inadequacy of some of their analytical tools, writers on the economics of international and interregional trade have not neglected situations where completely competitive conditions failed of fulfilment.   In fact, the distinguishing feature between national and international value theory has been the postulate of the latter that competition between the factors of production is confined to the region in which they happen to be localized.   In international trade, as Ohlin has put it, "The mobility of goods compensates for the lack of mobility of factors",[8] but, as the same author frequently points out, the compensation is not perfect, and factor prices in different countries tend towards, but usually do not reach, equality. Thus international trade theory is premised upon "imperfections" in the world market for factors.   An assumption of that type regarding the spatial separation of commodity markets has been regarded as a necessary, if not sufficient, causal element in a monopolistic situation.

Two important problems dealt with in traditional international trade theory are quite outside the scope of pure competition.

---

stitution ratio curves for group analysis.   The index number problem which arises if the number of commodities is increased beyond two presents all the difficulties associated with the general problem of quantity indexes constructed with the objective in mind of measuring real income in economic rather than physical terms.   Then there is the basic problem involved in any use of indifference curves for purposes of indicating the real income level of a group rather than one individual.   Unless a high degree of homogeneity is present in the demand schedules of the individuals composing the group, the group indifference curves, constructed by adding together the co-ordinates of the individuals' curves at points of equal tangency of the latter, will cross each other, and the usefulness of the device will be destroyed.   The difficulties associated with the concept of a fixed supply of factors despite changes in money wages are discussed by Professor Viner.   As adjustment is made by moving along the substitution ratio or alternative cost curve, an adaptation of the given supply of factors must be made by shifting them from industry to industry.   The perfection of this factor adjustment in practical life is usually a function of the time provided for the re-allocation.   This means that the slope of the cost curve will differ according to the duration of the time period over which our analysis extends.   This fact must be borne in mind with respect to any practical application of the device. These criticisms of this device are independent of the assumptions related to imperfect competition.

[8]*Interregional and International Trade*, p. 42.

These are popularly and scientifically known as non-competing groups among factors of production, especially labour, and price discrimination between national markets, or dumping. The large differentials between labour incomes, which play an important role in practical life, commanded the attention of Cairnes and later of Professor Taussig in their formulations of more realistic labour or real cost theories of value.[9] Only by the somewhat heroic assumption of uniformity in the stratification of labour groups in different countries was Professor Taussig able to bring into his very able formulation of the classical theory these rigid elements in the labour market.[10]

Dumping attracted much attention from theorists and practical legislators and administrators even before the intensive study of monopoly brought the question of discriminatory price policies to the fore.[11] Selling at different prices in different markets, if not accounted for by transport costs or other economic factors, is incompatible with the assumption of equality between costs of production and selling price, which is a necessary though not sufficient condition for perfect competition. As has been shown, the instruments devised to explain monopolistic practices on the domestic market are perfectly adapted for rationalizing dumping in foreign trade.[12]

II

Work done in the recent past provides us with a body of theory, adequate under certain conditions, for describing equilibrium when competition is limited on a closed market. Imperfect competition theory in its simpler formulation has assumed that the profitability of each firm's operations depends only on its own demand function and its organization of the factors of production, the supply prices

[9]See Haberler, *Theory of International Trade*, pp. 190-3, for a lucid explanation of the difference between the exposition of Cairnes and that of Taussig on non-competing groups.

[10]Taussig concluded that if the "hierarchy" of non-competing groups is uniform in structure between countries, the principle of comparative advantage is not violated by this rigid element in the labour market.

[11]We follow Viner, *Dumping—A Problem in International Trade* (Chicago, 1923), in excluding from our definition of dumping, price differences for causes such as tariffs, exchange depreciation, *etc.*

[12]T. Yntema, "Influence of Dumping on Monopoly Price" (*Journal of Political Economy*, vol. XXXVI, Oct., 1928).

of the factors being given for the individual firm, and the demand function for the product of the firm being independent of the price it charges or the rate of profit it earns. The last assumption is necessary if we are to have a workable demand function for the firm independent of its economies of factor organization and other elements which enter into its cost function. The dissimilarity of the different markets served by each firm engaged in international trade probably makes for a more extensive use of non-price competition and a greater degree of adaptation of the product to the specific market in this field than in purely domestic trade. For example, the motor cars and farm machinery exported from the United States and Canada to European markets are lighter and of smaller construction than those sold domestically. The tendency is strong to adjust the product to differences in income levels, taxation policies of foreign governments, and competition from substitutes, when the total market for a firm's output is spatially broken up into a number of fairly large units. The leading analyses of imperfect competition on the domestic market assume that the total demand function for the product of the firm may be represented by a single demand curve representative of the demand for the firm's output on a homogeneous market. This assumption cannot be validly applied to a firm selling on several foreign markets.

Orthodox international trade theory, whether of the type associated with the work of Professor Taussig or of Professor Ohlin, holds that the money prices of factors in a country are functions of their marginal efficiency in producing foreign trade goods. The theory of imperfect competition, in the main, adheres to the assumption that the individual firm is faced with given supply prices for its factors of production, an assumption inherent in most partial equilibrium analysis. However, if a firm is representative of an entire industry engaged in international trade, the supply prices of its factors, especially if they are fairly specific to the particular industry in which they are being employed, must react to any change in the money price of the product which they are producing for export. One cannot assume that a firm in a monopolistic position on the domestic market is driven out of production by the competition of another firm operating outside, because the initial money costs of the latter are lower. The actual process of trade may well result in a revision of these money cost relationships. The assumption of fixed supply prices of the factors in question would be an unwarranted extension of partial equilibrium analysis to a more general situation. A difficulty of this general type is attached to the argument which endeavours to show how a country may be driven into a less fortunate position by the opening of its markets in a domestically monopolized commodity, if its own factors are very efficient in the production of the commodity in question, relative to their efficiency in alternative products. Professor Haberler, for example, envisages a situation where a labour monopoly in a particular country is exceptionally efficient in the production of a certain commodity, and he concludes that it would be better, from the standpoint of that particular country, to allow the monopoly to exploit the domestic market and secure other goods, the alternative products of the factors producing the monopolized goods, from abroad at the international exchange rate.[13]   In his example commodities A and B are the alternative products which may be either produced domestically or obtained by trade from abroad. One unit of either commodity A or B requires the expenditure of one unit of labour for its production, but the labour producing B is organized and obtains double the wage of labour producing A.   The ratio of the price of A to the price of B is $1:2$ or the domestic exchange ratio between A and B is $1:\frac{1}{2}$ before trade is opened. The relative cost, or Haberler's substitution-ratio, is $1:1$. The international exchange ratio which presumably remains unaffected by the commercial policy of the individual country is $1:\frac{2}{3}$. Owing to the higher initial relative price of B at home than abroad, if imports of B are permitted, the country will specialize at first in the production of A, importing B.   As Haberler notes, this results in a loss of $\frac{1}{3}$ units of B, as the factors driven out of the production of B are only able to produce 1 of A for each unit of B sacrificed, and for this 1 of A only $\frac{2}{3}$ B can be obtained by international trade, whereas 1 B could be produced in place of 1 A if imports of B were prohibited by a tariff.

This of course assumes that the factors initially engaged in the production of B are willing to take a severe loss in money wages on their transfer to the production of A, rather than sacrifice their monopoly position in the production of B, a position which in any case is being destroyed by foreign competition.   If money costs

[13]Haberler, *Theory of International Trade*, p. 197.

were cut in the production of B, the country would undoubtedly specialize in that commodity, because the real cost ratio between the production of A and B (1:1) is lower than the international exchange ratio (1:$\frac{3}{4}$).   This example should serve merely to emphasize the quite obvious fact that a monopolistic situation on a closed market does not hold if the market is opened to foreign trade and that valid action under the former would not be sound tactics under the latter.

The points of distinction introduced into foreign trade theory by breaking down the assumption of perfect competition within countries, and its corollary, the assumption that marginal and average costs are equal for each producer, may be brought out by envisaging two firms, each of which has a monopoly on its own market, selling abroad and competing for the control of a third country which is not itself a factor in producing the commodity in question.   The classical theory would conclude that the firm in the country which has a comparative advantage in the production of the commodity would dominate the market in the third country. As we have shown, however, the phrase "comparative advantage" becomes ambiguous when marginal and average costs are not equal at the point of equilibrium.   We assume that one firm in each of the two countries has a complete monopoly on its own market which is surrounded by a tariff wall to prevent imports of the monopolized commodity.   We rule out differentiation of the product and unequal expenditures for advertising, and thus make possible the assumption that each producer is faced with a common demand curve in the foreign country.

The conditions for equilibrium for each firm, if it is to sell goods abroad on the neutral market, are that the marginal revenue from sales at home and abroad must be equal, and each must also be equal to marginal costs.   The point of equilibrium at which sharing of the third market is possible may not be reached.[14]   The country able to sell on the neutral market will likely be the one with lower marginal costs and marginal revenue at point of equilibrium on its domestic market, and not necessarily the one with lower average costs of production.   If we introduce the possibility of product differentiation and selling costs, it is quite possible that each firm may be able to exploit a share of the neutral market by moulding

[14]See algebraic illustration on p. 115

its own individual demand curve on that market to fit its cost and demand functions at home.

Figure 2, part 1, illustrates internal and external equilibrium for a single producer operating in country A. A has a sufficiently high tariff wall so that the producer may set his domestic price independently of foreign competition, actual or potential. Figure 2, part 2, illustrates the internal equilibrium for a single producer in country B who enjoys equal tariff advantages. The producer in B, despite his advantage over the monopolist in A with respect to average unit costs, does not participate in the foreign market. The OC curves indicate total costs in each country and the OR curves the total revenue. FO is the total revenue curve for sales on the foreign market. Average revenue, or price on each of the internal markets is indicated by the slopes of the OP lines, price abroad being the slope of MO, and average unit costs are represented by the slopes of the OQ lines. Internal marginal receipts are indicated by the slopes of the dd lines drawn as tangents to the OR curves at points of equilibria, external marginal receipts being indicated by the slope of $r_1 r_1$, and marginal costs are shown by the slopes of the cc lines drawn tangent to the OC curves. The conditions for equilibrium for the country exporting to the neutral market are that marginal revenues at home and abroad should be equal, and each should be equal to marginal costs, and exports should equal imports. These conditions are fulfilled in figure 2, part 1. For internal equilibrium, marginal revenue from domestic sales must equal marginal costs. This requirement is carried out in figure 2, part 2.

Since the slope of $O_1 Q_1$ is greater than the slope of $O_2 Q_2$, when each monopolist has attained his point of equilibrium production, we have a situation in which the firm with the lower average costs sells only in its domestic market, whereas the firm with the higher average costs sells at home and abroad. Total revenue and total cost curves have been used to simplify the comparison between total, average, and marginal costs and receipts. At no time would it have paid our producer in country B to have entered the foreign market, as marginal revenue from sales on his domestic market are greater than his marginal costs as well as marginal revenue abroad until quantity $O_2 A_2$ has been produced. On the other hand, it does not pay the firm in B to produce more than $O_2 A_2$ for purposes of export, as his marginal costs beyond that point (Q_2 on the cost

Country A

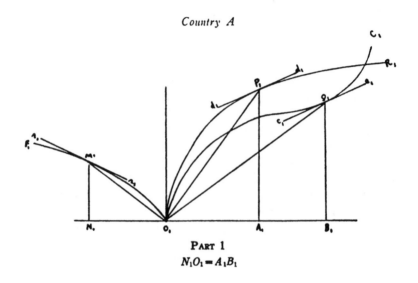

PART 1

$N_1O_1 = A_1B_1$

Country B

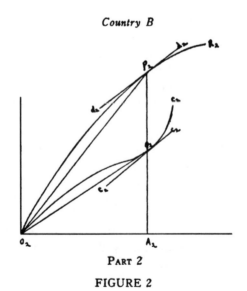

PART 2

FIGURE 2

curve O_2C_2) are greater than the marginal revenue for any unit of exports. That is, the slope of O_2C_2 beyond Q_2 is greater than the slope at any point on E_1O_1 in figure 2, part 1. The firm in A is, of course, dumping on the neutral market for economic reasons.[15]

[15]The problem of two monopolists with their productive equipment localized in different countries and selling in a third market, may be algebraically illustrated as follows: (x_1 is value of domestic sales, y_1 is value of product, and z_1 is value of foreign sales for country A.)

Let $f(x_1)$ be the total revenue function for the commodity in A.
" $f(y_1)$ " " " cost " " " " " ".
" $f(z_1)$ " " " revenue " " " " " the
third country.

If country A is selling abroad, and internal and external equilibrium is established without regard to country B, the following conditions are necessary and sufficient for equilibrium.

Marginal revenue at home equals marginal costs, and also equals a marginal revenue from sales abroad; and production less domestic sales must equal foreign sales.

That is; $f'(x_1) = f'(y_1) = f'(z_1)$
and $y_1 - x_1 = z_1$.

We have only two equality requirements for equilibrium, and since we have two independent variables, x_1 and y_1, a determinant solution is obtained.

Similarly for country B, if it alone is exploiting the third market, a determinant solution is reached at which $f'(x_2) = f'(y_2) = f'(z_2)$, and $y_2 - x_2 = z_2$.

If, however, the neutral market is thrown open to both A and B, another equality requirement is introduced, namely that the average revenue obtained in the neutral market for the sales of each monopolist must be equal, since a common price is supposed to prevail in the third country.

That is; $\dfrac{f(z_1)}{z_1} = \dfrac{f(z_2)}{z_2}$ = price of the commodity in the third market.

When two monopolists are selling abroad on a third market in which no possibility of a price differential between their respective outputs exists, we have five equality requirements which are not present when each seller is marketing his products only in his own country. These are: (1) marginal revenue from sales abroad must equal marginal revenue and marginal costs at home for country A's firm; (2) the same requirement for the firm in B; (3) A's exports must equal the amount the firm in A sells on the foreign market; (4) the same requirement for the firm in B; (5) the average revenue (price) at which the two firms sell in the third market must be equal. Since we only have four independent variables, namely each firm's output and sales on its domestic market, it would seem as though no determinant solution of this problem were forthcoming.

It has been suggested to the writer by Mr. V. F. Coe of the University of Toronto, that duopoly theory is the correct tool to use for the solution of this problem, but space limits forbid me from examining the question of equilibrium from that standpoint.

9

The problem will be readily recognized as a variant of the more general problem of dumping in international trade. The sale of goods abroad at prices below the domestic price is not necessarily a contributory factor in the monopolistic exploitation of the domestic market. The possession of monopoly power by firms selling on the domestic market is due to the attributes of the supply and demand functions for the goods in question on that market. Dumping abroad, as here defined, is unmistakable evidence of, but not a causal factor in, monopolistic practices in the domestic field. The effect of dumping upon the home market price of the commodity is a function of the slopes of the total revenue curve and the total cost or expenses curve which form the bases of figure 2. On this point Haberler concludes that if the elasticity of demand is greater in a newly opened foreign market than at home, discriminatory dumping will raise the home price regardless of the direction of change in marginal costs.[16]

A further interesting speculation is concerned with the volume of trade under discriminatory price policies as compared with perfect competition. On this point any generalization is of dubious value as each specific case demands special analysis. The valid assumption that the volume of domestic trade is reduced by monopolistic practices, except in some peculiar cases of discriminatory monopoly, cannot be entirely carried over into international trade. If the firm finds it expedient to restrict its sales volume on the world market because of a preferred position due to the ownership of international patent rights or a favoured quota position in foreign countries, the volume of trade in the specific commodity will be reduced. However, this does not preclude a greater flow of trade in the opposite direction which may be a direct result of the price maintenance policies of our monopolist, assuming the international demand curve for his product is less than unity. In any case, when international trading to a firm enjoying a monopolist's position on its own market means selling abroad at competitive prices or possibly at prices below the competitive level, it is not at once apparent that international trade must be less under discriminatory monopoly than under perfect competition.

[16]Haberler, *Theory of International Trade*, p. 313.

III

The implications for commercial policy of new elements in the theory of foreign trade have usually received minute examination from the proponents of free trade and protection alike, each striving to discover in the altered theoretical formulation new arguments for their particular case. Thus far the authority of theoretical economics has been on the side of the free traders. The latter, especially in the United States, have argued that, in a large part, monopolies were one of the joint products of closing the domestic market to foreign competition, especially in manufactured goods. Recent authors, however, have advanced the argument that in certain cases where market situations reflect the conditions described in the theory of imperfect competition, a carefully administered scheme of import restriction may be economically sound from the standpoint of the economy as a whole, as well as from the standpoint of the protected industry.

Several points raised by Miss Lovasy[17] relate to the effect of import exclusion upon the slope of the individual demand curve of the protected firm. For instance, she has suggested that if a firm has a fairly inelastic demand curve under free trade conditions when competing imports are absorbing income which might be spent on the firm's products, the elimination of substitutes from the domestic market may result in increasing the elasticity of the demand curve of the individual firm, and presuming that the firm's cost curve is negatively inclined throughout the relevant range, the new point of equilibrium for the firm serving the domestic market would be reached at a lower price than before the exclusion of the substitutes. This point is not without some theoretical validity.

Another possibility is that the entire demand curve for an industry may be shifted to the right by limiting the amount of substitutes that can enter the market. If the demand curve of the individual firm becomes more elastic and at the same time the demand curve for the entire industry shifts to the right, it would seem probable that the supply price of the product might fall under the cost conditions envisaged in the theory of imperfect competition. A carefully devised tariff would therefore be advisable. There are several circumstances which modify this result. In the first place it may be assumed that some loss in utility to the

[17]G. Lovasy, "Schutzolle bei unvollkommener Konkurrenz" (*Zeitschrift für Nationalökonomie*, vol. V, June, 1934).

community results from the restriction in choice that is imposed upon its members in the purchase of commodities if imports are excluded. Lower prices for a limited number of domestic goods may not compensate entirely, as far as consumers' welfare is concerned, for the loss of the opportunity to purchase foreign goods. There are, however, considerations of a more tangible character which indicate the doubtful expediency of such a policy. Although the entire demand curve for an industry may be shifted to the right if competitive commodities are excluded, if the supply of factors capable of adaptation to the production of substitutes in the domestic field is not limited, no pronounced shift or change in elasticity is likely to occur in the demand curve for the individual firm. In any case, instead of the price of the domestically produced commodity falling, under the influence of a tariff restricting the entrance of competitive commodities, the likelihood is that the sheltered firm will more fully exploit its strengthened position. Even though the cost ratio between a monopolized and a competitively sold commodity might decrease under the influence of protection of this kind to the former, there is a strong presumption that a similar decrease will not occur in the exchange ratio.

A factor of probably more significance than the shift in the demand curve is the possibility that the cost curve for the individual firm may shift downward if competition, actual or potential, is removed by a tariff. This may result from the lowering of selling costs incidental to the removal of pressure upon the individual sellers in the market. It is probably too much to assume that such a shift in the cost curve would lower prices, but we may be justified in concluding that it will be a factor in preventing them from rising by the full amount of the tariff.

In analysis such as that of Miss Lovasy, the use of the concept of a falling average unit cost curve is freely employed. Such a curve may be applied to either long or short run situations. It may be used as indicative of short run average total unit costs, in which case certain factors of production are assumed to be both "fixed" and "indivisible" relative to the time under consideration and the size of the output of the firm. These assumptions are basic to the use of the familiar U-shaped curve[18] for short run

[18]Economies resulting in a curve of this kind are due to technological rather than pecuniary factors.

analysis. The type of productive mechanism used and the organization of the factors of production are not independent of the possible or practical extent of the market that is being served, mainly, because of the lack of divisibility of certain mechanical units as well as units of highly skilled labour and management, a necessary and sufficient cause of internal economies of large scale production. For example, the type of productive organization and equipment engaged in the manufacture of motor vehicles in the United States is likely to differ in some particulars from that in use in Canada, because of the large capital expenditure involved in the purchase of certain units of productive equipment used in that industry. The ratio of fixed capital to labour used in the automotive industry proper is higher in the industry producing for the larger market, and the average cost of production somewhat lower, whereas if the same factor-ratio were employed in the smaller market, higher costs per unit of salable product would result than is actually experienced.

The concept of a cost curve for the firm that represents the long run equilibrium and that is negatively inclined requires more detailed investigation than the short run concept of increasing returns.[19] Since no reproducible factors are fixed in the long run and, at every point on the curve, the firm is presumed to have attained the most economical ratio between its technical factors of production with due regard for the size of its market, economies resulting in a negatively inclined cost curve are very likely to be external in origin.[20] Practically, the only type of external economy that is neither a product of long run historical change nor associated with internal economies in another industry[21] is the increased skill and productivity of labour which may respond to marginal investment in a particular industry. Of course the validity underlying any subsidy or protection to a particular

[19]See R. F. Kahn, "Some Notes on Ideal Output" (*Economic Journal*, vol. XLV, March, 1935); and J. M. Cassels, "Excess Capacity and Monopolistic Competition" (*Quarterly Journal of Economics*, vol. LI, May, 1937).

[20]We discuss the case below where an industry is applying varying amounts of non-specific factors to a fixed stock of natural resources. See p. 121.

[21]The infant industry argument, which is based upon the assumption of a non-reversible supply curve which in the long run tends to fall due to external economics of large scale production such as improved knowledge, the development of new sources of raw material, *etc.*, does not depend for its validity upon any aspect of the theory of imperfect competition.

industry rests upon the assumption that external economies generated by the investment of marginal units of resources differ for different industries. The effectiveness of private investment in improving the productivity of labour is usually hardly comparable with that of public investment for the same objective. Public investment in technical education will usually yield more substantial returns in lifting the standards of labour efficiency than public subsidy to increase the investment in, and output of, private industry. It seems doubtful, therefore, whether external economies of this type are worthy of state support.

IV

Despite the disapproval of economists, the United States has, at least since 1922, officially sanctioned the proposition that the tariff should be set equal to the difference between foreign and domestic costs of production. Far from being a scientific principle capable of any general theoretical defence, this practice, applied indiscriminately to the industrial production of a country, leaves the way open for unlimited protection to uneconomic industrial development. Disregarding the assumptions related to perfect competition both at home and abroad however, it is of interest to outline a situation in which the specialization induced by the free movement of commodities in foreign trade may not bring the universally beneficial results indicated by the theory of comparative advantage. If some warrant for the above-mentioned practice of tariff-making bodies is found in our results, it must be borne in mind that the latter depend entirely upon explicit assumptions. The argument is confined to two countries, designated A and B, and two commodities, which we call steel and corn. Country A is assumed to be quite large relative to country B. The assumptions regarding the cost functions are very important. In both countries steel is produced under conditions of internal economy of large scale production and its manufacture has become concentrated in the hands of a single firm which acts as a monopolist. (If we assume that production is in the hands of a group of firms with similar cost functions which act together in a monopolistic fashion, the argument is not impaired.) The economies leading to this concentration of output are technological rather than pecuniary, being the result either of better factor organization when the scale of output is large or of the existence in the productive mechanism of large indivisible productive equipment which can be profitably used only by very large factory units, as in the case of automobile production in the United States and Canada. The reduction in costs either before or after trade is opened may be considered as independent of any reduction in the prices of the factors of production in the two countries, although the vertical shift in B's average cost curve under free trade is attributable to the latter element in the situation.[22] Under the three situations of protection, free trade, and subsidy, which we have envisaged below, each of the numerical and diagrammatical representations of equilibrium have pretensions to long run stability, assuming the appropriate type of commercial policy is maintained.

The use of the U-shaped curve to describe the equilibrium average unit cost functions for the steel monopolists in both countries is based on technological grounds. The particular natural resources required in steel production are assumed to be limited in both countries, and they constitute the fixed, and for the most part, specific factors in the production function. They are only non-specific in so far as they could earn a certain return for their owners if they were employed in the alternative industry, agriculture. The average unit cost curves contain this "agricultural rent", as the opportunity cost for the natural resources, in addition to the prime cost of the labour units employed. The long and short run average unit cost curves have the same geometrical form due to the similarity of the roles played by plant and equipment, fixed in the short period, and natural resources, which may be assumed not to change even in the long run. Our results should be valid in either short or long run situations, although it is the latter which we have particularly in mind in our numerical examples.

In contra-distinction to steel, corn is produced under increasing costs in each country and free atomistic competition prevails on the corn markets of A and B. Immobility of labour between the two markets is assumed. All real costs are measured in labour-day units, the Taussig assumptions regarding the relation of capital to labour and the position of non-competing groups being followed.[23]

[22]See the diagrams on p. 130.
[23]See F. W. Taussig, *International Trade* (New York, 1927) for the assumptions necessary in the use of labour units as indexes of cost in realistic production functions, especially chapters on capital and interest.

We assume that the supply of factors is rigidly fixed in each of the countries, regardless of changes in money and real wages. Only average unit costs are used in the example that follows. The marginal cost and revenue curves, although basic to a determination of the monopolistic equilibrium, are not essential for total cost and total income computations. The following situation obtains before trade is opened, that is, when B prevents potential importers in that country from acquiring steel from A, *i.e.*, the protection case.[24]

Wages and Output in A

Factors available, 800 labour-days
Income rate in A, $5 per day per factor
Amount of corn produced and consumed, 1,000 units
Unit real costs of producing corn, 2/5 labour-days
Price of corn in A, $2/5 \times \$5 = \$2$ per unit

Amount of steel produced and consumed, 1,000 units
Unit real costs of producing steel, 2/5 labour-days
Unit money costs of producing steel, $2/5 \times \$5 = \$2$
Assume that the price of steel is set at $2.20 per unit.

Wages and Output in B

Factors available, 160 labour-days
Income rate in B, $4 per day per factor
Amount of corn produced and consumed, 200 units
Unit real costs of producing corn, ½ labour-days
Price of corn in B, $\frac{1}{2} \times \$4 = \$2$ per unit

[24]In this problem the factors of production are assumed to be fully employed at all times. Thus given the amount of one commodity produced and the unit labour-day costs of producing the commodities, it is a matter of simple arithmetic to calculate the amount of the other commodity that will be produced. Of course competitive forces are assumed to settle the rate of factor income in each country, and also the volume of agricultural products that are to be produced. The steel monopolists are assumed to set their volumes of output and their prices at point of monopolistic equilibrium after due regard for their cost and demand functions.

By measuring real costs in homogeneous labour-day units, we avoid complicating the problem with changes in the relative prices of different factors as industrial activity shifts from, say, manufacture to agriculture. The cost of labour would be expected to rise relatively to capital in that case. Since this assumption is not material to the theoretical results of this problem, we are not subject to the same criticism that Ohlin and Mason have directed at the theory of comparative advantage.

Amount of steel produced and consumed in B, 100 units
Unit real cost of steel production, 3/5 labour-days
Unit money cost of steel production, $3/5 \times \$4 = \$2.40$
Assume that the price of steel is set at \$2.50 per unit.

*Real and Money Incomes in A and B before Trade Is
Opened (under Protective Tariff on Steel in B)*

Money income in A = \$4,400
Money income of the hired factors in A = \$4,000
Real income in A = 1,000 corn + 1,000 steel

Money income in B = \$650
Money income of the hired factors in B = \$640
Real income in B = 200 corn + 100 steel.

Under each of the cases examined, namely protection, free
trade, and free trade with subsidy, the elementary requirements for
equilibrium in the economic system are fulfilled.   Total money
income is equal to total money expenditure in each country, and
costs of production plus profits is equal to selling price of the
product multiplied by volume of output.

As trade is opened between A and B, if we assume that
momentarily prices remain as before, the first movement will be
an export of steel from A, where its price is 30 cents per unit lower
than in B.   Corn will not move at first as its equilibrium price is
the same in both countries.   This unilateral trade from A to B
will cause a movement of specie from B to A, so that prices will
fall in the former country, and with them the price and costs of
production of corn, so that soon the trade will become bilateral,
corn flowing from B to A and steel from A to B.   For purposes of
simplification, we have assumed that country A is so large relative
to country B that the flow of specie into A, which occurred before
equilibrium in the commodity balance of trade was brought about,
has no influence on the money income of factors in A.[25]   This
assumption does not affect the theory, but it does materially
simplify the diagrammatical representation.   The cost curves in

[25]An alternative assumption may be made, namely that country A sterilizes
its specie imports so that they are not allowed to influence prices in that country.
Since, in this discussion, we are primarily concerned with relative and not
absolute money costs, the assumption that country A is very large relative to
country B or that country A sterilizes its gold imports is not necessary.   The
entire relative change in costs, consequent on the opening of trade, may be
imputed in the diagrams to country B's cost curves.

A remain fixed, regardless of the change in demand, or the shift in the cost curves in A.

The demand curves of the two monopolists undergo such a reorientation when trade becomes free that the single firm producing steel can no longer operate in country B in spite of the reduction in money wages which occurs in that country. The following wage and output positions result in the two countries from the establishment of free trade.

Wages and Output in A

> Factor income rate, $5 per day
> Amount of corn produced, 950 units
> Amount of corn imported, 110 units
> Unit real cost of corn production, 7/20 labour-days
> Price of corn, 7/20 × $5 = $1.75 per unit

> Unit real cost of steel production, 3/10 labour-days
> Amount of steel produced, 1,461 units
> Money cost of steel production, 8/25 × $5 = $1.60 per unit
> Assume that the new price of steel is $1.65 per unit
> Steel exports, 117 units

Wages and Output in B

> Factor income rate, $3.50 per day
> Unit real cost of producing corn, ½ labour-days[26]
> Amount of corn produced, 320 units
> Price of corn, ½ × $3.50 = $1.75 per unit

Balance of trade between A and B:

> A to B — 117 units of steel (117 × $1.65 = $193 *approx.*)
> B to A — 110 units of corn (110 × $1.75 = $193 *approx.*)

Income in A and B under free trade:

> Money income in A, $4,073
> Money income of the hired factors in A, $4,000
> Real income in A, 1,060 corn + 1,344 steel

> Money income in B, $560
> Money income of the hired factors in B, $560
> Real income in B, 210 corn + 117 steel.

---

[26]It will be noted that although the output of corn has increased in B by 120 units under free trade as compared with protection, the unit factor cost of corn production is assumed to have remained unchanged. This is due to the fact that we have assumed that the natural resources (land) no longer used in the production of steel in B, could be transferred to agriculture. This enlargement of the agricultural domain is assumed to have postponed the operation of diminishing returns per unit of labour-days employed in corn production.

Although no pretensions are made that this is a typical case, there seems to be no reason why the situation should not occur, granted the realism of the cost and demand functions we have postulated in the diagrams below. The results of trade are obviously beneficial to both countries as a comparison of the real incomes with the protection case reveals.

It is not, however, apparent that the real income in B is maximized under free trade. A logical plan would be to subsidize the steel industry in B before it is eliminated by competition from A's industry. The effect of this subsidy would be to induce A to lower its price, otherwise the steel industry in B would not only come to dominate its own market but to export to A. The demand curve for the product of A's steel industry is thus artificially shifted downward, until it becomes tangential to the industry's cost curve. In forcing A's demand curve down and to the right, a gap is opened between the demand curve and B's cost curve equal to the amount of the subsidy. This does not mean that trade between the two countries is eliminated by the subsidy to B's steel industry. An equilibrium point is re-established at which A will export some steel to B and B will export some corn to A. Granting the presence of perfect fluidity in the market, the final equilibrium reached would be a stable one. The subsidy would be equal to the difference between the average cost of production in A and B for steel at the point of equilibrium.

The following wage and output situation may be presumed to obtain in the case of subsidized output of steel in B:

Wages and Output in A

Factor income rate in A, $5 per labour-day
Amount of corn produced, 998 units
Corn imported, 40 units
Unit real cost of corn production, 3/8 labour-days
Price of corn, 3/8 × $5 = *$1.87 per unit*

Unit real cost of steel production, 7/25 labour-days
Amount of steel produced, 1,521 units
Unit money cost of steel production, 7/25 × $5 = $1.40
Amount of steel exported, 53.6 units
Price of steel, *$1.40 per unit.*

Wages and Output in B

Factor income rate in B, $3.60 per labour-day
Unit real cost of corn production, 13/25 labour-days
Amount of corn produced, 210 units
Unit money cost of corn production, 13/25 × $3.60 = *$1.87* (price of corn)

Unit real cost of steel production, 13/32 labour-days
Amount of steel produced, 130 units
Unit money cost of steel production, 13/32 × $3.60 = $1.46
Price of steel, *$1.40 per unit*
Subsidy to the steel industry, 6 cents per unit of output.

Balance of trade between A and B:
  A to B — 53.6 units of steel (53.6 × $1.40 = $75 *approx.*)
  B to A — 40 units of corn (40 × $1.87 = $75 *approx.*)

Income in A and B under the subsidy:
  Money income in A, $4,000
  Money income of the hired factors in A, $4,000
  Real income in A, 1,038 corn + 1,467 steel

  Money income in B, $576
  Money income of the hired factors in B, $576
  Real income in B, 170 corn + 183.6 steel.

In the last situation, when steel production in B is made possible by a subsidy, real income in that country is higher than under either of the former situations. The economy is better off than under free trade as at the sacrifice of 40 units of corn, 66.6 additional units of steel are acquired. As compared with the protection case, B has sacrificed 30 units of corn but she has gained nearly 84 units of steel. Since the unit value of steel is over 90 per cent that of corn in the equilibrium situation created by the subsidy, one may assume that the real income measured in terms of economic welfare reaches a higher level under the subsidy than under either protection or free trade. Of course a tariff, by careful adjustment, could be made to serve the same purpose as the subsidy. In A the subsidy arrangement is probably the most advantageous also, from the real income standpoint, while from her point of view, free trade is certainly to be preferred to complete exclusion from B's market, as under the first case. It is perhaps superfluous to emphasize that nothing definite can be said about the result, in terms of welfare, of altering the physical real income of a country by decreasing the available supply of one commodity and increasing another. In this example, A loses 22 units of corn and gains 123 units of steel under the subsidy as compared with free trade, and with an exchange ratio of steel to corn of over 9 to 10, the application of utility analysis would indicate that she is a net gainer from the subsidy arrangement.

By way of summary, the real physical incomes obtained by each country in the three situations may be noted:

For A

Protection (no trade case)..........1,000 corn + 1,000 steel
Free trade.......................1,060   "   + 1,344   "
Free trade with subsidy...........1,038   "   + 1,467   "

For B

Protection (no trade case).......... 200 corn + 100 steel
Free trade....................... 210   "   + 117 "
Free trade with subsidy........... 170   "   + 183.6 "

The diagrammatical exposition of this problem follows.

Figure 3, parts 1 and 2, illustrates the conditions for equilibrium in the increasing cost industry (corn production) in A and B before and after trade is opened between the two countries by the removal of B's protective tariff against steel imports from A. A_1B_1 and A_2B_2 are the domestic prices of corn before trade is opened. To simplify the exposition, these prices are assumed to be equal.[27] Under free trade, the supply and demand curves in B fall in response to the flow of specie to A, and corn flows from B to A. Under free trade equilibrium, P_1M_1 (equal to P_2M_2) is the international and domestic price of corn. M_1N_1 (equal to M_2N_2) is the amount of corn traded. The last step in this example, namely trade when a subsidy is being provided for B's steel industry, is omitted from figure 3. The reader may easily insert it for himself. Under the type of subsidy used in the arithmetical example, the curves in B (figure 3, part 2) would shift upward until the amount of corn exported from the corn surplus market (country B) just pays for the steel exported from A. In this example every adjustment which occurs in the steel industry in A and B reacts upon the equilibrium amount of corn production in the two countries.

Figure 4, part 1, illustrates three possible positions for equilibrium in the steel industry in country A, namely under protection for country B's steel industry, under free trade between country A and country B, and under free trade when a potential competitor in B is being subsidized by his government.

C_1C_1 is the total average unit cost curve for the single firm in

[27]The diagrams are not drawn to scale, but lines, theoretically of equal length are drawn as such.

Country A

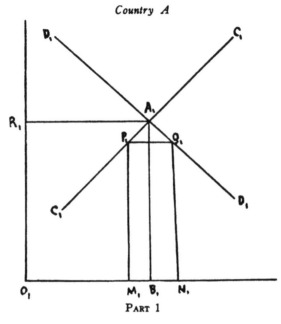

PART 1

Country B

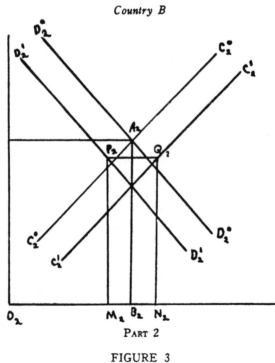

PART 2

FIGURE 3

A, as the C_2C_2 curves are for the firm in B under the three assumptions of protection, free trade, and subsidy mentioned above. The D_1D_1 curves in figure 4, part 1, are the demand curves facing the single producer in A under the three situations. The curve $D_1^\circ D_1^\circ$ relates only to the demand in A under no-trade conditions, but the other two curves $D_1^1 D_1^1$ and $D_1^2 D_1^2$ relate to the total market in A and B and are drawn up under the assumption that the steel producer in A is facing an actual or potential competitor in B. $D_2^\circ D_2^\circ$ is the demand curve for steel in country B in the initial position. P_1A_1 and P_2A_2 indicate the prices of steel in A and B in the initial position.

The demand curve $D_1^1 D_1^1$ is inserted in figure 4, part 2, to show that under free trade equilibrium, the steel producer in B is unable to meet the price $Q_1^1 B_1^1$ at which the firm in A maximizes its profits.[28] Regardless of the volume of output in B, that is, even if the firm in B produces at the optimum point on its own average unit cost curve, it will not be able to produce without sustaining a loss. This fact is implied in the construction of the curve $D_1^1 D_1^1$ which is drawn up to indicate what price the firm in A should charge in view of the potential competition from the firm in B.

$D_1^2 D_1^2$ is the demand curve for the output of the steel industry in A when B's industry is being subsidized by an amount per unit of its output equal to the difference between the average unit costs in B and A at the point of equilibrium production in the industry in each country. The approach to this equilibrium situation must be by experimental extension of the subsidy to the steel industry in B as long as the industry in A threatens it with extinction. The price cutting by the industry in A will stop when the curve $D_1^2 D_1^2$ becomes tangential to A's average cost curve. We assume that the slope of $D_1^2 D_1^2$ is greater than the slope of the cost curve for the firm in B at the point M in figure 4, part 2. This assumption is necessary to ensure that there will be no undercutting the equilibrium price (AB) by the steel industry in B. L is a point of stable equilibrium for A's industry as point M is for B's. ML_2

---

[28]Recalling our numerical example, the unit labour-day cost of steel in B under the subsidy was 13/25. The industry in B was not then producing at the optimum. If we assume the lowest average unit cost of steel production in B to be 12/25 labour-days, at a \$3.50 wage rate in that country, B could not meet A's free trade price of \$1.65 for steel. (\$3.59 $\times$ 12/25 = \$1.68.)

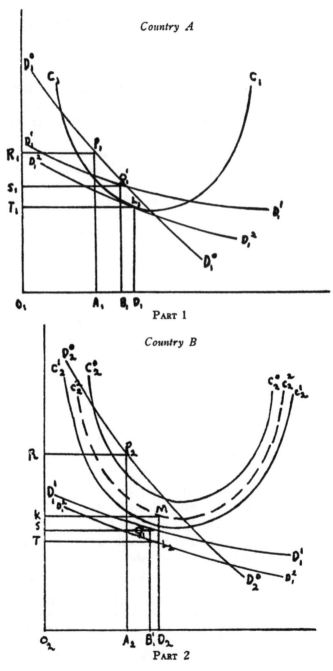

Country A

PART 1

Country B

PART 2

FIGURE 4

is the amount of the subsidy and L_2D_2 ($=L_1D_1$) the international price of steel.

The strength of the argument illustrated by this example obviously depends upon the validity of constructing demand curves such as $D_1^{'}D_1^{'}$ and $D_1^{'}D_1^{'}$. The sequence of events in reaching the equilibrium indicated in the subsidy case may be presumed to be a payment of a subsidy by the government in B when its steel industry is incurring a loss, a resulting fall in the demand for the product of A's steel industry, and a consequent cut in price by the latter. This cut in price would have to be followed by an increase in the subsidy in B and so on until the industry in A is no longer making monopoly profits, and the stable equilibrium described above is attained in both industries in each country. The curve $D_1^{'}D_1^{'}$ is drawn under the assumption that the actual demand curve for the output of the industry in A is a function not only of the international demand for steel, but of the output of the industry in B, that is, if the industry in A set its price above the lowest average cost of producing steel in B, the latter country would again become a factor in the steel market. In view of the relative smallness of the industry in B, the slope of $D_1^{'}D_1^{'}$ as drawn does not show any marked irregularity, but no claim is made for its validity if the firm in A substantially reduces the volume of its output. In view of the relative money costs in A and B, however, such a move would be a very unprofitable one.[29]

The points raised above cast some doubt upon the adequacy of our analytical apparatus for dealing with international trade situations when the monopolistic and discriminatory practices treated by modern value theory are extended to foreign trade. The solution to many problems will probably be found in breaking

[29]The nature of the demand for the product of the steel industries in A and B would probably be much more complicated than the simple elastic demand curves of our diagram. If for example A reduced its output drastically, B's capacity to take up the slack would be limited despite extensive subsidies owing to the small actual and potential capacity of its industry. Consequently under a drastic cut in output by A, the demand curve for steel would enable sales to be made at a higher price than is indicated in the diagram. At the same time if A tries to meet the competition from the subsidized industry in B and produces as indicated in the diagram, as indeed the cost situation there indicated would oblige him to do, the total demand curve for steel would become practically horizontal over the part of its range in the vicinity of the point of equilibrium indicated.

down the distinction between international and domestic value theory, although the particular problems of international price equilibrium will have to be faced when doing so. It should be made clear that there is little in the formal theory of imperfect competition to preclude the occurrence of the price level adjustments upon which equilibrium in the international balance of payments depends. Because it is profitable for monopolists, or those who sell upon an imperfectly competitive market, to maintain rigid prices and curtail output when their inelastic demand curves shift to the left during depression, is no economic reason why their prices should not be adjusted to changes in costs and prices of related parts of the economy in response to general credit changes as a result of international monetary transactions. Of course, if prices are arbitrarily established without regard to their short run profitableness, the old concept of a fluctuating regional or national price level breaks down. In that case the burden of adjustments which must be made in the balance of trade will be thrown on non-monopolistic export and import industries.

ON THE STUDY OF POLITICS IN CANADA

C. B. MACPHERSON

"ANY attempt to make Politics more worthy of the name of a science has met with little academic collaboration. The metaphysician dislikes its empiricism, the natural scientist suspects its human uncertainty, the historian abhors its attempt to theorize; each makes a peace offering of it to the others. It has been left to the unsympathetic guardianship of the moral philosopher, to the unappetizing nourishment of local and arbitrary fact served up by the lawyer, to the occasional help of the suspect follower after psychological opinions, and to the unscrupulous attentions of men of affairs."[1] The vigour of these remarks flows from their author's position as advocate of a special type of political science which at the time of writing had yet to make its way in the academic world. Yet they are not entirely irrelevant to the study of politics in its broadest sense in Canadian universities. There politics has had a chequered career, in uneasy union with its neighbours—economics, law, and history. And while the work of Canadians in political science has produced a valuable nucleus of scholarship, yet we find frequent complaints[2] of the paucity of work done in studying the actual operation of political institutions in Canada. Further, the amount and range of graduate work in political science in the last decade or so, compared with that done in history or economics, have been small.

These facts present a problem to Canadian political scientists which it is the object of this essay at least to state. From a survey of the development of the teaching of political science in Canadian universities and of graduate and published work by Canadian students of the subject, an attempt is made to discover the factors which have brought it to its present position in Canada; and in the light of this analysis some possibilities for its future development are considered.

[1]G. E. G. Catlin, *The Science and Method of Politics* (New York, 1927), p. 94.

[2]*Cf.* the prefaces of R. A. MacKay's *The Unreformed Senate of Canada* (Oxford, 1926) and R. McG. Dawson's *Constitutional Issues in Canada* (Oxford, 1933).

The content of political science and the boundaries between it and the related subjects of law, history, economics, and philosophy have changed considerably over the last fifty years; this means that "politics" or "political science" (the terms are here used interchangeably) cannot be rigidly defined in advance. In general, however, it may be said that in early (nineteenth-century) usage political science meant the study of the politically organized community in every aspect, and so included what modern usage terms constitutional history, constitutional law, jurisprudence, economic theory, economic history, and political science. Political science in modern usage is understood to include the study of political ideas and of government, the latter differentiated from constitutional studies by emphasis on the processes of actual government and on the extra-constitutional factors in this process.

A survey of the teaching of political science, based on the calendars of Canadian universities over the last fifty years, will serve to give a general picture of its growth and present position in relation to other social studies.

Whereas economics appeared in university curricula as early as 1878 at Queen's and 1881 at Dalhousie, a start was not made with politics until ten years later. The first courses in politics were given at Toronto in 1888 and at Queen's in 1889. Previous to this the nearest approach to a course in politics in any Canadian university was a course in ethics dealing, among other things, with the ethical aspects of property, the family, the civic community, and the state, given at Queen's in 1876 by Professor John Watson.[3] In 1888 W. J. Ashley was appointed professor of political economy and constitutional history at Toronto, and an honour department was in-

---

[3]A similar course in philosophy went before the study of politics at Dalhousie, where a course on moral institutions, on the basis, nature, and function of the state in relation to morality, was given from 1895 to 1901; history and economics began in 1912 and politics in 1923. At Toronto as early as 1854 the curriculum included "The Elements of Political Philosophy and Economy" in the pass work of the second year, Paley's *Political Philosophy* in the third year, and Mill's *Political Economy* in the fourth year; in the *Calendar* of 1860-1 a course in ethics, metaphysics, and civil polity was included but civil polity was not taught. Edward Blake founded scholarships in 1877 "for the promotion and encouragement of the study of the Science of Politics, Political Economy, Civil Polity and Constitutional History". But at no time until 1888 does any instruction appear to have been given in any of these subjects.

augurated under the title of "Political Science". The subjects comprised the history and criticism of political ideas from Aristotle to Green, the constitutional histories of England and Canada, constitutional law of England, Canada, and the United States, history of Roman law, general jurisprudence, international law, political economy based on Walker and Mill, history and criticism of economic theories, and economic history.

In terms of modern practice only the first of these could be described as political science. But a new discipline such as this course was intended to be had naturally to draw largely from all the contributory subjects and attempt to weld them into a whole. Political science was indeed at this period a discipline *in posse* rather than *in esse*. Ashley in his inaugural lecture[4] defined it as "systematic knowledge concerning the state or political society". He relied on constitutional history and law to examine "the manner in which public authority is constituted and the legal limits of its power", and on a comparative study of constitutions to lead to a consideration of the merits, demerits, and possibilities of different forms of government. Then, since the underlying causes of constitutional differences and changes would be found to be economic, the study of political economy and economic history was the natural complement of constitutional studies. Finally, since moral judgments could not be dispensed with and since "the final test in any matter must be the welfare of the state", some training in political philosophy was necessary to complete the course. Thus was unity to be established between these four subjects, a unity which was justified in Ashley's mind by the need of a broad training in citizenship to avoid the perils of the new and ignorant democracy.

But no sooner was this unity conceived and its realization attempted than disintegrating tendencies became apparent. The legal, constitutional, and economic subjects began to move away in directions of their own. In 1889 the teaching staff in political science was appointed to be, in addition, the teaching staff in the Faculty of Law, which now became a teaching faculty; the result was an increasing emphasis on legal subjects in the political science course, the first three years of the law course being made identical with the second, third, and fourth years of the political science course. After the appointment of Professor Mavor as professor of political economy

---

[4] *What is Political Science?* (Toronto, 1888).

and constitutional history in 1892, the number of courses in law and history increased, while the single course in political philosophy (now from Plato to Green) remained.

By 1894, besides this one course in politics there were two in history, two in constitutional history, five in economics, three in constitutional law, and five in other law subjects. In the following year some enlargement in the scope of the study of politics is seen, in that the course in the history and criticism of political theories was changed, being now based on Sidgwick's *Elements*, Pollock's *History of the Science of Politics*, Bonar's *Philosophy and Political Economy*, Ritchie's *Principles of State Interference*, Seeley's *Introduction to Political Science*, Mackenzie's *Introduction to Social Philosophy*, and Barker's *Plato and Aristotle*.

No substantial change was made in this course or in the whole arrangement of courses until 1911, when a course in comparative government, based on Lowell's *Government of England*, his *Governments and Parties in Continental Europe*, Bryce's *American Commonwealth*, Cromer's *Ancient and Modern Imperialism*, Jebb's *Colonial Nationalism*, and other works, was added to the curriculum. In addition, a course in public administration was established for students in commerce and finance. In the same year the teaching of constitutional history was transferred to the History Department where it proceeded to develop along lines of its own, while still a constituent of the political science course. The economics teaching had been steadily increasing and becoming more specialized. Already in 1911, therefore, the old compound political science was separating to a considerable extent into its elements, and although politics was now directly represented by both political theory and comparative government the bulk of the students' work was still in economics, law, and history.

In 1924 an attempt was made to allow political science greater scope than it had so far enjoyed in its conjunction with economics. The union of politics with economics was broken, and the political science course was made over into two divisions, one in politics and law and one in economics. This arrangement continued until 1929, when further expansion of the law teaching resulted in the establishment of a separate honour course in law, but political science was subordinate to law throughout this period. Some expansion of political science was observable, however; after 1927 there were three courses in politics, namely, comparative politics, history of political theory, and advanced political theory (the theory, functions, institutions, and limits of the modern state). With the withdrawal of all the law subjects from the political science course, politics was reunited with economics, and in the joint course economics was, and remains, preponderant. In the next few years experiments were made with courses in the structure of the modern state but this, together with comparative politics, has not found a permanent place in the curriculum. At present (1936-7) the teaching of politics at Toronto consists of three courses, one in the development of political ideas, one in advanced political theory (dealing with contemporary theories of the state and the process of government), and one on the state and economic life.[5]

Thus the development at Toronto displays a consistent subordination of political science to one or more of the related subjects with which it, in the beginning, formed a single whole planned as one self-contained intellectual discipline. The other three parts of the whole, with their increasing specialization, expanded and began to be self-sufficient intellectually before any such movement was discernable in political science. The causes of this are discussed later, but we may note here the peculiar result it has had. For some time after economics, history, and law had ceased in effect to be parts of one discipline and had become each one discipline in its own right, they were still taught in union with politics. Thus while the intention remained what it was at first—that these others should with politics form one coherent system of studies—the result has been rather the overshadowing of politics by the others.

The development at Queen's University has been somewhat different. We have already noted that the ethical aspects of certain social and political institutions were dealt with by the Department of Logic, Metaphysics, and Ethics as early as 1876, and it was within this same department that a course in economics first appeared in 1878, the arrival of the new subject being signalized two years later by a change in the title of the subjects of study to "Mental and Moral Philosophy and Political Economy". In 1890, after the appointment

[5]Since this was written a new development has begun (1937-8) by which three courses in government (dealing with Canadian, British, and American and European governments) are being added to the three courses mentioned above.

of Adam Shortt as lecturer on political science, we find the subjects of study redivided, political science being made separate from mental and moral philosophy. The term political science was used to include both politics and economics, and in the new Department of Political Science we find the emphasis almost equally divided between the two. No law courses were given for any Arts degree. The first courses in politics were established in 1889, and in the early years the approach to politics was largely philosophical, as was to be expected from its parentage.[6] The "Regular" or pass course was "a critical examination of leading theories of the State, and a discussion of the nature of Social and Political Relations", being based on class-room study of Plato's *Republic*, Hobbes's *Leviathan*, and Locke's *Civil Government*. The honours courses, on "Society and the State", were based on Aristotle's *Politics*, Mill's *Representative Government*, Maine's *Ancient Law*, Carlyle's *Sartor Resartus* and *Past and Present*, and Montague's *Limits of Individual Liberty*, and, for the second year, Bluntschli's *Theory of the State*, Holland's *Elements of Jurisprudence*, Arnold's *Culture and Anarchy*, and Rae's *Contemporary Socialism*.

By 1905 a shifting of interest towards the study of government becomes noticeable with the inclusion of such books as Wilson's *The State, Historical and Practical Politics,* and Lowell's *Governments and Parties in Continental Europe* in the basic texts for the honours course. The new emphasis became more pronounced with the reorganization of the whole political science curriculum after Dr. O. D. Skelton had succeeded Adam Shortt as professor of political science in 1908. The course in the history of political theory remained as a pass subject, but the other theoretical courses gave way to the study of government, with particular attention being given to Canadian and imperial structure and problems.

In 1919 the political science curriculum was again reorganized and the scope and number of courses in politics considerably increased. Besides an introductory course dealing both with theories of the state and with the process of government, courses were

[6]The Queen's tradition in general was that of the Scottish universities. John Watson, who introduced both political philosophy and political economy as branches of moral philosophy, was a product of the philosophy school at Glasgow, and Adam Shortt, who subsequently built up the teaching of politics and economics, was trained at Queen's itself and at Glasgow and Edinburgh.

included in modern political theory, the government of the United Kingdom, the government of Canada, Canadian constitutional law, Canadian national problems, modern democracies, international law and organization, new democratic constitutions of Europe, imperial relations, imperial problems, and political parties. Only a few of these were given each year, but the extent to which Queen's was developing its teaching on the governmental side is strikingly indicated by this listing. As before, politics was carried on in conjunction with economics.[7]

Since 1932 it has been possible for an undergraduate to take an honours degree for which the major part of the work is done in politics. This was made possible by the virtual separation of economics from politics. Within the politics course the relative importance of constitutional law and history has increased and the emphasis on the structure of government is, therefore, somewhat greater than before. The present scope of the teaching of politics may be indicated by the list of courses offered (1935-6): introduction to politics, modern political theory, Canadian government and constitutional law, English constitutional history and law, international law and organization, the British Commonwealth of Nations; and reading courses in comparative government, English constitutional history and law, and contemporary political problems.

The development of the teaching of politics at Queen's can be seen to have differed from that at Toronto in that politics has taken for itself a somewhat wider field, and has given more attention to the study of government, and particularly to Canadian and imperial government, and less to political ideas. The greater scope of politics teaching at Queen's demands some explanation further than the superficial fact of its departmental organization separate from economics. Perhaps that explanation is to be sought in the contrast in the early development at the two universities. At Toronto, law and history, as well as economics, were regarded from the first as integral parts of the scheme of studies which was called political science and which was created out of nothing with the arrival of a professor from England. In this complete scheme politics, apart from law and history, was a minor element. At Queen's, on the other hand, both economics and politics emerged gradually from

[7]In 1912 the name of the course was changed from "Political Science" to "Political and Economic Science".

moral philosophy and, as a branch or descendant of philosophy, politics enjoyed in its formative years an importance of its own which prevented it being displaced by law or history, which, as at Toronto, at first might be substantial parts of a political science, but afterwards would grow into specialisms of their own and leave politics inadequately provided for.[8]

At Dalhousie University the teaching of politics has a shorter history than at Toronto or Queen's but it now occupies as important a place. Dalhousie was fortunate in having a chair in government and political science established at the relatively late date of 1923, for this meant that the study of politics could begin in an atmosphere free from the memory of previous subordination to its neighbour subjects.[9] By that date politics was recognized as a subject having sufficient content to constitute a separate department, and it was organized as such. From the outset a scheme of six courses was arranged including: (1) government of the British Commonwealth, based on Anson, Bryce, Dicey, Keith, Lowell, and Kennedy; (2) general political science, based on Sidgwick's *Elements of Politics,* supplemented by Seeley, Bryce, Bluntschli, Wilson, Willoughby, *etc.*; (3) history of political theory, from Plato to Bolshevism, based on Dunning and the original texts; (4) social theory, based on Giddings; (5) constitutional history of England; (6) international law. In this scheme we see theory well represented while the structure of government is approached through comparative government, constitutional history, and law.

After the appointment of Professor MacKay as professor of political science in 1927 the curriculum was expanded with the admission of courses in international relations, and since then this subject has gained an established place. At present (1936-7) the Department of Government and Political Science offers the following scheme of seven courses: (1) government of the British Commonwealth; (2) international relations and problems; (3) the modern state, its theory, constitution and functions (especially social

[8]In terms of origin the difference is that between the Scottish tradition represented by Watson and Shortt at Queen's, and the Oxford historical tradition represented by Ashley at Toronto. With Ashley it was the historical method rather than the application of it to any particular branch that was important, though his own interest lay chiefly in its application to economic phenomena.

[9]*Cf.* n. 3.

and economic), based on Laski's *State in Theory and Practice*, Finer's *Theory and Practice of Modern Government*, Slichter's *Modern Economic Society*, Buell's *New Governments in Europe*, and Brady's *Canada*; (4) constitution and government of Canada, based on Dawson's *Constitutional Issues in Canada* and Kennedy's *Statutes, Treaties and Documents of the Canadian Constitution*; (5) municipal government and administration; (6) introduction to law and legislation; (7) constitutional and administrative law. Three additional courses are available for honours and M.A. students, namely, (8) problems of the British Commonwealth (seminar); (9) international law; and (10) history of political theory. In general the development at Dalhousie has been similar to that at Queen's in recent years, and has produced up to now a rather similar curriculum. Politics has achieved a fairly substantial place, in this case a separate departmental organization; its relations are closer with law than with economics; the scope of its teaching is fairly wide; and there is more emphasis on the structure and process of government than on political theory or the history of political ideas.

At McGill University the teaching of politics began with the establishment of the Department of Economic and Political Science in 1901, and has since developed largely under the influence of Professor Leacock who brought to the whole subject the American approach exemplified in the Chicago system. In 1903 an honour course in history and economics was offered, in two divisions: (1) history and politics, and (2) economics and politics; and politics appears to have developed ever since largely in conjunction with economics and history. While various experiments have been tried in more advanced or more specialized fields, the core of the teaching has been in three courses: (1) elements of politics, including general principles and comparative government; (2) government of Canada, from a constitutional approach; and (3) history of political theory. The latter course only achieved a secure position in the curriculum after 1919. The emphasis on the whole has been on government rather than on political thought, and Canadian and imperial problems and policy have been given considerable attention, more especially in courses for graduate students.

A Department of Political Science was established at the University of Saskatchewan in 1911 and the teaching was from the first closely related to the teaching of history. Apart from an introductory course on the elements of politics, the emphasis was upon British and Canadian constitutional history and law, though courses in the structure and process of government and in the history of political theory were given intermittently. In 1928, following the appointment of Professor R. McG. Dawson, a wider scheme of courses was inaugurated and since that time courses have been given in general political science and government of Canada, governments of the British Empire, governments of the United States and Europe, and problems of modern democracy, with seminar courses, for advanced students, in Canadian government and in imperial and foreign relations of the British Empire. Courses in the history of political ideas have been offered intermittently, but the emphasis throughout has been on the structure and process of government and especially of Canadian and British government. At the University of British Columbia politics has been taught since 1920 under Professor Angus. The basic courses have been those in constitutional government and in legal history and jurisprudence, with additional courses in imperial problems and problems of the Pacific. In the other universities in general less attention is given to political science than in those mentioned above, although the Universities of New Brunswick and of Western Ontario both provide comprehensive groups of courses in government and political theory.

From a survey such as the foregoing certain general characteristics regarding the teaching of politics in Canada are apparent. The most noticeable is that politics has consistently had a less substantial place than might have been expected in view of the growth of the other social studies. As to its content, in its origin and early years it was treated from a philosophical angle to which was added a considerable study of constitutional law and history; where, later, the teaching of politics has expanded it has done so in the direction of the study of the structure and process of government rather than of ideas and political philosophy; and, within this trend, an increasing emphasis on Canadian government and political problems has been noticeable. All these facts require explanation, and it is not difficult to see them as related in the first instance to Canadian academic development, and, more broadly, as resulting from Canadian social requirements.

When social studies were first introduced into Canada, the Canadian universities were modelled on the older British universities.

Their Arts faculties offered chiefly rounded disciplines based on classical, philosophical, or mathematical studies. The nineteenth century was not an age of intellectual specialization and in England the newer social studies were slow in gaining university recognition because they were not thought to be a necessary part of the education of a statesman, a civil servant, or a gentleman. In the British universities what we now understand as political science was neglected until well into the present century; before that, politics was studied only in so far as it was either a part of classical studies, a branch of moral philosophy, or an aspect of constitutional history or law.[10] Economics, on the other hand, had earlier attained an independent respected place.[11]

In these circumstances it was natural that politics should have appeared at first in Canadian universities in a minor position and limited to political philosophy and constitutional studies. The study of the Canadian and United States constitutions was added to the traditional study of the English constitution, but such politics as was taught was, at first, as in England, simply part of a curriculum arranged in accordance with the educational ideal of an all-round training.

However, the requirements of Canadian life were different from the English. A young and rapidly developing community, Canada had little time for the leisured intellectual pursuits which the more

[10]The first chair in political science was established at Oxford in 1912, following a readership established in 1910. A chair was established at Cambridge in 1927. At London politics has been taught since 1896 at the School of Economics where chairs were established in public administration in 1913 and in political science in 1915.

[11]Senior was appointed to the Drummond chair of political economy at Oxford in 1825; McCulloch became professor of political economy at University College, London, in 1828, a position later held by such men as Cairnes and Jevons; at Cambridge, Fawcett was the first professor in 1863, followed by Marshall in 1885. At the Scottish universities by the middle of the nineteenth century economics was being studied as a subject in itself and not merely as a branch of moral philosophy, although chairs were not established until 1870 at Edinburgh and 1896 at Glasgow. The establishment of chairs is, at Oxford and Cambridge at least, no evidence of the strength of a subject's position, but in general economics was ahead of political science in obtaining recognition. The flowering of political philosophy at Oxford in the nineteenth century may be thought an exception to this—certainly it held a more honoured place than economics—but, as under Green and Bosanquet, it was more a branch of philosophy than what is now understood as political science.

stable society with its steady surplus income could afford. Ashley at Toronto in 1888 had justified the new system of studies partly on its own intellectual merits and partly as a necessary training in citizenship. But the direction in which these studies were to move was foreshadowed more clearly by J. G. Bourinot in an address to the Royal Society of Canada in 1889.[12] It was the practical usefulness of political science which appealed to him. He commended the new courses in the universities for their practical value in training future generations of politicians, administrators, judges, lawyers, and other public men to deal competently with the constitutional and economic issues which had arisen and would arise in Canadian political life. With usefulness as the criterion, it was natural that constitutional history and law, and economics, should come to the forefront. And it may be noted that in a rapidly expanding economy law is not only the most lucrative of all the professions but also the most likely route to eminence and power in public life. The resulting prestige of the lawyer in the community was reflected in the increasing prestige of legal and constitutional studies within the universities, and legal and constitutional studies absorbed much of the attention which in a more developed country might have gone to political science.[13]

As long as, and to the extent that, the English university ideal remained, little attempt was made to relate courses to Canadian needs. For some decades the addition of Canadian constitutional history and law to the typical English university course was the whole extent of the adaptation. The appearance of courses on government after 1900 is probably a reflection of the growth of United States influence in Canadian academic life,[14] for the American universities early emphasized government rather than political ideas, and before 1900 courses on the structure and process of government, distinct from constitutional history and law, were well developed there. The study of specifically Canadian government (apart from Canadian

[12]"The Study of Political Science in Canadian Universities" (*Transactions of the Royal Society of Canada*, sect. 2, 1889, pp. 3 ff.).

[13]As it was doing by this time in the United States, which had previously had the same experience.

[14]The study of government was first introduced in Canada with American texts: Wilson's *The State*, and Lowell's *Governments and Parties in Continental Europe*, although English studies such as Bryce's *American Commonwealth* and Dicey's *Law and Public Opinion in England* were soon added.

constitutional history and law) was not seriously attempted until 1910, and even then grew slowly for want of material for undergraduate study. The study of its own government is a natural subject for the political science of any country, and its comparatively late appearance, and that of suitable material, may be attributed partly to the late development of a Canadian national consciousness and partly to the fact that the similarity of the Canadian to the English and United States systems of government made a specifically Canadian study seem relatively unnecessary.

Political science has had a continuous history of fifty years in Canadian university teaching, but the amount of published work and graduate work has been small compared to that in economics with its only slightly longer career. Moreover, the work which has been done has been largely confined to the last fifteen years.[15] Professor

[15]A few earlier works must not be overlooked. Alpheus Todd's *On Parliamentary Government in England* (vol. I, 1867; vol. II, 1869) was an attempt to elucidate the actual working of parliamentary government, and in particular the relations between crown and Parliament and the development and functions of the Cabinet, through a systematic analysis of the laws, usages, and traditions of the various branches of the British government. The author, the librarian of the Canadian House of Commons, did not attempt to conceal the purposes of his work: to assert the principle of executive authority against the encroachments of the democratic element which "is everywhere gaining the mastery, and is seeking the overthrow of all institutions that are intended to be a check upon the popular will" (vol. I, p. x), and to guide the statesmen of the newly-formed Dominion in the true principles of British government.

J. G. Bourinot, besides his descriptive lectures on *Federal Government in Canada* (Baltimore, 1889), published some studies in political science such as the three papers entitled *Canadian Studies in Comparative Politics* (Montreal, 1890), and his *Local Government in Canada* (written as a paper for the Royal Society of Canada in 1886 and published in the Johns Hopkins University series of Studies in History and Political Science in 1887), a review of the origin and growth of the municipal system of Canada considered as a part of the movement towards self-government. While little more than historical description, this study broke new ground. Twenty years later interest in local government was evinced by the work of Morley Wickett (see *Municipal Government in Canada*, edited by him, Toronto, 1907) and can be seen in the first meeting of the Canadian Political Science Association in 1913. With this exception these early studies in political science were not productive of more work in their field. The many sections dealing with political institutions, parties, and policies, in *Canada and Its Provinces* (ed. by A. Shortt and A. G. Doughty, Toronto, 1914-7) are mainly historical and descriptive, not analytical.

MacKay's *The Unreformed Senate of Canada* (Oxford, 1926), Professor R. McG. Dawson's *The Principle of Official Independence* (Toronto, 1922) and his *Civil Service of Canada* (Oxford, 1929), Professor MacIver's *The Modern State* (Oxford, 1926), and Professor Brady's *Canada* (Toronto, 1932), may be mentioned as outstanding Canadian contributions to political science. All but one of these deal primarily with Canadian affairs, although in the special studies the bearing of Canadian experience upon the general theories of their subject-matter has not been neglected. Significant recent tendencies have been an increasing interest in public administration and in the effects upon government of state participation in, and control of, economic enterprise. Recent graduate work in Canadian universities and by Canadian students in other universities has the same characteristics; it is comparatively small in amount and is directed mainly to Canadian problems. Imperial and external relations and the party system in Canada are the subjects which have attracted most attention.

A superficial explanation of the small amount of work done in political science is suggested by the fact, mentioned above, that it has been mainly confined to the last fifteen years. What was called political science in the early decades of its teaching was, as we have seen, preponderantly constitutional law and constitutional history. And just as these related subjects supplied most of the substance of political science, so most of the published work which could be brought under the head of political science was in that period done by the constitutional lawyers and historians. The relatively small place held by political science in graduate work and publication cannot, of course, be explained entirely by attributing it to the relatively small place held by political science in university teaching especially in the earlier decades, nor by the fact that constitutional law and history supplied the major substance of that political science which was taught. The parallel is, however, too obvious to be overlooked, and it is to be expected that graduate work in political science will not be so directly encouraged when it has been little taught or taught by those whose approach is primarily that of history or law and who will communicate their own enthusiasms to their students.[16]

[16]The Canadians who have made the chief contributions to political science in recent years have all received advanced training at British or American

But a further explanation may be suggested. At the beginning of social studies in Canada their whole intellectual equipment was taken over from England and Scotland. The subjects, the approach, and the literature were all British. As the consciousness of nationhood which was evident in Canada early in this century began to be felt in the universities, interest was stimulated in the investigation and interpretation of those things which seemed most essentially Canadian. In the social studies attention was concentrated on those things which most clearly set Canada apart from other nations and the elucidation of which was plainly at the core of an understanding of Canadian national life. Two such things immediately met the eye: first, the Canadian federal system of government, and second, the fact of Dominion self-government within British imperial unity. Since both these phenomena are embodied in, or at least depend on, the constitution, it was natural that they should attract the attention of constitutional lawyers and historians first of all the students of the social sciences, and that research on these lines should be the first to be stimulated.

These issues are, indeed, natural focal points; for the constitutional lawyer because they constitute the peculiarly Canadian contributions to constitutional law and as such require interpretation and elucidation beyond the traditional theories; and for the historian because the development of Dominion autonomy and of federal government is the most clearly apparent general tendency around which the political history of Canada may be integrated. Thus Canadian history has been mainly concerned with the development towards Confederation, with the struggle for responsible government, and more recently with the new position of the Dominion within the British Commonwealth of Nations, as in such works as Professor Trotter's *Canadian Federation* (Toronto, 1924), Professor Burt's *The Old Province of Quebec* (Toronto, 1933), Professor New's *Lord Durham* (Oxford, 1929), and Professor Martin's *Empire and Commonwealth* (Oxford, 1929). Similarly, Canadian constitutional law has largely concerned itself with the structure of the federal system of government and with the development and present

---

universities: Professor Angus and Professor Brady at Oxford; Professor Dawson at London under Graham Wallas, Professor Leacock at Chicago, and Professor MacKay at Princeton. Professor MacIver came to Canada as a graduate of Edinburgh and Oxford.

meaning of Dominion autonomy and imperial unity. For many years the books were confined to purely descriptive works such as Bourinot's *Federal Government in Canada* (Baltimore, 1889) or technical treatises such as Lefroy's *Canada's Federal System* (Toronto, 1913). More recently, notably in Professor Kennedy's *The Constitution of Canada* (Oxford, 1922), an additional point of view more akin to that of political science has been represented.

The same two issues would appear to be natural focal points for the Canadian political scientist, if it is in these that the essentially Canadian experiments in government, the deviations from the traditional British democratic system, are to be discovered. Some consideration of this suggests, however, that they are a less fruitful field for the political scientist than for the constitutional lawyer and the historian. The latter have shown that their methods are well able to elicit the general tendencies and general principles that can be discovered in these developments considered as constitutional developments and constitutional facts; beyond this it has seemed only possible, when considering the issues thus broadly, to indulge in speculative generalities about underlying forces—the British democratic and freedom-loving tradition, Canadian national unity, the fellow-feeling of English-speaking peoples—which make these systems, constitutionally anomalous as they are, function as well as they do.[17]

The task of the Canadian political scientist, as far as the understanding of Canadian government and political life is concerned, has, therefore, properly lain not in the study of federalism and of Dominion self-government as such, but in the investigation of institutions and political habits and ideas which have grown up beside and within the framework so established. To the extent that the historical and legal fundamentals have been established, this work by political scientists has become at once more profitable and more desirable. It is, therefore, not unnatural that research in Canadian political science

[17]It may be noted that most of this work has in the past been done in a spirit of implicit or explicit eulogy of Canadian institutions and has displayed an almost teleological belief in the progress of the Canadian people. The same situation was apparent in an exaggerated form in the United States in the second half of the nineteenth century, where it was a reflection of the uncritical spirit of a period of national prosperity and growth. *Cf.* W. J. Shepard, "Recent Tendencies in American Political Science" (*Politica*, vol I, Feb., 1934).

should have begun only fifteen years ago; and with the larger constitutional fundamentals laid bare and with the development of political science in other countries, notably the United States, we may look for more and more investigation of the Canadian political structure and process by Canadian students of political science.

Certain prospects for political science in Canada are suggested by this analysis of the trend up to the present. There is no doubt that interest in it and the amount of time devoted to it in the universities have been increasing in recent years; and with the increasing rate of political change and the growing demand by governments, government boards and commissions for men trained in political science, this growth may be expected to continue. Equally clearly, most of this new interest has gone into the study of government and the concrete aspects of politics, and it seems probable that this trend will continue. The influence in this direction of contemporary American scholarship is not to be overlooked. And recent developments in the Canadian political system, as in other countries, require further study. In the problems raised by the emergence of the positive state and the consequent growing importance of the administrative function, in the matter of Canada's external relations, and with regard to the place of the church, of labour organizations, and of other associations in relation to the state, for instance, we clearly have not reached the limits of knowledge. And as more work is done in this field, the attention devoted to the undergraduate study of the process of government in general and Canadian government in particular may be expected to increase. Further, it may be surmised that if political science is to continue to expand in our universities it may be at the price of more and more concentration on the concrete aspects, for the utility of the results to be obtained in this direction is more immediately apparent than is the case with political theory.

There is a danger in this trend that in the midst of it theory may be overlooked. The danger foreseen here is not that the new political science will become merely descriptive;[18] on the contrary, it generally

[18]Though the teaching of it may become so. The temptation to become descriptive is as great as the temptation to become exclusively Canadian in emphasis. If the former temptation is unduly indulged, it will mean the further weakening of political science, as of any subject which is put on a descriptive level. Students must be made to discover and to face the principles behind the machinery of their government; unawareness of such principles

aims at discovering inductively from new facts, or from fresh analysis of old facts, new principles or necessary modifications of old principles. When undertaken in this spirit its value to theory is undoubted; constant work of this kind is required to keep theory where it ought to be, abreast of practice. Yet it is doubtful if it can continue to have such value if our undergraduate training proceeds to a neglect of the study of political ideas in favour of the study of government and the actual political process in the modern state. For nothing in the modern state is to be fully understood unless that state is seen as a product of the interaction of men's ideas and men's actions and the circumstances from which these have arisen and with which they have been confronted. This understanding must be sought in the study of the history of political ideas, considered not as abstract philosophies but as, at each stage, both cause and effect of political, social, and economic situations and activity. With such a basic training, future graduates will be able to analyse with a surer touch the special problems of concrete politics which await them.

And a further prospect appears. By making such a study of political ideas the centre of the teaching of politics, it may be possible to build up anew a coherent intellectual discipline such as political science aspired to be fifty years ago. Then, the attempt was made to build up a political science from heterogeneous elements and without as yet a sufficient principle of unity; now the study of the development in interaction of political ideas and concrete political facts offers a new principle of unity. And the other elements of which such a political science must be composed or on which it must rely are more homogeneous now. History has been moving steadily towards the wider study of social development as a whole; economic history has more to contribute towards an understanding of political change; and in place of the constitutional studies in which the legal approach was generally predominant we have now a body of knowledge and methods of research about the actual working of government which forms an integral part of political science.

The emphasis on political ideas need not be confined to undergraduate teaching. As a field of research it is of equal importance

---

means a too ready acquiescence in any development that may take place in the machinery, a fact which such men as Ashley and Todd saw and stated for their day (cf. p. 135 and p. 145, n. 15). That some of the students will subsequently occupy positions in government adds weight to this consideration.

with the concrete aspects of politics.   The more we can discover
about the relation between what has been thought and what has been
done in the realm of politics, and between all this and the social
structure and movement which is inseparable from it, the more clearly
we shall be able to comprehend the process of development which has
formed and is forming the society and the states we have to-day.
And if we can discern any principles underlying this process, in their
light and in the knowledge of future possibilities and impossibilities
which they disclose, we may be able to move more intelligently towards whatever ends we desire.   If the study of political science is
to be more than a mental puzzle, this is probably the best purpose it
can set itself to serve.

THE ORIGINS AND DEVELOPMENT OF FASCISM

LORNE T. MORGAN

NATIONS throughout the world to-day might not unfairly be divided into pro- and anti-Fascist camps. Yet in the whole field of political economy there is probably no other term which has caused as much controversy and confusion as Fascism. Is Fascism a more or less accidental intrusion, or an inevitable result of economic development? Is it a transitory stage as its opponents maintain, or does it, as its followers vociferously assert, offer a permanent solution to the economic problems facing the nations of the world? A brief consideration of a few definitions by authorities will show the complete absence of unanimity of opinion among writers on the subject. According to Mussolini, "Fascism conceives of the State as an absolute, in comparison with which all individuals or groups are relative, only to be conceived of in their relation to the State". Hitler sees the Fascist state as "the organisation of a community homogeneous in nature and feeling, for the better furtherance and maintenance of their type and the fulfilment of the destiny marked out for them by Providence". Palme Dutt, one of its ablest critics, summarizes Fascism as "a movement of mixed elements, dominantly petit-bourgeois, but also slum-proletarian and demoralised working class, financed and directed by finance-capital, by the big industrialists, landlords and financiers, to defeat the working-class revolution and smash the working-class organisations". Professor Robert A. Brady, impartial American investigator, in an authoritative work on German Fascism defines it as "monopoly capitalism become conscious of its powers, the conditions of its survival, and mobilized to crush all opposition. It is capitalism mobilized to crush trade unions, to wipe out radical and liberal criticism, to promote, with the sum total of all its internal resources, economic advantage at home and abroad." Gentile, Fascist philosopher, describes it as a "wholly spiritual creation". Gregor Strasser included among the elements of Fascism

167

"the Prussian officers' system of selection by achievement; the incorruptibility of the German official; the old walls, the town hall, [and] the cathedral of the free Imperial city"(!). In the light of such widely divergent opinions, it becomes necessary to observe the developments of Fascism in relation to the *forces which produced it* before coming to a conclusion that can claim any validity whatsoever. Within the very limited space at its disposal, this essay is an attempt at such a study and evaluation.

The economic crisis facing the world to-day provides the soil from which Fascism springs. The rapid expansion characteristic of nineteenth-century and pre-war capitalism is in sharp contrast to the situation as it exists to-day. According to a League of Nations report,[1] "If the line of trend from 1860 to 1913 is extended to 1932, the rather startling conclusion is reached that the index of world production, on the hypothesis that nothing had occurred to alter its regular upward trend for the fifty preceding years, would to-day be rather more than twice as great as it actually is". Palme Dutt,[2] surveying the situation from a quite different angle, arrives at a similar conclusion: "the modern development of technique and productive powers has reached a point at which the existing capitalist forms are more and more incompatible with the further development of production and utilisation of technique." The highly theoretical and sharply disputed explanations of that phenomenon do not concern us here. The fact remains that there is a crisis; and the further fact that the usual attempt at solution has, under existing economic relationships, but increased the discrepancy is admitted in even the most orthodox circles. The resultant threat to economic security is basic to the development of Fascism.

Political repercussions to economic crises have undoubtedly played an important part in the development of Fascism. Governments have come and gone. It has mattered little whether they were Conservative, Liberal, or Social-Democratic; they have met the same fate. They rolled into office on one wave of mass discontent and they tumbled out on another. Not infrequently political stalemate prevented even an attempt to function. In Austria the Nazis, the Heimwehr, and the Social-Democrats effectually offset Dollfuss's

[1]*World Economic Survey, 1932-33*, p. 82.
[2]*Fascism and Social Revolution* (New York, 1934), p. 14.

Social Clerical group. His cold-blooded slaughter of the Socialists was an effort to work his way out of this impasse. In Italy the Catholic and Socialist parties fought to a draw at a time when Mussolini could collect but 4,000 votes to his Socialist opponent's 180,000. In Germany economic chaos, numerous political parties, and proportional representation combined to produce as ill-assorted a group as ever slept in a common cabinet bed. The marvel is that democracy lasted in Germany until 1930.

The result of futility and stalemate was an ever-increasing dissatisfaction on the part of the masses with parliamentarianism. This was particularly true when a Social-Democratic government had failed, for it was generally believed that such a government really had the welfare of the masses at heart. At this point it becomes necessary to consider in some detail the relationship between Social Democracy and Fascism. That the former has definitely contributed to the success of Fascism in Austria, Germany, and Italy is an established fact. Whether that contribution was *deliberate* or simply the result of misunderstanding, consistent bungling, and lack of courage, is still disputed.

Social Democracy is a collective term including all those groups who, professing Socialism as their ultimate goal, believe they can achieve that end through the use of *existing* political, legal, and economic institutions. Its approach is, therefore, essentially *constitutional*. The British Labour party, the Social Democratic party of Germany, and the Austrian and Italian Socialists come under this heading. One might also include the Coöperative Commonwealth Federation of Canada. What is perhaps the most penetrating analysis ever made of the historical role of Social Democracy appeared in two "confidential" bulletins of the Federation of German Industry.[3] This analysis, expressed through the official organ of large scale German industry, shows clearly that German Capitalism knew it had nothing to fear from Social Democracy. Lack of space precludes more than a bare summary of the views put forth, but they should be read in their entirety for a full appreciation of their significance.

According to the bulletins, the threat of revolution after the World War placed German Capitalism in a precarious position. Military force alone was too dangerous a weapon for maintaining

[3]Quoted at length in *ibid.*, pp. 171-4.

the *status quo*. The only alternative was to *split* the working-class, form an alliance with one section of it, and by this means keep the other, and more revolutionary element, in check. The Social Democratic party was the tool used to effect this split: "Social Democracy brought into the system of reconstruction at that time . . . the organized working-class, and *while paralysing their revolutionary energy chained them fast to the bourgeois State*" (italics mine). The price paid for such allegiance consisted of greater economic security to *organized* labour and a liberal social policy. Unfortunately the severe economic crisis through which the world was passing rendered it impossible for German Capitalism to continue those payments for services rendered. In the resultant decline in the popularity of Social Democracy, Communism again threatened. The situation was such that "the only possible means of saving bourgeois rule from this abyss is to effect the splitting of the working-class and its tying to the State apparatus *by other and more direct means* [italics mine]. Herein lie the positive possibilities and the tasks of National Socialism." The political ramifications of this development are clearly elucidated in the following words: "A bourgeois regime based on a liberal bourgeois constitution must not only be parliamentary; it must rely for support on Social Democracy and allow Social Democracy adequate achievements. A bourgeois regime which destroys these achievements must sacrifice Social Democracy and parliamentarianism, must create a substitute for Social Democracy, and must go over to a *restricted social constitution*" (italics mine). The bulletin then draws an interesting parallel between Social Democracy and Fascism: both promised the masses a revolution and then "led them to the new formation of bourgeois rule". The conclusion is, naturally enough, that "National Socialism has taken over from Social Democracy the task of providing the mass-support for the rule of the bourgeoisie in Germany". Such is the opinion of German Capitalism on the role of Social Democracy.

One thing is certain: Social Democracy has failed lamentably in every case in which it has been actually confronted by Fascism. That failure lies in the *means used* to carry out its programme. As Mowrer asks, "What can be said for a republic [under Social Democratic rule] that allows its laws to be interpreted by monarchist judges, its government to be administered by old-time functionaries brought up in fidelity to the old regime; that watches passively while reactionary school teachers and professors teach its children to despise the present freedom in favour of a glorified feudal past; that permits and encourages the revival of the militarism which was chiefly responsible for the country's previous humiliation?"[4]   In Austria Social Democracy proved just as egregious a failure.[5]   In 1919 it could have socialized the very "pivot of Austrian industry", but it failed to do so.   It "socialized some of the luxuries of life but none of the necessities", and eventually lost out to Clerical Fascism "because of its own decency".   Bauer, its leader, was a fine theorist and an able debater, but utterly helpless in the face of unexpected realities.   In 1933 a bold stroke would have ended the Dollfuss menace to Social Democracy but Bauer hesitated, negotiated, and lost.   Too late he saw it and confessed: "It was a mistake—the most fatal of all our mistakes."   And the story of his incompetence on the very eve of Dollfuss's massacre of Vienna workers is the tale of an even more tragic blunder.

In Italy it was exactly the same story.   In the fall of 1920, northern industrial workers seized a large number of industrial units, and were prepared to operate them.   Effective opposition at that particular time did not exist.   Here was the greatest opportunity ever offered Social Democracy, and it again failed miserably.   Lack of courage, complete bankruptcy of leadership, and the total absence of a plan prevented what would undoubtedly have been a successful and bloodless revolution.   The following year the Social Democrats ousted their really active minority, and then proceeded to carry on in their usual manner—debating inconsequential trifles in a scholarly fashion.   Salvemini, noted historian and anything but a revolutionary, describes the situation as follows: "Had the leaders of the General Confederation of Labour and of the Socialist Party wished to strike a decisive blow, here was the opportunity. . . .   The bankers, the big industrialists and big landlords waited for the social revolution

---

[4]E. A. Mowrer, *Germany Puts the Clock Back* (London, 1933), p. 17. See also R. A. Brady, *The Spirit and Structure of German Fascism* (New York, 1937), pp. 16-7; H. Lichtenberger, *The Third Reich* (New York, 1937), pp. 6 *ff*.; F. L. Schuman, *Hitler and the Nazi Dictatorship* (London, 1936), p. 172.

[5]See John Gunther, *Inside Europe* (New York and London, 1936), pp. 283-5.

as sheep wait to be led to the slaughter. If a Communist revolution could be brought about by bewilderment and cowardice on the part of the ruling classes, the Italian people in September, 1920, could have made as many Communist revolutions as they wished."[6]   If any further proof is necessary, consider the words of the secretary of the General Confederation who, two years later, remarked: "But after we had the honour [!] of preventing a revolutionary catastrophe— Fascism arrived."[7]

The ghastly tragedy being enacted in Spain to-day can certainly be partly attributed to the policy pursued by the Social Democrats. From 1931 to 1933 the Azaña government did many important things.   It disestablished the church, nationalized its property, completely separated it from both the state and education, and dissolved the Jesuit order.   Thousands of army officers were pensioned off; primary school education was made free and compulsory; the nobility lost their titles; women were given the franchise; Catalonia gained its practical independence; a thorough-going land reform project was proposed and considered though never carried out.   But no mere parliamentarianism could revolutionize the Spain of that period, as Gunther clearly saw when he wrote: "If he [Azaña] had only been less legalistic! But he chose a democratic parliament as a weapon of revolution—and failed."[8]   The Lerroux-Robles reaction produced a revolt which was crushed in bloodshed—twenty-five thousand progressives were in jail at the close of 1935.   All this *should* have taught the Social Democrats much, but it taught them nothing.   Returned to power early in 1936, they pursued almost exactly the same "constitutionally radical" policy that had ended in failure in 1933. In 1936 the Social Democrats still had illusions, but the *extreme right* had none.   Reforms that would have been grudgingly tolerated by a more enlightened group in a more advanced country were anathema to them.   *They* struck viciously in defence of their own interests, and tossed "constitutionalism" to one side as if it had never mattered. The only thing that could have prevented the present Fascist rebellion in Spain was a revolution which would definitely have ended the

[6]G. Salvemini, *The Fascist Dictatorship* (New York, 1927), vol. I, p. 64.
[7]*Daily Herald*, April 12, 1928; quoted by Palme Dutt, *Fascism and Social Revolution*, p. 119.
[8]See also Brady, *The Spirit and Structure of German Fascism*, p. 17.

economic control of the landed nobility, the church hierarchy, large scale industrialists, financiers, army leaders, the civil service, and the civil guard. Social Democracy's halfway measures made Fascism possible in Germany; they made a bloody counter-revolution inevitable in Spain.

Further illustration of the weakness of Social Democracy is unnecessary. The above is not to be construed as a criticism of *all* parties who do not produce revolutions! It is a criticism of a party which, in the light of the promises it makes, the philosophy it espouses, and the goal at which it aims, fails to comprehend in the face of repeated failures that *only a revolution* can produce the things for which it ostensibly stands. If this criticism at first seems a bit harsh, one has only to reflect upon the attitude of Social Democracy in the Anglo-American countries to-day. It does criticize the groups more orthodox than itself, but its real attack is reserved for those to its left. This attitude is probably the result of a sub-conscious realization of where its true allegiance rests. Social Democracy, judged solely on the basis of what it has actually done, and the part that it has played in the development of Fascism, cannot be considered a left-wing party. It is not without reason that Schuman refers to the "cowardice and treachery" of Social Democracy. Monopoly capital in the older industrial countries trusts Social Democracy and uses it as long as it serves its purpose. Monopoly capital in Spain, the United States, and Canada, seeing fundamental issues less clearly, is still suspicious.

A usual concomitant of mass disillusionment with parliamentarianism is an increase in the numbers and power of the extreme *left*. This development instils fear of revolution into the more conservative elements of capitalist society.[9] In such circumstances embryonic Fascism appears.

To begin with Fascism is a petty middle-class movement. Small traders, small landowners, independent artisans, technicians, members of the professions, the "white-collar" group, and others of similar economic status are its earliest recruits. To them can usually

[9]The Communists of Germany polled 590,000 votes in the election of 1920; 3,230,000 in 1928; 4,500,000 in 1930; and 5,980,939 in 1933. See Brady, *The Spirit and Structure of German Fascism*, p. 16; and *cf.* Schuman, *Hitler and the Nazi Dictatorship*, p. 159.

be added certain "de-classed" groups including sections of unorganized labour, clerical trade unions, and the army. At first, curiously enough in view of what invariably happens later, this motley group is vigorous in its condemnation of monopoly capital interests such as large scale industrialists, landlords, financiers, and the owners of department and chain stores. Their own economic security seriously threatened, they demand protection against the so-called Big Interests. This fact accounts for the critical and often socialistic nature of the Fascist programme in its earliest phase. For example, consider the official Italian Fascist programme adopted in October, 1919. It advocated, among other things, a republican form of government; decentralization of the executive power and the right of popular initiative, referendum, and veto; universal suffrage; the abolition of the Senate, political police, caste-titles, conscription, speculation, and stock companies; the confiscation of "unproductive" revenues and landed estates (which were to be distributed among the peasants) ; and finally promised labour a direct voice in the operation of industry ! The British Labour party in its rashest moments, if it has ever had rash moments, would never have had the temerity to consider such a programme. That adopted by the German Nazi party in 1920, and re-affirmed in 1926 as "unalterable", was even more socialistic.[10] The reasons for the radical aspects of such programmes are obvious: Fascism *originates* in social unrest, and mere criticism is not nearly enough; also, since the movement must have a *mass basis* in order to achieve success at the polls, its net must be cast far and wide; lastly, Fascism must of necessity compete with Socialism for many of its early following, and therefore finds it necessary to steal numerous Socialist planks. In the case of Germany, it has been necessary to steal the very name itself, and National Socialism and Fascism are synonymous terms to-day.

There are other elements in the early Fascist programmes, elements which are completely inconsistent with those outlined above, and clearly demarcate the Fascist from the real Socialist programme. They are, first, a fanatical and often violent nationalism, and, secondly, a cult of mysticism. The former is so well known as to need no elaboration. The latter is most clearly brought out by

[10]*Cf.* Schuman, *Hitler and the Nazi Dictatorship,* pp. 15-21; also Konrad Heiden, *A History of National Socialism* (New York, 1935), pp. 3-8.

quoting from the speeches and writings of the various Fascist leaders. Doriot considers it necessary "to forge a collective soul". Colonel de la Rocque, leader of the French Croix de Feu, talks vaguely of restoring "the *mystique* of sacrifice for the fatherland". Mussolini writes: "The Fascist State, the most potent and highest form of the personality, is a force, but a spiritual one, which sums up all the forms of man's moral and intellectual life. . . . It is an interior form and norm and a discipline of the whole person; it permeates the will like the intelligence. Its principle, a central inspiration of the human personality living in the civic community, descends deeply and lodges in the heart of the man of action as well as the thinker, of the artist as well as the scientist: it is the soul of the soul." Hitler writes of "the destiny marked out for them [Germans] by Providence". Mosley considers "Fascist organisation is the method of world peace among nations bound together by the universal Fascism of the twentieth century". All in all it may be fairly said that the earlier programmes are masterpieces of inconsistency, ambiguity, contradiction, and mysticism. How much of them is downright obfuscation, how much the result of sheer muddle-headedness, it is hard to determine. But when one remembers the object of such a platform—the acquiring of mass support—one suspects there is more than a bit of deliberate misleading. Conservatism, Liberalism, Socialism, and Communism have their more or less distinct economic and political philosophies, although they may and do overlap at times. No such philosophical unity exists in early Fascism, as Mussolini makes clear in the following words: "Doctrine, beautifully defined and carefully elucidated, with headlines and paragraphs, might be lacking; but there was to take its place something more decisive— Faith." Faith in what? The LEADER. That is why a *Führer* or a *Duce* is essential to the rise of Fascism. Only the blindest devotion to a given leader can explain an ever-increasing following in the face of the inherent and glaringly apparent inconsistencies and contradictions which clutter up the Fascist band-wagon. Spell-binding and rank opportunism are the essential qualifications for such leadership. Adolf Hitler, Benito Mussolini, and Oswald Mosley are the three greatest political athletes alive to-day; and all three have the same specialties—political hurdling, and the economic hop-step-and-jump. The mere fact that Mosley has not succeeded in gaining power detracts in no way from his peculiar abilities. Given the German or the Italian situation, it is quite possible that he would have had success comparable to that now enjoyed by his German and Italian *confrères*. In summary, Fascism develops out of economic crisis and disillusionment with parliamentarianism; it is originally a *petit-bourgeois* movement with a polyglot programme, and is held together by a blindly accepted leader.

Fascism in Italy and Germany succeeded to power when it finally received the support, surreptitiously or otherwise, of the monopoly capital elements whose interests it *originally* criticized and even threatened.[11] This is not as astonishing as it may seem on the surface. Opportunism has already been mentioned as one of the cardinal qualifications for Fascist leadership. If the party is to continue to expand its membership, it must continue to travel to the *right* because, if it did otherwise, it would soon lose its identity in the parties of the extreme *left*. So, bit by bit, the quasi-socialistic elements in the programme are quietly shed, and others adopted. In other words, National Socialism becomes more and more national-ist and less and less socialist. It finally emerges as a thorough-going nationalist party which finds its logical and natural enemy in that genuinely socialist group some of whose planks it had previously pretended to espouse. This metamorphosis is by no means either perceived or understood by the petty rank and file of the Fascist group, some of whom doubtless remain under the delusion that they are members of a reform party. But it *is* clearly perceived and thoroughly understood by monopoly capital interests, especially when those interests find themselves confronted by the possibility of Com-munism or loss of political control. This is exactly what took place in Italy and Germany. Mussolini, openly derided, scoffed at, and scorned by both Capitalist and Socialist factions in 1919, "marched on" Rome in 1922 in a *wagon-lit*, backed by industrialists, large land-owners, and financiers, with the tacit consent of the army, the neutrality of the church, and the twice-repeated (once oral, once written!) "invitation" of the king of Italy.[12] Hitler, a foreign trouble-maker, was ridiculed, shot at, and jailed in 1923. Ten years later,

[11]See Brady, *The Spirit and Structure of German Fascism*, pp. 20-1; and Schuman, *Hitler and the Nazi Dictatorship*, pp. 182-8.
[12]See Brady, *The Spirit and Structure of German Fascism*, p. 363.

with the connivance of von Papen and Hugenberg who undoubtedly influenced poor old von Hindenburg, Hitler became chancellor of the German Reich; and that *after* his party had recently lost both prestige and votes at the polls. Thus Fascism comes into power through a union of what might be called Big and Little capital interests.[13]

This marriage, like so many others, has its elements of incompatibility. The impossibility of harmonizing the mutually antagonistic economic interests of the two parties involved in the union is one of the most baffling problems confronting Fascist governments to-day. Monopoly capital interests have invariably won out, and Fascism has come to be synonymous with Monopoly Capitalism. The danger remains, however, that the dissatisfied element may understand what is happening and transfer its political allegiance to genuine left-wing groups, thus endangering, if not wrecking, the mass basis so essential to control as long as *political* democracy exists. Consequently, dictatorship must accompany Fascism. The speed at which the transformation takes place depends upon existing circumstances. In Germany it was almost automatic, for practical absolutism had existed for over two years before Hitler became chancellor. In Italy the development came much more slowly. For more than two years, Mussolini kept, partly at least, within constitutional limits. The election of 1924 and the Matteotti "incident" frightened him and showed him the danger of such a procedure. Out and out dictatorship followed, although it was months before he recovered the nerve necessary to take the final steps. Pathetically incompetent leadership on the part of the opposition, far more than any action on the part of *Il Duce* himself, spelled the doom of democracy in Italy. But Fascist dictatorship offers no solution for the economic problems of the rank and file within the party. One needs only to glance at the recent labour and social legislation of both Italy and Germany to understand how firmly Monopoly Capitalism is in the saddle. Dissident Fascist groups have been shown scant mercy. Undoubtedly one reason for the official murders in Germany of June 30, 1934, was the "liquidation" of certain S.A. leaders. As one writer has put it, that bloody purge "ended finally 'radicalism' in the party". The

[13]*Cf.* C. B. Hoover, *Germany Enters the Third Reich* (New York, 1933), p. 83.

12

Rossoni group in Italy has caused the government a bit of embarrass-
ment at times, but so far drastic measures have been unnecessary.

A technical and detailed analysis of Fascism in maturity does not
fall within the confines of this essay. A brief survey of its economic
essentials will suffice to show that it is simply Capitalism in crisis
and carried to the logical extreme. Private ownership of the means
of production and distribution, and production for profit, are the
cornerstones of Fascist as well as of laissez-faire Capitalism. There
has been some attempt at economic planning, but this is not distinctive
of Fascism. Current attempts at economic planning and state regulation have been carried even further in the United States and Great
Britain; and those two countries are still democracies. Political
absolutism is a necessity to the Fascist state; but it alone is not
definitive, for the old Russia and Germany, and Spain up to 1931,
though they were undemocratic, were *not* Fascist states. The term
Corporate state is a mystical alias.[14] The best possible reference for
such a statement is Mussolini himself. On the legal establishment
of twenty-two corporations in November, 1934, he proclaimed: "It is
as yet premature to say what developments the Corporative System
may have in Italy and elsewhere from the point of view of the production and distribution of goods. Ours is a point of departure, not
of arrival." On another occasion he declared: "Corporations are
the instrument which, under the aegis of the State, actualises the
integral, organic and unitary discipline of the productive forces, with
a view to the development of the wealth, the political power and the
well-being of the Italian people." Rossoni is equally enlightening:
"The Corporation is not to be defined in legal terms. The Corporation is a state of mind. It is one big family." Undoubtedly the more
radical among Italian Fascists visualize as a goal a sort of State
Capitalism under which employer and employee work for the common good of the state. This is what might be called the "mystical
uplift" group. The owning group has no such illusory dreams. It
realizes clearly that the government can do much for it, can assist
it, make investigations, collect statistics, act for it abroad, look after
the strictly political end of things, keep labour in its place, and, in
general, provide those services which every government except one
of the purest laissez-faire variety (existing in text-books only) has

[14]See H. Finer, *Mussolini's Italy* (New York, 1935), pp. 492 *ff.*

always performed. But it wants, and will tolerate, no *serious* interference. Mussolini's position is unquestionably between the two
groups. "Mystical uplift" has done a lot for him, and he likes it as
an idea. But he is too close to reality to be able to visualize a government *in vacuo*, existing only in and for itself. He knows full well
that every government represents many interests in general and
certain interests in particular. At times he may chafe at the thought
of any form of control, just as monopoly capital may worry a bit
concerning his fiercely individualistic outbursts; but both know that,
for the time being at least, their interests are identical.

So far there would seem to be no essential difference between the
Capitalism of, say, Great Britain and that of Italy. Such a conclusion
would be quite false. British Capitalism is democratic, that of Italy
autocratic. Democratic Capitalism implies two rights which are non-
existent in Fascist countries to-day: first, the working-class is allowed
to form *its own* economic organizations, and, secondly, it is allowed
independent political activity. These two essentials clearly demarcate
Democratic from Fascist Capitalism. There is another, though
minor, distinction which merits a passing reference—the difference
in emphasis on nationalism. Though, under Democratic Capitalism,
states have fought to preserve their national interests, they have,
nevertheless, usually treated the rights of other nations with respect.
Fascist states, however, employ the same draconian ruthlessness in
their foreign relations that is so characteristic of their purely domestic
policies. The difference is one of degree only, but it does serve to
demarcate further Democratic from Fascist Capitalism. With these
distinctions in mind, we may attempt a definition of Fascism. Fascism
is simply *Undemocratic Capitalism*[15] whose sole purpose is the maintenance and furtherance, at home and abroad, of the interests which
placed it in power and which it represents. To achieve that purpose,
the Fascist machine establishes an absolute control over "all activities
and all thought, ideas and values" of the entire nation. The slightest
criticism is ruthlessly repressed. Freedom of speech, of assembly,
and of the press go by the board. Independent working-class organizations are completely smashed. The church must choose between
selling its soul and suffering bitter persecution. It has chosen one
course in Italy and Spain, the other in Germany. Science degenerates

[15]*Cf.* Schuman, *Hitler and the Nazi Dictatorship*, p. 501.

into "pseudo-scientific nonsense". Above all, the Fascist nation girds itself for war, war being the logical and inevitable outcome of failure in the blind pursuit of rampant economic nationalism.[16] Binding treaties do not exist in the eyes of the Fascist state, and the *declaration* of war has become an anachronism. Fascism

believes neither in the possibility nor the utility of perpetual peace. It thus repudiates the doctrine of Pacifism—born of a renunciation of the struggle and an act of cowardice in the face of sacrifice. War alone brings up to its highest tension all human energy and puts the stamp of nobility upon the peoples who have the courage to meet it. All other trials are substitutes, which never really put men into the position where they have to make the great decision—the alternative of life or death. Thus a doctrine which is founded on this harmful postulate of peace is hostile to Fascism.

So writes Mussolini. It is no accident that Fascist nations to-day are, literally, nations in arms.

The question now arises: since Fascism is the result of Capitalism in crisis, is it not logical to expect its appearance in other countries when they face a similar crisis? The answer is: *Yes*.[17] When Fascism was an almost purely Italian monopoly, it was blithely dismissed elsewhere as a development which could take place only in "backward" countries. It was frequently suggested, also, that the "Latin temperament" had something to do with it. The rise to power of Fascism in Germany struck these glib explanations a heavy blow, for Germany is one of the most highly developed countries; and even the most superb rationalist finds it difficult to equate German and Italian "temperaments". Clearly, another explanation is necessary. The reason why Fascism struck Italy and Germany is that, because of certain specific developments, Italian and German Capitalisms encountered the crisis earlier, and in a more severe form, than any of their contemporaries. The truth of such a statement is self-evident from even a casual survey of the economic conditions confronting those countries on the eve of Fascism.

Italy is, from the standpoint of economic essentials, one of the most unfortunately placed of all countries. Her paucity of raw materials is notorious. Italy proper is one-third the size of Ontario and has twelve times its population. Forty per cent of her land is

[16]*Cf. ibid.*, p. 504.
[17]*Cf. ibid.*, p. 500.

incapable of cultivation. The result is that she is forced to import about 20 per cent of her food. She possesses no manganese, tin, rubber, tungsten, nickel, chromium, mica. She is also forced to import over 90 per cent of her cotton, coal, mineral oil, and copper; and over 80 per cent of her wool, iron, and steel. She is largely agricultural; such industry as she has developed has been forced to compete with that of nations better situated or more highly industrialized than herself. Her textile industry faces ruinous competition with that of Britain, the United States, and Japan. Her wines compete with those of France, Spain, and Germany. Substitutes have hurt her olive oil industry. Her silks fight a losing battle with those of France, Japan, and China, and silk substitutes are an ever-growing menace. Her market for marble is disappearing; Texas has wiped out her sulphur monopoly. She has few foreign investments, sells no financial services, and subsidizes her shipping. The result has been one of the lowest standards of living in Europe and a high percentage of illiteracy. Add to all that the huge losses, increased national debt, and heavy inflation due to the World War, the financial crash of 1919, complete political stalemate, and the constant fear of Communism described previously, and the capitalist crisis in Italy is fully understandable.

The case of Germany is so widely known as to need no more than a reference. Practically single-handed she fought the most powerful nations of the world with the losses one would expect under the circumstances. The peace terms further denuded her, reduced her to military impotence, and practically took away her sovereign rights. The Weimar constitution guaranteed political instability. The marvel of it all is that Germany did not develop either Fascism or Communism long before 1933.

In Italy and Germany, as well as in Austria, Monopoly Capitalism found itself backed to the wall by forces over which it had little or no control, faced with grave political instability and the ever-present menace of extinction by Communism. Fascism and Communism were the only alternatives. Monopoly Capitalism could control Fascism and, if necessary, twist it slightly to make it conform absolutely with its own interests. And this it proceeded to do.

Elsewhere, the hope of escaping similar developments depends upon avoiding a continuance, or a deepening, of economic crisis. Few economists, even the most conservatively inclined, are at all sanguine regarding long-run prospects. Mr. Keynes, than whom no greater theoretical influence (Douglas included) exists in Canada, is already eyeing 1939-40 with apprehension. How long can the present awe-inspiring armament race continue without producing war or bankruptcy? And if this suicidal race *were* abandoned, what would be the effect upon heavy industry and employment, both of which are fundamental to a nation's economic well-being? Economic magicians (theorists in general) may scoff at such an "elementary" analysis, and glibly mention several ways out. The truth is that in the past innumerable economic rabbits, pink and otherwise, have been produced from innumerable theoretical hats, without solving the world's economic maladjustment. In short, economic crisis, present "prosperity" notwithstanding, is still with us, and the remaining democracies will yet be confronted with developments similar to those witnessed in the Fascist countries.[18]

The reasons why Britain, France, the United States, and Canada, among others, have so far escaped as lightly as they have, are not far to seek. In some cases, that of Britain in particular, priority over others in industrial and imperial development produced an economic "back-log" that has so far rendered invaluable service. Her chronic unfavourable visible balance of trade has been much more than offset by the income from her investments abroad and the sale of shipping, financial, and other services to her Dominions and to foreigners. The resultant inflow of great wealth enabled her most fortunately situated group to live in luxury, while it guaranteed the lower middle class solid comfort and undeniable respectability, the two great perquisites of that most important stratum of English society. Even the working-class had but little to complain of in the past. It was fed, clothed, and sheltered in a fashion rarely approached in the rest of Europe. It was educated, given the franchise, and allowed to form its own economic and political organizations. On two occasions it was permitted to govern the country, though under the supervisory eye of another party. Under such circumstances extreme radicalism made little headway in Britain, and is still of

[18]See Brady, *The Spirit and Structure of German Fascism*, part III, for a detailed discussion of the same point.

minor importance. The British working-class is industrious, law-abiding, patriotic, cautious; it may and does grumble at times; but it knows its place and its betters. Under such conditions, Democracy was inevitable. Britain was wealthy enough to afford it; it worked with a minimum of friction; it became a *tradition*. But the economic foundation upon which this democracy rests is increasingly threatened to-day. Competition in the world market is becoming ever keener, and that market is growing ever smaller through the rapid advance of economic nationalism abroad. The inflow of wealth has been seriously curtailed in the last two decades, although that curtailment passed unnoticed by the layman until the crash. Unemployment has become a permanent problem: the chances of reaching an irreducible minimum below a million in time of peace are admittedly small. Stanley Baldwin, in a parliamentary address in 1934, stated that Britain had gone about as far as she could by *domestic* measures alone; further improvement depended upon outside factors. (This was before Britain entered the rearmament race.) And the world situation to-day is an ominous one for a nation whose whole economic structure is built upon, and tied to, world markets. A curtailed economy will affect first of all the British working-class. And, as implacably stolid and as utterly immovable as it appears to be to-day, it will react exactly as did others· when the shoe begins to pinch. Will British "traditions" prevent British workers from action taken to protect themselves, or British monopoly capital from defending its interests by whatever means are necessary? It is utter nonsense to believe it.

What is probably one of the greatest unexploded political myths of all time is that the British ruling class has only one method of accomplishing anything—to "muddle through". Walter Page, former American ambassador to Britain, was not deceived by this popular superstition: "They call these old Tories 'Diehards'. It's a good name. They use military power, social power, financial power, eloquence, learning, boundless impudence, blackguardism—everything —to hold what they have; and they fight—fight like tigers, and tire not."[19] The last three elections which have produced Conservative (or National) governments support the above shrewd observation. 1924 witnessed the questionable Zinovieff letter episode. 1931 saw

[19]Quoted in Palme Dutt, *Fascism and Social Revolution*, p. 258.

an election to "save the pound", and the pound got short shrift when the desired result had been attained. The 1935 election was won on a promise of supporting the League; yet Baldwin has since confessed that his government knew at the time of the election that it intended to betray the League as soon as re-election was confirmed. For months the Simpson case had been flamboyantly featured in the American press; not a single British paper ventured to bring up the subject. The most popular sovereign in British history, the "idol of the masses", was handed an ultimatum, and practically forced to abdicate. Each one of these episodes may in itself have been understandable, even laudable. The important thing to remember is that probably no governing group in the world can and does act more swiftly, decisively, and ruthlessly in an emergency than the British ruling class. One has but to glance at the record of the present government in foreign affairs to realize just how cold-bloodedly materialistic that class can be. Even Lord Eustace Percy, one of its recent Cabinet members, remarked from a public platform that it was a record in which he himself could take no pride.

Another myth currently believed in Canada is that the present government has somehow led Britain out of the depression without interfering with the management of private enterprise. Nothing could be further from the truth. As a British professor has pointed out:[20] "The changes made during the depression, however, represent a departure from traditional policy comparable in magnitude with, though much less discussed than, the 'New Deal' of the United States." British finance, industry, commerce, and agriculture are controlled to-day as never before in time of peace since the close of the mercantilistic era.

From the above it is apparent why Fascism has made so little progress in Britain. *There has been no need for it.* British monopoly capital has so far been able to afford the luxury of a democracy, to accomplish its purpose (protecting its own interests) without the necessity of direct and undemocratic control. But even in Britain a significant change in the method of governing has been taking place. The use of so-called "stampede elections" has been referred to, as has the indirect control of the press. Less noticeable, because

[20]J. H. Richardson, *British Economic Foreign Policy* (New York, 1936), p. 7.

less spectacular, has been the weakening of Parliament as a policy-making body, and a corresponding increase in the power of the executive.   Emergency Power legislation, the increasing deputation of power to various commissions, the extension and militarization of police power, the Trade Union Act of 1927, the Incitement to Disaffection Act, the Political Uniforms Act, the Means Test, and other similar developments are all significant when one considers the basic concepts of the type of democracy under which most of us were reared.   If and when the crisis deepens, parallel developments to those which have occurred on the continent will take place in Britain.

And not only in Britain.   France, old, wise, an empire, and almost fanatical in the tenacity with which her people cling to individualism and the democratic ideal, escaped the probability of Fascism only by developing a United Front against it.   The retention of Democracy depends upon the ability of that Front to remain united. How long can Radical Socialist (middle-class Liberal) support be relied on?   Will its defection, if it occurs, be offset by increased membership in the parties on the left?   Democracy in France is to-day threatened as never before in her recent history.

The majority of people in the United States and Canada long ago convinced themselves that, while they were *in* the world, they were not, *of* it.   The recent years of depression shook that conviction, but did not destroy it.   On the surface, there was much to warrant such a feeling of superiority—for, whether or not they admitted it, it was a feeling of superiority.   The thousands of miles of water that separate North America from its nearest predatory neighbour engender a feeling of security.   Canada, besides distance, has also the protection of the British Empire.   In addition, Canada has one of the largest air forces, navies, and armies in the world.   True, it flies the American flag and costs her nothing, but it belongs to her just as much as it does to the United States.   In the light of the recent remarkable developments in aviation, the loss of a single foothold on Canadian soil is just as much of a menace to the United States as it is to Canada.   In fact it is more so, for she has more to lose.   *Ipso facto,* whether Canada likes it or not, she is assured of American protection.   And she is under no obligation for it, for her protection is only incidental to that of the United States.   That country is now fortifying the Aleutian Islands—over a thousand miles to the west of the northern British Columbia coast. All Canada falls naturally within that ambit of defence. It is the result of a happy geographical accident, and a mere iota of that grim realism that characterizes British foreign policy to-day will enable Canada to view her situation with equanimity and without loss of pride.

But the superiority long felt, and sometimes displayed, by Canadians and Americans rests on much more than a feeling of physical security. An abundance of land, ample resources, a rapidly growing domestic market, and a chronic shortage of labour were long characteristic of their economy. The net result was general well-being and a relatively high standard of living. Naturally there was, for a long period of time, little incentive for labour to organize economically and politically, and practically no demand for social insurance and other such protective devices commonplace in industrialized European countries. A curious paradox resulted: Canadian and American labour, while it enjoyed comparative luxury, was much more defenceless in adversity than its European counterpart; and adversity slowly developed. Cheap land has disappeared in the United States and become a drug on the market in Canada. Chronic shortage of labour has been more than offset by immigration, natural increase, and the development of the machine. Canada's resources are being gutted to-day just as successfully as were those of the United States yesterday; and, with prices of primary materials at unusually low levels, she is getting little in return. There is nothing much she can do about it for she must sell those materials on a world market over which she has no control. Finally her industrial development has overhauled existing effective demand. All this has been going on for some time; but it has only recently become obvious. The results are now known to all. The United States has had, during the last five years, more people unemployed and more people on relief (known as the "dole" before it struck North America) than all of the industrial countries of Europe together! Moreover, American labour in 1929 was practically unorganized, and hardly knew the meaning of the term "social insurance". It has paid and is paying a terrific price for its "rugged individualism". The difference between the conditions of the American and Canadian worker is due chiefly to the economic size of the two countries.

There is another difference between the working class of Europe and that of North America. The former, in the main, has been satisfied with little more than subsistence. The more active element emigrated. Those who remained seldom questioned economic distinctions of long standing. The North American is different. From earliest childhood he has visualized the day when he would become a Roosevelt, a Mackenzie King, a Rockefeller, a Holt, or a Capone. He was not particular about his field of endeavour—he simply took it for granted that he would excel. His home environment, his church, and his school, had taught him that. It is not surprising that he believed it. Unemployment, destitution, private charity, and public relief momentarily stunned him and smashed his pride. He is now recovering from the double blow and is becoming restive. As he realizes that he is likely to remain a worker earning a more or less precarious living in an economically unstable society, he will react exactly as his European brothers have done before him. He will build his own economic and political organizations and will take action to assure his economic well-being. When he finds that he is definitely handicapped in solving his problems under the *status quo,* he will challenge existing society itself. Already he is beginning to do so. As yet the issues are by no means clear to him. They will be in the future. In other words, the difference between the European and North American worker is due to differences in economic environment and in time. The North American has lagged in taking political and economic action for the plain and simple reason that he did not need them, but he will be forced to use both in the future. Likewise, there is little reason to doubt that monopoly capital will pursue the policies here that it has pursued elsewhere in defending its interests. Since labour on this continent must perforce start from scratch, and since it is still only dimly aware of the forces at work, Fascism must be given better than an even chance of success. It will not be called that, for Fascism abroad has earned too unsavoury a name, and it will not be as direct, as open, or as brutal for "we don't do those things". But it will be Fascism.

Certain Canadians are fond of proclaiming that "Canada is a middle-class country". They labour under the delusion that a *state of mind* can offset the *economic forces* that are at work here as elsewhere. Admittedly, class lines in Canada have been, for reasons already mentioned, less rigidly drawn than in Europe. The fact that the average Canadian worker still considers himself either actually or potentially a member of the middle class proves only that he is blissfully unaware of what is going on around him. His relatively high standard of living in the past has lulled him into a sense of security that is at variance with the present facts of the situation. As the issues become clearer, class lines will be more sharply drawn. It does not necessarily follow that class interests automatically determine political philosophy—the rank and file of Fascism *prove* that. The very fact that such a large percentage of North Americans fail to correlate their own economic interests and their political philosophy is a positive guarantee that Fascism here will not lack the mass basis so necessary for its rise to power. Any ostensibly radical party that formulates its economic philosophy and chooses its political platform on the assumption that "Canada is a middle-class country" is foredoomed to political impotence and eventually to extinction. As economic crisis sharpens, such parties are invariably split asunder. The smaller, more active, and class-conscious group will move to the left. The larger, more inchoate group, including most of its present leaders, will lose its identity by moving to the right where it logically belongs. In other words, it will share the fate that Social Democracy has inevitably met elsewhere. A denial of this inevitability based on the assumption that Canada "is somehow different" is not only proof positive that its leaders do not understand the issues at stake; it is also ample evidence that they cannot learn.

Writers on the extreme left wing have frequently maintained that Social Democratic leaders are thoroughly conscious from the beginning of the role they are to play, and that their every action is a deliberate betrayal of the working-class. There is undoubtedly some evidence which compels one to suspect the sincerity and integrity of certain Social Democratic leaders, but to maintain that as a group they are nothing less than scheming charlatans is simply fantastic. The truer explanation is that they are, in the majority of cases, misguided idealists who fail to see that what they really want can only be obtained by means which they abhor and so repudiate. They are men of debate rather than of action, and their task involves the tearing down of stone walls with bare hands. Naturally enough they fail.

Capitalism has so far survived, not so much because of its leaders, as in spite of their blindness, stupidity, and downright blundering. Its own inherent strength plus the ignorance and apathy of the class it must exploit in order to exist are the explanation of much of its ability to survive. If its representatives were but half as diabolically clever as certain extremists believe them to be, the nations of the world would not now be confronted with the spectres facing them on half a dozen fronts. Roosevelt is no Social Democrat, but to describe his New Deal as representing "the most comprehensive and ruthless attempt of finance-capital to consolidate its power with the entire strength of the State machine over the whole field of industry, to hold the workers in subjection under extreme and intensified exploitation with a universal lowering of standards, to conduct on this basis and on the basis of the depreciated dollar a world campaign for markets, and to prepare directly the consequent inevitable war"[21] is to give a completely erroneous picture. One statement alone will refute it—President Roosevelt is by no means so clever. While it is true that the New Deal may eventually *produce* those results, the statement that it was so *planned* is absurd. And so with the Social Democrats—*they* plan but *other factors* determine.

Granting the inevitability of the *appearance* of Fascism, does it logically follow that it must *come into power*? The answer is an emphatic *No*. Calm acceptance of the opposite implies an economic fatalism that even Karl Marx (popular opinion notwithstanding) spent much of his life and efforts refuting. The temporary prevention of Fascism depends upon a *united stand* of all genuinely liberal elements against it. That common cause does *not* necessarily imply the adoption of a common programme *except on that one issue*. For Canadian Social Democrats to refuse to co-operate with more radical elements because they "can't depend on them" is palpably hypocritical in the light of Social Democracy's record of failure (if not betrayal) elsewhere. If Canadian Fascism, now but a latent possibility, ever comes into power because its opponents fail to unite against it, the blame will lie at the door of Social Democracy.

The permanent solution of the Fascist menace can result only from the liquidation of those interests for whose protection Fascism is created and maintained. At present, a "middle-road" exists, though it is becoming perceptibly narrower. Another world-wide war will blast it, along with many other things, into oblivion. The chances of permanent peace leave even the most conservative pessimistic to-day.

In summary, Fascism is Undemocratic Capitalism. It results from economic crisis, a decline in parliamentarianism, and the threat

[21]Palme Dutt, *Fascism and Social Revolution*, p. 267.

of Communism. It originates as a petty middle-class movement with a nondescript programme, the obfuscations, ambiguities, and contradictions of which are mystically welded into a dazzling halo about the head of a blindly-followed LEADER. It comes to maturity through a union of Big and Little capital inspired by confusion and alarm. Its appearance upon the political stage is *via* a quasi-constitutional entrance, and scene 1 of the play witnesses a consolidation of power along loosely interpreted democratic lines; scene 2 is one long war —a series of battles fought along numerous fronts: against unemployment, destitution, adverse trade balances, declining gold reserves, the machinations of jealous foreign nations, renegades within the state, Pontine mosquitoes, and Jews—and ends in a glorious Pyrrhic victory; scene 3 presents the deification of a shadowy figure, the *Corporate State*, and the worship of the Holy Trinity of Fascism— Political Absolutism, Religious Mysticism, and Economic Nationalism. As the curtain falls on act I, the Fascist army, composed of all able-bodied males over the age of eight, marches forth to smash its natural foe—Democracy.

THE ARGUMENTS FOR CENTRAL BANKING IN THE BRITISH DOMINIONS

A. F. W. PLUMPTRE

FOUR of the British Dominions are sufficiently similar, in their economics and politics, to permit comparisons and generalizations. All four of them have introduced central banking; the necessary legislation having been adopted in South Africa in 1920, in Australia in 1924, in New Zealand in 1933, and in Canada in 1934. This paper recounts the arguments which were generally used in favour of the innovation, and describes some of the more *immediate* influences which, *within* the Dominions, promoted the same end. There is little discussion of the fundamental influence of the trend towards state intervention. There is no discussion of the influence which was exerted from England.

Intelligent, Unified Monetary Control

"The observer cannot but be impressed by the absence in Canada of any single banking authority. . . . To what extent and through what organizations should the volume of credit and currency be regulated? On what body should lie the primary responsibility for maintaining the external stability of the country's currency? To what institution may the government most suitably turn for informed and impartial advice on matters of financial policy? In the great, and increasing, majority of countries the answer to these questions has been found in the existence or the creation of a central bank."[1] So ran the report of a Canadian royal commission in 1933. The same line of argument was followed by the finance minister in each Dominion when he sponsored central banking legislation. "Decision and settled policy are essential. Divided counsel and clashing interests of individual bankers must in the end be fatal to good credit

[1]*Report of the Royal Commission on Banking and Currency in Canada, 1933* (Ottawa, King's Printer), pp. 61-2.

191

management", said the Australian.[2] "Our forefathers got along reasonably well with very primitive forms of barter. . . . The central bank merely represents another stage in the evolution of monetary science. . . . [It is] a national institution to co-ordinate and control our banking system", said the New Zealander.[3]

It was broadly true to state that the commercial bankers in the various Dominions did not consciously formulate or implement a "national monetary policy". In each of the Dominions there were a very few commercial banks, occupying a position which facilitated a certain amount of collective activity. Such action sometimes concerned the movement of interest or exchange rates, but was usually taken rather unwillingly, under the pressure of circumstances, with an eye to profits but without much cognizance of its general economic effects. This was particularly the case in Canada[4] (where the exchange rate was free to fluctuate and not a "quoted rate") ; but it was also largely true of the other Dominions.

Nowhere is the decline of laissez-faire and the trend to state control seen more clearly than in the mistrust of self-seeking and divided banking counsels. Time was, not so very long ago, when the absence of a single unified purpose was considered to be at any rate presumptive evidence in favour of the existing state of affairs ; individual self-interest producing, under the Divine Hand, activity for the general good. Time was, too, when it was presumed that the government, intervening with the best of intentions, would do the job in such a bungle that the last state would be worse than the first. But the proponents of central banking, of conscious, intelligent control, have scarcely had to pay any attention to such views for they are held only by a decreasing minority. Certainly, if the proponents of central banking had been swimming against the tide instead of with it, they would have found themselves in considerable difficulties. They could not even answer the simple question : What policy should

[2]The Hon. Earle Page, *Speech in the House of Representatives, June 13, 1924* (Melbourne, Government Printer), p. 2.

[3]The Rt. Hon. J. G. Coates, *The Reserve Bank Proposal* (Wellington, Government Printer, 1933), p. 12.

[4]A. F. W. Plumptre, "Canadian Monetary Policy" (in *The Canadian Economy and Its Problems* ed. by H. A. Innis and A. F. W. Plumptre, Toronto, 1934, p. 159).

your central bank follow? Individually, of course, they could reply: but collectively their voices were babel.[5]

PRIVATE BANKERS' MONOPOLY

In addition to the statement that the banks did *not* adopt a common policy in the public interest, another was made that they *did* adopt one in their own. In both contentions there was, of course, a measure of truth, although the great size of most of the banks made them such easy political targets as to invite exaggeration of their monopolistic activities. In all the Dominions there were groups who saw, in the introduction of a central bank by the state, a means whereby the bankers' monopoly might be broken. These groups fell into three classes. One class was of a radical, perhaps socialistic, turn of mind; and regarded the operations of the private bankers as broadly anti-social and predatory. Another class was of small business men, farmers, and other clients of the banks who had reason, real or imagined, for dissatisfaction with the treatment which the banks had accorded them. The third class consisted of civil servants and members of governments who were similarly dissatisfied.

The radical and progressive groups did not have much to do with the final establishment of the central banks. It is quite possible, however, that the part they played in earlier years by means of continual speeches inside and outside Parliament was ultimately of considerable significance.[6] When the more conservative members of the countries

[5]Vera C. Smith, *The Rationale of Central Banking* (London, 1936), p. 167.
[6]*Round Table,* vol. XXIV, 1933-4, p. 622. The following members of the Canadian Progressive group made motions in favour of central and national banking (dates and pages of *Hansard* in parentheses): Mr. Irvine (May 1, 1922, p. 1289; Feb. 26, 1923, p. 627); Mr. Shaw (May 21, 1924, p. 2371); Mr. Woodsworth (March 4, 1925, p. 753; April 14, 1926, p. 2416; Feb. 13, 1928); and Mr. Coote (1931, p. 1547). At an even earlier date Mr. W. F. MacLean spoke in favour of the creation of a "Bank of Canada as I would call it. It would be a bank of rediscount . . . and emission of a national currency" (*Hansard,* 1916, pp. 1814-5). The earliest suggestion for a central bank was no doubt that of the governor-general, Lord Sydenham, in 1841. A friend of Lord Overstone, he proposed the introduction of legislation similar to Peel's Bank Act of 1844. It is probably fortunate that Canada, in its subsequent rapid developments, was not encumbered with the strait jacket of a bank of issue strictly bound by the Currency Principle. See R. M. Breckenridge, *The Canadian Banking System, 1817-1890* (New York, 1895), pp. 109-13.

and the legislatures had become favourable to the project, those who held more advanced opinion had travelled ahead and looked back suspiciously. They were apprehensive lest a prop of their platform should be removed by the erection of an ineffectual and all too conservative central bank.[7] In South Africa the enthusiasts for broader measures of state banking were actually hostile to the establishment of the Reserve Bank.[8] In Canada they opposed the form rather than the fact of the proposed central bank, arguing that its powers were too limited and that private ownership was merely a thin veil behind which the management of the bank would slip into the hands of vested financial interests. Large numbers of people in Canada and New Zealand had been taught by Major Douglas and others that central banks were merely the instruments by which international financiers executed their nefarious schemes. They, of course, were opposed; although in Canada they had no parliamentary representation when the central bank was in process of formation. In general, advanced and radical monetary opinion gave very qualified support to the actual central banking bills when they were introduced.

In Australia such opinion was also disappointed, but in a different way. The Commonwealth Bank of Australia was founded by a Labour government, and it gained support from the rank and file of the party largely in order to "break the ring" of private banks. But the left wing of the Labour party was never satisfied; for the governor of the new bank, chosen from one of the other banks, followed a co-operative rather than a combative policy. This dissatisfaction increased as the bank gradually assumed the role of noncompetitive central banking.

Amongst advanced and radical groups there were various shades of opinion regarding the nature of the monopolistic operations of the commercial bankers. Some regarded these institutions as profiting greatly from their privilege to issue notes;[9] and in Australia, South Africa, and Canada the bankers lent confirmation to this suspicion by objecting most strenuously to its loss. (Actually it is very doubt-

[7]Arnold Plant, "The Relations between Banking and the State in the Union of South Africa" (in *London Essays in Economics in Honour of Edwin Cannan* ed. by T. E. Gregory, London, 1927, p. 99).

[8]Arnold Plant, "The Future of Central Banking in South Africa" (*The Banker,* London, vol. V, March, 1928, p. 385).

[9]*Ibid.*

ful whether the privilege was as valuable even as the bankers themselves thought.[10] The New Zealand bankers seem to have recognized that the issues were of little value, considering that heavy taxes removed most of the profit.[11]) Other groups were suspicious of the banks' control of credit; believing that they were consciously expanding and contracting in order to manipulate prices and, in times of deflationary contraction, obtain control through bankruptcy of the hard-earned wealth of private manufacturers and primary producers. Still others believed that, by keeping credit scarce they were reaping a rich reward of usury; keeping others poor in a world of potential plenty. It was usually made clear, therefore, by the more conservative groups which were responsible for the introduction of central banking, that the new institution was *not* designed to promote inflation or to meet such situations as the radicals pictured.

Some similar disillusionment (but not too much) had to be imparted to the second group which hoped to see the bankers' monopoly broken: that is, to the individuals who were dissatisfied with their treatment by the banks. Their complaints were numerous and their knowledge of accepted central banking was limited.[12] The New Zealand minister of finance did go so far as to say that "the setting up of a central bank in New Zealand will undoubtedly lead to cheaper credit . . . for farmers and traders generally".[13] As a statement by a responsible minister this was exceptional; but amongst the voters there was some support to be won for a central bank by dwelling on the grievances against the banks—high interest rates, excessive charges for small services, unduly wide spreads between buying and selling rates for exchange, and a number of other extortions, real or imaginary.

We now turn to the third and most immediately powerful of the groups which challenged the entrenched position of the banks. In

[10]See article by "Economist" in *Financial Post*, Toronto, Dec. 16, 1933.

[11]New Zealand Monetary Committee, 1934, *Minutes of Evidence* (Wellington, Government Printer), p. 39.

[12]A. F. W. Plumptre, "The Evidence Presented to the 'Canadian Macmillan Commission'" (*Canadian Journal of Economics and Political Science*, vol. II, Feb., 1936, p. 58). Also *Report of the Royal Commission on Banking and Currency in Canada, 1933*, ch. vii. Also Plant, "The Future of Central Banking in South Africa".

[13]Coates, *The Reserve Bank Proposal*, p. 4.

the governments and civil services, as among the academic economists, there was not much credence given to the idea that the bankers were monopolistically manipulating the total volume of credit for their pernicious purposes. Indeed, in those circles the view was more widely held that the bankers simply did not understand how bank credit and deposits, viewed in the aggregate, came into being, or what the effects of variations in these factors might be upon the national economy. The influence of academic economists has been considerable throughout the central banking movement in the Dominions. It started in 1924 when an American professor, E. W. Kemmerer, was invited to make suggestions, *inter alia*, for the improvement of the Reserve Bank of South Africa. It reached a high point in Canada in 1933-4. In 1931 the newly elected Conservative administration was openly hostile to the proposals for central banking which emanated from Progressive and later from Liberal quarters.[14] About the same time C. A. Curtis and other economists in Queen's University were sponsoring a central bank. In 1932 one of their number, Dr. W. C. Clark, who had practical financial experience in the United States, was appointed deputy minister (under-treasurer) of finance. In 1933 the prime minister disclosed that he had adopted the cause of central banking, even before he had appointed a royal commission to investigate the matter.[15] In 1934 the necessary legislation was devised, presumably in the Department of Finance, and passed through Parliament; and a young banker with known academic sympathies was appointed governor. In 1935 the bank began operations.

The Dominion governments (other than the Australian) established their central banks in defiance of the advice of the commercial banks and in part as a method of escape from them. Governments and their administrators felt handicapped and irritated by their dependence upon a small cohesive group of large extensive banks for their short term accommodation, their long term issues of bonds and their supplies of foreign exchange. As the needs of government grew, the dependence naturally became more irksome; particularly

[14]See discussion by Mr. Bennett and others of Mr. Coote's resolution "That a nationally owned central bank be established" (*Hansard*, 1931, pp. 1547 *ff.*).

[15]*Financial Post*, Toronto, Oct. 21, 1933. On another occasion the same paper called Dr. Clark "the godfather of the Bank of Canada".

as the banks often seemed to be using their monopolistic, creditor position to drive hard bargains. However, the extending conceptions of state control brought, together with the new burdens, an avenue of escape; and this was the foundation of a central bank, endowed with the necessary financial machinery to facilitate government operations but shorn of the profit motive and dedicated to the public good. With the growth of nationalism it seemed *infra dig.* that the central government and other public bodies should be dependent upon, and sometimes even thwarted by, a group of private institutions. In Canada, at any rate, it was hoped in some quarters that the new central bank would become the banker, not only of the Dominion, but of provinces and municipalities.[16]

The nature of the clash between public authority and financial authority has been delineated as follows:

> The present conflict between governments and financial institutions is not in practice a simple conflict between debtor and creditor or labour and capital (although it undoubtedly arises from the fixed claims to income associated with certain forms of private property) but a conflict between governments and salaried trustees. These trustees who are officials of insurance companies, trust companies, banks, and investment banking companies constitute a small and powerful financial bureaucracy. It is their business to defend the assets under their administration and they may be expected to resist any [downward] adjustment of interest charges which is not forced upon them by overwhelming odds.[17]

Controversy over the establishment of central banks was, in Canada and New Zealand, closely associated with conflict over the course and control of interest rates. There were some financiers, familiar with modern monetary thought, who were willing to see interest rates fall in the years succeeding 1929. But most of them were persuaded by tradition, self-interest, and distrust of a policy which seemed to facilitate the accumulation of government debt, to fight reductions step by step. It was into this scene that the governments of New Zealand and Canada introduced proposals for the establishment of machinery, central banks, to control interest rates.

The conflict between public authority and private finance arose,

[16]Plumptre, "The Evidence Presented to the 'Canadian Macmillan Commission'", p. 57.

[17]D. C. MacGregor, "The Problem of Public Debt in Canada" (*Canadian Journal of Economics and Political Science,* vol. II, May, 1936, pp. 186-7).

even more acutely, over the proposals that the central banks should take over the commercial banks' local stocks of gold at the old statutory price instead of at the substantially higher market price.[18] At this suggestion even the bankers who were liberally disposed towards central banking were very annoyed. And yet, as in the case of interest rates and the establishment of the central banks themselves, the victory went in the end to the governments in both New Zealand and Canada.

ESCAPE FROM "FOREIGN" DOMINATION

One of the arguments upon which the Canadian prime minister laid considerable stress, in public speeches favouring a central bank, was that it would free the Canadian dollar from American domination. Earlier in his term of office he had found his budget considerably burdened by the "extra" cost of servicing debt, payable in American dollars, out of depreciated Canadian ones: and he had, apparently, gathered that the exchange rate between the two currencies was in some way determined in New York, beyond Canadian borders and Canadian control. Nobody operating in the foreign exchange market would describe the situation in this way. Nevertheless Mr. Bennett was anxious to remedy the condition as he saw it; and what is significant is that he considered the matter one of sufficient importance to be used as an argument in favour of a central bank.

Likewise in New Zealand, it was found that the exchange rate was managed from abroad and without consideration of the country's interests. A statement by the New Zealand Treasury, made shortly after the Reserve Bank was established, ran as follows:

Four of the six banks carrying on business in New Zealand, from the point of view of their operations, are primarily Australian institutions. Australia is operating on a sterling-exchange system very similar to that of New Zealand, and the London balances to finance the trade of both countries, so far as these four banks were concerned, really formed one fund. In fact some of the banks themselves did not know how much of their London funds had accrued from

---

[18]The Rt. Hon. J. G. Coates, *The Reserve Bank of New Zealand and the Gold Question* (Wellington, Dec., 1933). Also Select Standing Committee on Banking and Commerce, House of Commons (Canada), 1934, *Minutes of Proceedings and Evidence,* pp. 897-914, evidence given by S. H. Logan, acting president of the Canadian Bankers' Association, and pp. 917-32, by W. C. Clark, deputy minister of finance.

New Zealand business and how much from Australian business. [Rates of exchange between New Zealand and London were thus largely dependent upon the position of Australia; the larger country being subject to much wider climatic and economic variations. This situation] worked unfairly to the people of this Dominion.[19]

Just as Canadians chafed under the charge that their dollar was controlled in New York, so people in the other three Dominions fretted when they heard that their respective pounds were controlled in London. (In New Zealand some people held that the local currency was governed in London and some in Australia.) It is doubtful whether this nationalistic feeling had very much to do with the establishment of the Reserve Bank of South Africa immediately after the war, or with the transformation of the Commonwealth Bank of Australia into a central bank. It undoubtedly had not a little to do with the South African government's refusal to follow sterling off gold in 1931. It even found a place among the arguments for the establishment of a central bank in New Zealand, that most British of Dominions.

INTERNATIONAL AND INTRA-IMPERIAL CO-OPERATION

A certain argument was made out in favour of central banking on grounds of international and intra-imperial co-operation. In all the Dominions, except in South Africa which obtained its central bank at an earlier date, it was possible to quote from the resolutions of the financial conferences at Brussels (1920) and Genoa (1922) which commended central banks to the governments of such countries as still lacked them.[20] A similar statement came from the World Economic Conference of 1933. The recommendations of various Imperial Conferences to the same effect were also serviceable, and the more tardy Dominions were specifically urged to catch up with the others.[21] Further, the cause of internationalism was actually supported by an appeal to national pride, for it was said that no country could be considered to have attained maturity until it had given birth to a central bank.

[19]New Zealand Monetary Committee, 1934, *Minutes of Evidence,* p. 12.
[20]*Report of the Royal Commission on Banking and Currency in Canada, 1933,* p. 62.
[21]*Ibid.,* p. 64. See also Sir Josiah Stamp, *Central Banking as an Imperial Factor* (University of Nottingham, Cust Foundation Lecture, 1934).

Co-operation was not a cry to evoke great public enthusiasm in the Dominions. In certain parts it was possible to gain applause for anything which appeared to strengthen the ties of the British Empire, and the proposals for central banks received pontifical approval from the City of London. But in the Dominions it is probable that this approval was more often regarded as part of a predatory plot than as an infallible pronouncement. Those who urged co-operation seldom, if ever, explained in any detail what forms it would take and wherein its benefits would lie. Their broad generalities no doubt appealed to enthusiastic imperialists and internationalists. But even amongst this intelligentzia the question sometimes arose why it should be necessary to establish a certain type of financial machinery, called a central bank, in order to secure co-operation.

There was another objection to the argument of internationalism which was sometimes made, and this was that it was difficult to see tangible evidence of existing co-operation. A Canadian royal commissioner, who had been minister of finance throughout the war, wrote as follows in his dissent from the recommendation for a central bank: "Expressions of opinion by international conferences no longer, I am sorry to be obliged to say, carry weight with the public in any part of the world. History records no more tragic futilities than the deliberations and resolutions of these all too numerous gatherings from the Treaty of Versailles to the present day."[22]

Unsatisfactory Currency Legislation

In each of the Dominions the argument for a central bank was supported by, indeed may have originated from, the discovery that the existing legislation upon note issue was unsatisfactory. In all four countries the regulations had undergone appreciable changes under the stress of war. After the war the law was discovered in Australia to be too rigid; in South Africa and Canada to be too lax; and in New Zealand to be out of touch with actuality.

In South Africa[23] until 1920 all paper money was supplied by the

[22]*Report of the Royal Commission on Banking and Currency in Canada, 1933*, p. 90.

[23]See C. S. Richards, "The Kemmerer-Vissering Report and the Position of the Reserve Bank of the Union of South Africa" (*Economic Journal*, vol. XXXV, Dec., 1925, p. 558). Also Sir Henry Strakosch, "The South African Reserve Bank" (*Economic Journal*, vol. XXXI, June, 1921, p. 172). Also

commercial banks. Their notes were not legal tender and had to be redeemed in gold. At the very beginning of the war a ban was placed upon gold exports. Thus, without immediate danger to their gold reserves, the banks supported war-time inflation by expansion of their notes and credit. When, after the war, exchange rates were unpegged, a high premium developed and gold began to be withdrawn from the banks and smuggled abroad. Runs on the banks occurred. The bankers were thus as anxious as anyone to change the existing situation as soon as possible, although they certainly did not urge the establishment of a central bank as the remedy.

In Australia,[24] where the note issues of the private banks had been taxed out of existence shortly before the war, the government note issue was gradually increased under the pressure of war finance, the ratio of gold reserves being maintained by tempting or cajoling the banks to surrender their stocks. An attempt was made to impart some direction and elasticity to the issue by the establishment in 1920 of a Notes Board which had to hold certain gold reserves and was permitted to invest in trade and treasury bills. The Notes Board eked out an unhappy existence during the post-war deflation and revival (for which, of course, it was held responsible in some quarters) and latterly there was actually a note shortage arising out of an insufficiency of approved local collateral. This unsatisfactory state of affairs was a factor in precipitating the reconstitution of the Commonwealth Bank in 1924. Under these provisions the note issue was finally handed over to the bank; and sterling assets might be held, although not yet among the minimum reserves, in its note issue department.

In New Zealand[25] the entire paper circulation consisted until 1934 of the issues of the private banks. In war time the banks' powers of issue were greatly extended and even after the lapse of

---

E. H. D. Arndt, *Banking and Currency Development in South Africa* (*1652-1927*) (Cape Town, 1928), part II, ch. xii, "The Rise of Central Banking".

[24]Page, *Speech in the House of Representatives, June 13, 1924.* Also L. C. Jauncey, *Australia's Government Bank* (London, 1933), ch. ix.

[25]See B. C. Ashwin, "Banking and Currency in New Zealand" (*Economic Record*, vol. VI, Nov., 1930, p. 188). Also New Zealand Monetary Committee, 1934, *Minutes of Evidence*, pp. 1-13, statement by the Treasury, and p. 34, bankers' evidence. Also Coates, *The Reserve Bank Proposal.* Also Sir Otto Niemeyer, *Report on Banking and Currency in New Zealand* (Wellington, 1931).

certain war-time privileges they could still issue up to the limit of their coin and bullion, and their holdings of public securities of New Zealand, the United Kingdom, and the Commonwealth and States of Australia. The power to issue against this wide selection of bonds might have permitted an indefinite expansion. Actually, however, the banks' statements usually showed their issues to be far less than their eligible assets would allow. One of the incentives to expand the issues was removed by heavy taxation upon bank notes. Moreover, the banks had other criteria than their cash and marketable securities in New Zealand (notably their balances held in London) upon which to base their credit policies. With New Zealand, in fact, operating on a sterling-exchange standard, the existing currency legislation, which presumed a gold standard with gold coinage in circulation, was clearly out of touch with reality. Redemption of notes in gold had been suspended during the war, and bank notes made legal tender. The latter provision had survived, but was to lapse in 1932. Two years in advance English advice was secured, and it recommended the recognition of the sterling standard together with the establishment of a central bank.

In Canada[26] the system of note issues was most complex. For many years before the war government notes (known as Dominion notes) for one and two dollars used to circulate side by side with bank notes of five dollars and upwards. Both issues were subject to fairly rigorous legal limitations, and Dominion notes were backed by gold on a fiduciary issue basis. With the advent of war not only was the fiduciary issue expanded, but under special emergency legislation[27] the banks were permitted to borrow Dominion notes from the Department of Finance; and no limitation such as a proportional gold reserve was placed upon the issue of notes in this manner. The

[26]See C. A. Curtis, "The Canadian Monetary Situation" (*Journal of Political Economy*, vol. XL, June, 1932). Also by the economists of Queen's University, "The Proposal for a Central Bank" (*Queen's Quarterly*, vol. XL, Aug., 1933). Also A. F. W. Plumptre, six articles in *Financial Post*, Toronto, Oct.-Nov., 1932; reprinted in pamphlet form, under the title *A Central Bank for Canada*. Also *Report of the Royal Commission on Banking and Currency in Canada, 1933*, pp. 57-60.

[27]The Finance Act, 1914, c. 3, 5 Geo. V. The sections relating to borrowing of Dominion notes by the banks were re-enacted, almost unchanged, in c. 48 of 1923. They were consolidated into the Revised Statutes of Canada, 1927, as c. 70.

objective of this measure was to protect and strengthen the banking system, which was faced by runs, and generally to facilitate finance during the war. The banks soon became fairly accustomed to borrowing Dominion notes of large denominations, and used them as a basis of reserves for extension of credit and bank-note issues. The government exercised little or no restriction over the banks' use of this privilege; and the natural result, in a competitive commercial banking system, was a substantial expansion in boom times (*e.g.*, 1920 and 1929) and an equally substantial withdrawal of note issues and contraction of the basis of credit in subsequent depressions. In academic circles this unregulated elasticity of the note issues was made the crux of the case for a central bank. A similar case was made in the report of the Royal Commission on Banking and Currency in Canada, 1933.

CONCLUSION

In all countries, and particularly in those which are democratically governed, any important change of government policy will be supported by a great diversity of argument. So it was with the introduction of central banking. Sometimes the proponents of central institutions were to be found arguing that the existing banks were exploiting a monopolistic position at the expense of the public and the government; sometimes arguing that the banks were good enough in their way, and needed only unified and intelligent leadership; some argued that a central bank was needed to protect national interests against the dominance of foreign financiers; some argued that it was needed to cement imperial and international ties; and still others supplied grist to the political mill by their disclosures of the difficulties and dangers attached to the existing currency legislation.

The central banks are now established and are taking their places in the political and economic life of the four countries. Like the Bank of England, they will probably live to serve purposes far other than those which were originally put forward in their support. But before the tumult and the shouting dies away it is worth while to make some record of it.[28]

[28]Worth while, if for no other reason, as a comment upon "The Role of Intelligence in the Social Process". *Cf.* Professor Urwick's article of that title in the *Canadian Journal of Economics and Political Science*, vol. I, Feb., 1935, p. 64.

PROBLEMS OF THE DROUGHT AREA IN WESTERN CANADA

W. J. WAINES

$\mathbf{E}$ IGHT years of drought in the Prairie Provinces have served to revive doubts as to the ability of the short-grass prairie lands of Western Canada permanently to support a population of some 900,000 persons predominantly dependent, directly or indirectly, upon agriculture. These doubts are as old as the exploration of the plains and various opinions are recorded respecting them. The servants of the Hudson's Bay Company, familiar with the country but not entirely unbiased, argued that lack of fuel, inferior soil, lack of moisture, the frost hazard, and difficulties of transportation imposed fairly rigid limitations on agricultural settlement. Captain John Palliser, on behalf of the British government, explored the region west of Lake Superior during the years 1857-60 and he considered "Palliser's Triangle" as an area of semi-arid desert and unfit for agricultural development. Professor H. Y. Hind, who explored portions of the West in 1857 and 1858, agreed in general with Palliser's conclusions.[1] John Macoun, botanist to the Sandford Fleming expedition in 1872, and to the Selwyn expedition in 1875, was more optimistic. In 1879 he investigated the causes of the supposed aridity of the southern area. "I found a parched surface, dried and withered grasses, and, in short, every appearance of the existence of much aridity; but closer examination showed that these indications were illusory." At Blackfoot Crossing "where the consequences of aridity appeared the strongest, I came upon ground broken up in the spring, bearing excellent crops of all kinds—oats being four feet high, while on the land outside the fence the grass was burnt up and all other vegetation withered. From this I argued that the rainfall in the district was evidently ample for the requirements of vegetation, but that, until the baked crust was broken, it could not percolate the ground as rapidly as it fell and so a great portion was

[1]W. A. Mackintosh, *Prairie Settlement: The Geographical Setting* (Toronto, 1934), ch. xi.

evaporated by the dry atmosphere and lost. Thus the apparent
aridity vanishes before the first efforts of husbandry."[2] His optimism
was partly responsible for the shift of the projected route of the
Canadian Pacific Railway from the "fertile belt" in the north to the
semi-arid region of the south.[3] This optimism grew and culminated
in the phenomenal expansion after 1900.

Shortly after the opening of the decade of the eighties, settlers
penetrated the second prairie level and there began a battle against
the hazards of frost and drought.[4] Evidence suggests that during
the period 1883-96 there were years in which precipitation was as low
as it has been since 1929, and that there was in addition considerable
frost damage.[5] In consequence, settlement for agriculture was inter-
mittent in spite of the inducements offered by the railway, the coloni-
zation companies, and the government.[6] Ranching developed rapidly
between 1880 and 1900, and in the latter year covered a large portion
of the prairies. With the rapid increase in settlement after 1900, the
greater part of the country was rapidly converted to wheat growing
and the area of the open range declined.[7] Hazards of drought and
frost stimulated attempts to conquer the physical handicaps through
improved techniques. Red Fife, an earlier maturing wheat than the
Red River variety, was introduced. The government established the
system of experimental farms under the direction of William Saunders
and the search for Marquis was begun, and, after 1895, from the
station at Indian Head, Angus Mackay began his propaganda for dry-
farming methods. The decade 1901-10, as Professor Morton points

[2]John Macoun, *Manitoba and the Great North-West* (Guelph, 1882), p. 144.
[3]A. S. Morton, *History of Prairie Settlement* (Macmillan, in press), p. 51.
[4]*Ibid.*, chs. iv and v.
[5]E. S. Hopkins *et al.*, *Soil Drifting Control in the Prairie Provinces* (Ottawa,
1937), pp. 50-1; A. S. Morton, *History of Prairie Settlement*, chs. iv and v; S. D.
Clark, "Settlement in Saskatchewan, with Reference to the Influence of Dry
Farming" (University of Saskatchewan, M. A. Thesis, 1931).
[6]*E.g.*, the following figures (from Clark, "Settlement in Saskatchewan",
p. 49) for the Qu'Appelle–Regina–Moose Jaw district illustrate the point:

	1885	*1891*
Occupiers of land	2,593	2,502
Acreage of improved land	99,112	75,142

[7]R. W. Murchie *et al.*, *Agricultural Progress on the Prairie Frontier* (Toronto,
1936), ch. v.

out, "stands in sharp contrast with the previous ten years. The problems of farming in a semi-arid region were partially solved. . . . The precipitation of these ten years proved less variable, and prices of wheat were good. . . . Immigrants were pouring in."[8]

The rapid rate of development after 1895, which led to unwise utilization of certain areas of land, was possible because of a coincidence of favourable factors. Wheat prices were rising and transportation costs were falling owing to the development of new techniques and their rapid adaptation to western conditions under the stimulus of government assistance. The rapid industrialization of other countries and the ease with which the industrial and agricultural techniques of older countries, as well as the money with which to purchase the capital equipment, could be borrowed were contributing factors. Dry farming, early maturing wheat, barbed wire, the windmill, and the land speculator spelled the doom of the open range. Railways required traffic and purchasers for their lands; the homestead and immigration policies provided both. To the middle of the decade 1901-10 there had been little invasion of "Palliser's Triangle" by the wheat grower, but, during the following years, and especially after 1907, much of the arid region was converted from the range to the farm. The high prices of the war and immediate post-war period, together with government propaganda, induced a rapid extension of wheat acreage in spite of frequently unfavourable climatic conditions. It has been said with respect to the dry area in Alberta "that most of the area was either used for ranching purposes or was unused prior to the big influx of settlement in 1911. From 1911 to the outbreak of the war in 1914 the invasion of this area by the wheat farmer was not serious, but from 1914 onwards the area was rapidly brought under the plough. The land was easily and inexpensively cultivated, the wheat produced was of extremely high quality, prices were good, and the bumper crops of 1915-16 made this area seem a veritable Eldorado."[9] The extent of this invasion by the wheat farmer is evident in an examination of the wheat acreage in south-central and

[8]*History of Prairie Settlement*, p. 119.
[9]*Report on the Rehabilitation of the Dry Areas of Alberta and Crop Insurance, 1935-36* (Edmonton, 1936), p. 25. (Hereafter referred to as *Drought Report.*)

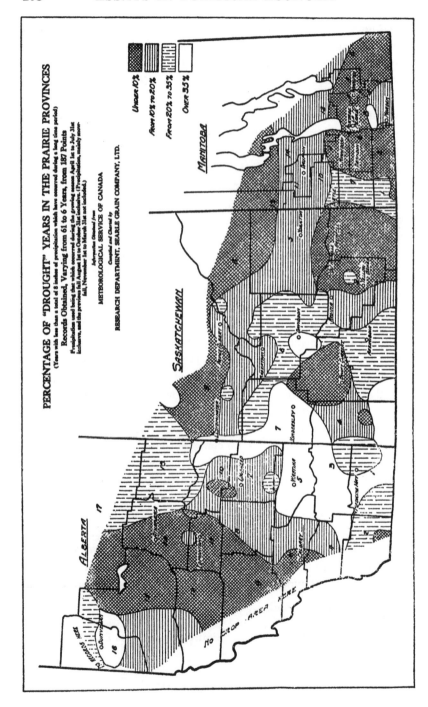

south-western Saskatchewan.[10]   In the south-central district the wheat acreage in 1916 was nearly 1.5 millions; in 1921 over 3 millions; in the south-western district the acreage increased from 298,000 acres in 1916 to over 1 million acres in 1921. At present in the "grazing country"[11] of approximately 24 million acres, the major activities are cattle ranching and wheat farming while some 2 to 3 million acres are occupied by specialized sheep ranchers.

The area subject to drought conditions varies considerably from year to year, as illustrated in the table[12] showing the population and number of farms included within the drought area in the Prairie Provinces. The "Drought Area", specified for rehabilitation under the Prairie Farm Rehabilitation Act, is indicated on the map as including the whole of the short-grass prairie plains and encroaching

[10]Wheat Acreage in 1916 and 1921 in Certain Crop Districts in the Province of Saskatchewan

	1916 acres	1921 acres
Crop district no. 1 (south-eastern)	1,083,652	1,062,863
" " " 2 (Regina-Weyburn)	1,356,605	1,607,763
" " " 3 (south-central)	1,476,257	3,193,377
" " " 4 (south-western)	298,644	1,142,636
	4,215,158	7,006,639

Compiled from *Reports on Crop and other Statistics* issued by the government of the province of Saskatchewan, Department of Agriculture (mimeo.). Crop districts 3 and 4 include the driest regions in the province.

[11]The National Development Bureau has defined the grazing area as that region in which "grazing leases predominated and wheat acreage constituted less than 16% of the total area". See *Drought Report*, p. 27.

[12]Population and Number of Farms Included within the Drought Area, 1929-34

	Population	Number of farms
1929	524,743	85,144
1930	283,336	43,888
1931	699,026	103,146
1932	182,837	30,221
1933	586,044	93,411
1934	646,290	95,157

From Sanford Evans Statistical Service, Winnipeg, *Drought Areas of the Prairie Provinces, 1929-1937*.

NOTE: Population figures include urban population.

upon the southern edges of the park belt. The foothills of the Rocky Mountains form its western boundary; the international boundary from the foothills to, roughly, longitude 98 degrees west, marks its southern limit. From this point the line is drawn in a north-western direction to a point just south of Lloydminster on the Alberta-Saskatchewan border in latitude 53 degrees north. The boundary line then runs in a south-westerly direction to the foothills north-west of Calgary. The total area of this block is about 60 million acres, of which about 45 million acres are occupied and 20 million improved. The occupied acreage in the area is about one-half the occupied acreage of the three provinces, and the improved acreage is about one-third of the total for the provinces. The bulk of this region is devoted to grazing and wheat growing, though mixed farming is common in eastern Saskatchewan and in Manitoba. Grazing is prevalent in south-western Saskatchewan and southern Alberta. The table[13] showing the population of the drought region in certain of the census years since 1901, indicates the very rapid rate of increase between 1901 and 1921, the much slower increase between 1921 and 1931, and the decline between 1931 and 1936. The density of the population of large sections of the area was, in 1931, five or less persons to the square mile and in the dryest portions of the region, less than two.[14]

This generalized picture of the region, while indicating the potential drought area, is not sufficiently detailed to suggest effective lines of approach to the problem. There are portions of the drought area that are subject to frequent severe periods of dry weather, while other parts are less vulnerable. In the prairies, climate is the main controlling factor both with respect to land use and agricultural tech-

[13]POPULATION OF THE DROUGHT AREA, 1901-36

	1901	1911	1921	1926	1931	1936
Manitoba.........	78,000	93,000	98,000	101,000	104,000	101,000
Saskatchewan.....	43,000	314,000	494,000	532,000	580,000	542,000
Alberta..........	29,000	200,000	299,000	292,000	336,000	331,000
Total..........	150,000	607,000	891,000	925,000	1,020,000	974,000
Total Prairie Provinces.....	419,512	1,328,121	1,956,082	2,067,393	2,353,529	

Compiled from the *Census Reports* using the population figures of the census divisions roughly corresponding to the drought area as defined.

[14]Mackintosh, *Prairie Settlement*, p. 68.

nique—in the north, temperature, and in the south, precipitation. The climate[15] is continental in character. The mid-northern latitudinal location of the region, the mountain barrier on the west, and the direction of flow of air currents imply low and varied precipitation, and great extremes of temperature. The problem is fundamentally one of adapting the agricultural economy to this physical environment if it is to become the basis of permanent and successful settlement— an adaptation which must be made with respect to land use, agricultural techniques, and social, financial, and governmental organization. Climatic conditions are never far from the critical point for agricultural production. This, together with the fact of variability from year to year, are the significant facts in the history of settlement and agriculture in the West, and will determine in the end, the successful lines of attack on the economic problems of the area. If the region had always been a desert it never would have been settled, but ranging, as it does, between desert and abundance, settlement has occurred with little regard to the environment.

Professor Mackintosh considers an "annual precipitation of less than 12 inches" as "insufficient for the production of crops",[16] and the critical growing season precipitation as 7½ inches. In the worst of the drought region annual average precipitation is, in general, 15 inches or less. In the section north-west of Medicine Hat it is 11 inches. Not only is average precipitation low, but the range between high and low is extreme.[17] Precipitation varies everywhere from year

[15]For a more detailed discussion of the geography of the area, see *ibid.*, chs. i, vi, and ix; and University of Saskatchewan, College of Agriculture, *Reconnaissance Soil Survey of Saskatchewan*, Soil Survey Report No. *10*, May, 1936.

[16]Mackintosh, *Prairie Settlement*, p. 175.

[17]AVERAGE ANNUAL PRECIPITATION AND THE RANGE BETWEEN HIGH AND LOW FOR REPRESENTATIVE POINTS IN THE DROUGHT AREA

(*The periods covered range from 25 to 53 years*)

	Average	High	Low	Range
				per cent
	inches	inches	inches	of mean
Saskatoon, Sask.........	14.35	21.28	10.38	75
Rosthern, Sask.........	14.59	22.67	10.13	72
Scott, Sask............	13.31	20.79	6.63	106
Swift Current, Sask.....	15.21	24.55	9.66	98
Medicine Hat, Alberta...	12.83	25.28	6.38	147
Lethbridge, Alberta.....	15.51	27.92	7.63	130
Calgary, Alberta........	16.28	34.57	7.91	163

From Hopkins *et al.*, *Soil Drifting Control in the Prairie Provinces*, p. 50.

to year, but where the normal rainfall is abundant no very serious consequences ensue. Where the normal precipitation is scanty, extreme variation means years of drought and years of plenty. Frequency of rainfall deficiency over a long period of time is in many ways more significant than average precipitation, or its variability. Recently prepared charts,[18] showing the percentage of years with less than a total of 8 inches of precipitation during the growing season and the previous fall, indicate that over the driest of the region in more than 35 per cent of the years for which there are records, annual precipitation was less than 8 inches, and that over a great part of the dry section of Alberta and Saskatchewan, and in the southwest part of Manitoba, 20 per cent or more of the years studied were deficient in precipitation.

The causes of such variation are only partially known. "Rain is due to the cooling *en masse* of air which contains water-vapour. Apart from local and temporary conditions there are two principal methods by which this cooling may be brought about. The air may flow to colder latitudes or it may rise to greater altitudes where both temperature and pressure are less. In either case there will be a tendency to produce rain."[19] A mountain range obstructs the easy passage of vapour. The air, being forced upward, expands and cools and so precipitates some of its moisture as rain or snow.[20] Thus the Rocky Mountains force the westerly winds to lose their moisture on the western slopes and pass across the prairies comparatively dry. Hence

the occurrence of rain in appreciable amounts in the Prairie Provinces is dependent upon the advance southward of relatively cool air-masses from the northeast and northwest . . ., in such a way that while warm air-masses carrying water-vapour from the south are invading the grain belt, they are surrounded in their further advance by an environment of relatively cool dry air of septentrional origin. In this environment the vapour-bearing air-masses ascend, expand and cool to such a temperature that they are no longer able to retain all their moisture. . . . Too rapid an advance of cool air from the northeast across Manitoba, cuts off the supply of moisture-bearing air coming from the south, so that rain fails to occur in western Manitoba, or Saskatchewan,

---

[18]Research Department, Searle Grain Company, Ltd., Winnipeg. It should be noted that these charts are not based on effective precipitation, because differences in the rate of evaporation are not taken into account. See p. 208.

[19]Philip Lake, *Physical Geography* (Cambridge, 1933), p. 100.

[20]*Ibid.*, p. 111.

although heavy rain may occur in the western United States on the margin of this cool, northeast polar front. Failure of the cool air-masses to advance from the northwest allows warm air to sweep north over the grain-belt. During these hot spells the amount of moisture carried in the air is often enormous but since there is no interference with the northward movement no precipitation occurs, and very often very little cloud forms. The combination of strong sunshine and great heat in these rainless spells rapidly depletes the soil moisture.[21]

Land elevations, such as the Cypress Hills, cause a greater precipitation in their immediate vicinity than in the surrounding area. The irregularity in the movement of air currents suggests that considerable variation in rainfall is to be expected over the west within the same year, as well as variation from year to year for the same place. Unless the polar and tropical air currents meet over the region, "it is utterly impossible to get rainfall of any account. . . . Thus when drought conditions appear, either one or other of these currents is very weak, and generally this is the polar current, so that the prairies are largely under the domination of the tropical or warm air current during years of drought; this being the case, there is usually more moisture in the air per cubic foot than there is in years of good rainfall, but as there is no means by which the ascension of the air can be forced, there is in consequence no precipitation."[22] It is a matter of record that in dry years there are prevailing south-west and west winds, whereas in wet years there is a prevalence of north-west winds.[23] Why this should be so is still unexplained, but it apparently accounts largely for marked differences in precipitation.

Actual moisture efficiency is a function of temperature and wind velocity as well as of precipitation, as these factors affect the rate of evaporation and transpiration. It is also dependent on the type of crop grown. Hot, dry winds of high velocity are frequent in summer, and it is not uncommon that a satisfactory amount of precipitation in one season is quite inadequate in another due to variations in wind velocity. Recent investigations show that for the points studied wind

[21]W. B. Hurd and T. W. Grindley, *Agriculture, Climate and Population of the Prairie Provinces* (Ottawa, 1931), p. 11.
[22]John Patterson, "Precipitation in the Prairie Provinces" (*Engineering Journal*, vol. XVIII, April, 1935, p. 178).
[23]*Ibid.*, p. 179.

velocities are frequently very high, for example, at Swift Current, often exceeding sixteen miles an hour.[24]

Climate has a direct bearing on the type of vegetation and the character of the soil of a region. The drought area as defined by the Prairie Farm Rehabilitation Act includes the whole of the true prairie region and extends into the park lands.[25] The natural vegetation of the short-grass prairie region is a thin stand of relatively short grasses and sagebrush, cactus and grease-wood. Trees are found only in some valleys and in certain portions of the hilly country. In the intermediate prairie region the stand of grass is heavier and taller, and there are clumps of poplar and willow. In the park land, on the other hand, where the climate is sub-humid, vegetation is more luxuriant—tall grasses prevail, and "bluffs" of poplar and willow are common. Since soils are the product of the original material composing the surface of the region, and of climate and vegetation, it follows that soil types and vegetation are an accurate indication of the climatic conditions over a long period of time. Palliser, in fact, deduced the climatic conditions of the prairie region from the vegetative cover. The soils expert would now deduce the long-run climatic conditions from the nature of the soil. The soils of the true prairies, like the vegetation, are of two general types. There are the brown prairie types with relatively low organic content because of the sparse vegetation, and the dark brown prairie types with a relatively higher organic content. Beyond the true prairie are the black soils which correspond roughly with the park vegetation. Moreover, the depth of the lime carbonate concentration in a soil is a particularly good index of the amount of precipitation. It tends to be nearer the surface in a dry region than in a humid one. In the brown soils it tends to be nearer the surface than in the black soils.[26] These factors are considered particularly important because they seem to provide the most useful approach to the problem of land utilization, which is a significant aspect of the problem of rehabilitation.

The region between the Rockies and the Precambrian Shield consists of a series of plateaus sloping toward the east and north-east. The elevation ranges from 1,000 feet on the eastern edge of the

[24]A. J. Conner and C. C. Boughner, "Prevailing Direction of Wind in Periods of Dust and Drought" (*Report of the National Committee on Soil Drifting*, 1935).

[25]See map, p. 208.

[26]See *Reconnaissance Soil Survey of Saskatchewan*, p. 120.

drought area to 5,000 on the western. The surface is undulating to rolling, but there are several very level districts, and other areas that are extremely rough and badly eroded. Exterior drainage is mainly toward the north-east and east through the Saskatchewan and Assiniboine-Red river systems. A small area in the extreme southern part of Alberta and Saskatchewan is drained into the Mississippi. Large sections are not drained to the exterior but through small creeks into local depressions and lakes which usually become dry in the summer, and in periods of prolonged drought, large lakes may become mere beds of alkali.[27] Analyses made by the Dominion Water Power and Hydrometric Bureau show that the only fairly consistent run-off in the prairie region is from mountain sources. An average of approximately 80 per cent of normal flow has been maintained from these sources during the last six years, while the mean of the run-off from prairie sources has been from 20 to 30 per cent of normal during the same period.[28]

The preceding examination is intended to suggest the significant geographical controls with respect to which policies for the future must be determined. In the Canadian West, in the past, scant respect has been paid to geography, with unfortunate consequences. That long-run climatic changes do occur is admitted, but it seems safe to assume that they occur so slowly that they have little bearing on the immediate problem. Agricultural techniques have intensified the effects of deficient rainfall. "Physical alteration of the soil and loss of organic matter through deterioration and erosion bring about increased moisture losses through surface run-off and evaporation and reduce the amount of moisture that remains available for plant growth."[29] It follows that attention must be paid to cultural practices if progressive deterioration is to be avoided. Climate is beyond man's control. He must adapt himself to it. Adaptation involves the two-fold problem of the uses to which land is to be put and the techniques that are to be applied to it. Adjustments in land utilization will in turn involve adjustments in the distribution of the population and in social and governmental organization.

[27]See P. C. Perry, "The Surface Waters of the Canadian Prairie" (*Engineering Journal*, vol. XVIII, April, 1935, pp. 204-11).

[28]J. T. Johnston, "Surface Water Supply and Runoff of the Prairie Provinces" (*Engineering Journal*, vol. XVIII, April, 1935, pp. 181-93).

[29]*Report of the Great Plains Committee* (Washington, D.C., 1936), p. 32.

A significant implication of the analysis of geographic factors is that the drought area is not uniformly arid. Some portions present an extremely serious problem, while others, though severely affected on certain occasions, are, on the whole, much less subject to an extremely dry climate. No one solution can be applied uniformly to the whole area. Certain portions of the prairies have been devoted to growing wheat which should never have been so used. For example, in seven municipal areas within the Special Municipal Areas in Alberta there were, at the peak of settlement, some 2,400 families. Fifteen years later there were fifteen.[30] The Special Municipal Areas Board, convinced that the region will support in a permanent fashion only a small population, is reclaiming and restoring it to grazing. Probably the bulk of that portion of the brown soils area located in the region of most serious drought should be used for purposes other than wheat growing, those lands most suitable for agriculture being devoted to growing fodder, in some cases possibly under irrigation. This in turn involves the problem of resettlement of people resident in these areas, and the acquisition and allotment of land. In the re-allotment of land, water supply for the stock, grazing capacity of the land, and ability to ensure a reserve of fodder for dry years must be considered. The carrying capacity of the range varies from 40 to 120 acres per head of stock.[31] Consequently the ranch unit must be large. Some portions of the area have been over-grazed or cultivated, and are badly drifted and must be reclaimed. The problem of resettlement is the most difficult, because it involves the task of finding land on which the settlers may eventually become self-supporting.[32]

The 900,000 people resident in the drought area cannot all shift to other regions, but a redistribution of some part of the population in the worst of the region appears to be essential to provide stable agricultural organization in the dry areas, a fact which the enthusiastic advocates of large-scale immigration apparently fail to take into account. Moreover, they generally over-estimate the amount of suitable land available for settlement. Improper utilization of land,

[30]*Drought Report*, pp. 44-5.

[31]*Ibid.*, p. 38.

[32]*Report of the Commissioner of the Northern Settlers' Re-Establishment Board, October, 1937* (Regina, 1937). It should be noted that this branch is not engaged in moving people from the drought area, but in re-establishing those who have moved from there, or from other parts of the province.

unplanned settlement, and an unsuitable system of land survey are obstacles which must be overcome in the process of rehabilitation. While it seems reasonably clear that if some portion of the population were to shift they would, in the long run, be better off as individuals, as would also those who remained in the dry region, there is at present sufficient capital equipment in the form of railways, schools, roads, and other public facilities to accommodate a larger population. To carry this burden requires a larger rather than a smaller population. The financial costs of resettlement are not merely those connected with moving and establishing the people in new homes, but also those involved in the overhead of equipment which will be less completely utilized and will be reflected in government deficits, and in defaults. The problem is whether, in the long run, it is more or less profitable to write this off and attempt an adjustment of existing institutions to a permanently smaller population.

In so far as wheat is to be grown in the West, it is necessary to adopt, as far as possible, cultural practices which are suitable to the environment and will preserve the crop-producing abilities of the soil. It is necessary to adopt practices which conserve the maximum amount of moisture, and, at the same time, do not predispose the soil to drifting. Wind erosion has been serious in some parts of the West in recent years. "In many instances farmers have lost their entire crop and have had the fertility of their land enormously reduced, certainly for many years and possibly permanently."[33] This problem is being attacked, largely through the Experimental Farms, in an attempt to devise cultural practices which combine dry farming and prevention of wind erosion.[34]

The problem of water conservation is also of considerable importance, the limiting factors being amount of water available, topography, and (a factor not unrelated to the first two) cost. Topography is such that it seems doubtful if large-scale irrigation projects are possible, except at great cost. There remain the small-scale water conservation projects, such as small irrigation schemes, dug-outs for stock watering, and so on, which are now being developed under the

[33]Hopkins et al., *Soil Drifting Control in the Prairie Provinces*, p. 6.
[34]For some account of these methods, see *ibid.*; *Drought Report;* G. E. Britnell, "The Rehabilitation of the Prairie Wheat Economy" (*Canadian Journal of Economics and Political Science*, vol. III, Nov., 1937, pp. 511-7).

Prairie Farm Rehabilitation Act. The main object of such developments is to provide the greatest degree of self-sufficiency for the farm or ranch unit.

Moreover, the problem of financial adjustment, with respect to the individual farmer, must not be ignored. Income is variable, while costs are relatively inflexible. Variability of gross income is due in part to the prevalence of drought conditions, in part to the fluctuations in price. Relative fixity of costs implies a net income which is even more variable than gross income. Inflexible costs arise mainly out of the institutional structure of the Canadian economy. It is this fact that has given rise to proposals for a more flexible instrument of finance than the mortgage, for the provision by the individual, or by the government through taxation, of reserves, and for crop insurance, and has led to the various schemes of debt adjustment in operation. In addition, the problem of rehabilitation implies an estimate of the market potentialities with respect to Western products. In short, rehabilitation in Western Canada involves consideration of the methods and difficulties of internal and financial adjustment and some assumptions concerning future trends of development.

THE ECONOMIC FORCES LEADING TO A CENTRALIZED FEDERALISM IN CANADA

LEO WARSHAW

THE title of this paper implicitly suggests the contrast between the centralized federation into which the British North American colonies became moulded in 1867, and the decentralized confederation welded by the thirteen American colonies less than a century before. The causes of centralization in Canada were internal and long-run, basically economic. Their roots lay buried deep in the history of British North America, and Confederation crowned a continuous socio-economic development of at least a century of "fur imperialism" followed by some half-century of a sort of colonial mercantilism in timber and flour, and by land monopolism, supported by colonial preference under Britain's timber duties and the Corn Laws. They blossomed forth with the coming of the railway and the factory to Canada. Lord Strathcona, "Labrador Smith", and Sir A. T. Galt, "the architect of our Canadian constitution", vividly and tersely epitomize the transmutation of fur and land into railways, and it is largely the railways, or rather their financing, that welded the British North American colonies into a centralized federal system.

The fur trade stamped itself on our present national personality: "It is no mere accident that the present Dominion coincides roughly with the fur-trading areas of northern North America. The bases of supplies for the trade in Quebec, in Western Ontario and in British Columbia represent areas of the present Dominion. The North West Company was the forerunner of present Confederation."[1] From a trade subsidiary to the fishing industry on the Atlantic coast in the early part of the sixteenth century, the fur trade rapidly rose to independence and supremacy with the revival of the beaver hat fashion in Europe in the latter half of the century. Feudal France in its mercantilist stage of development opened up the interior of Canada. It was the precious beaver that enticed the merchant adventurers and their financial backers (including Cardinal Richelieu)

---

[1]H. A. Innis, *The Fur Trade in Canada* (New Haven, 1930), p. 37.

just as it was mainly its feudatories that lured a few of the landed nobility. But the fur trade was the fundamental basis of New France and to it every other aspect of life was subordinated and adjusted. The seigneurs of New France and the crown of Old France wanted a maximum of settlers in the colony. But the fur trade stood in stark antithesis to settlement, for settlement signified the destruction of the habitat of the beaver and increasing danger of interloping in the trade: therefore settlement was kept at a minimum. On the other hand, the trade needed supplies for its hunters and traders so that a minimum of settlement was a necessity. And had the settlers not been planted under the feudal set-up naturally carried over from their land of origin, something closely resembling it would doubtless have been instituted, for the fur trade required that the settlers be tied to the soil to produce supplies and to keep out of the trade. The feudal customs, decrees, and authority, armed with the seigneur's sway and the priest's perennial suasion, if they could not eliminate the *coureurs de bois,* could keep them down to a not too disquieting minimum. It was much harder to keep the seigneur, the priest, and the missionary out of the profitable trade. Frontenac, not an unbiassed observer it is true, remarked in a letter to Colbert in 1672 that the priests "think as much about the conversion of Beaver as of souls; for the majority of their missions are pure mockeries". But if the fur lord could not keep the feudal nobility from sharing his profits of the woods, he could, and did, share their prestige and profits in the clearings by setting himself up as lord of seigniories. With the growth and north-westward extension of the trade, settlements increased to supply its growing needs. As the gains of the fur lord and the seigneur were consolidated the forces of settled civilization were allowed to press ever harder on the heels of the fur trader, but even then the eastern and southern peripheries of the beaver's westward-shifting domain were by law and force closed by the fur lords against trespass.

The Hudson's Bay Company was chartered by Charles II in 1670, largely to give his cousin Prince Rupert a field for exploitation in the north similar to that which the Duke of York enjoyed in New England. The twenty-two nobles and merchants incorporated under the charter were offered a monopoly of the fur trade in, and absolute ownership and regency over, the territory vaguely defined as lands drained by rivers flowing into Hudson Bay and including everything east, north, west, and south of the bay, to about the 49th parallel. Rivalry with the French from the St. Lawrence continued to be violent until 1763.

The royal proclamation of that year fixed not merely eastern and southern, but northern and western, boundaries as well, for the "Government of Quebec". The quadrilateral, worked out to hem in this colony, was given Lake Nipissing as its north-westernmost vortex. The fur trade continued to be protected by the feudal set-up in Quebec which was retained by Britain for that very purpose and because seigniorial tenure was profitable. As for the remainder, some 90 per cent or more, of present-day Canada, it was declared to be "just and reasonable, and essential to our interests" that the lands be reserved to the Indians "as their Hunting Grounds". The Hudson's Bay Company's vast preserves were shielded from encroachment by the settler or the American trader.

Most of the French traders and many nobles sold out their interests on the St. Lawrence after 1763 and left. Fur merchants from Detroit and Albany, who had been coming in since the closing years of the war, took over the trade routes and bought up seigniories. They succeeded, through consolidation into the North West Company, in establishing themselves as the ruling force in the British colony on the St. Lawrence and the exclusive monopoly concern to rival the Hudson's Bay Company. The Constitutional Act of 1791 placed a large measure of the imperial government's power in the hands of the fur lords of the St. Lawrence and their French seigniorial collaborators. The measure had a great liberalizing effect on the trading activities of the St. Lawrence, and the rivalry of the two monopolies became more intense.

The province of Upper Canada created by the Constitutional Act had as its first lieutenant-governor John Graves Simcoe, who wrote on September 11, 1794, in a letter to the Board of Trade and Plantations: "The Fur Trade has hitherto been the staple of Canada and the protection of it, until the Establishment of Upper Canada, seems to have been the primary object of all the Military Arrangements and consequent settlements in the Upper Country."[2] It did not cease to be the primary concern, not merely in the matter of

[2]E. A. Cruikshank (ed.), *The Correspondence of Lieut.-Gov. John Graves Simcoe, with Allied Documents relating to his Administration of the Government of Upper Canada* (Toronto, 1923-31), vol. III, p. 52.

military arrangements and settlement, but also in general economic and social, as well as political, arrangements. Settlement and Indian policy were directed and roads built in support of the trade. In his letter to Lord Dorchester, on March 9, 1795, Simcoe suggests ways and means of intercepting the Indians on their way to the American fur-trading posts so that they "may be preserved from becoming the property of the United States, whenever they shall possess Detroit".[3] In Upper Canada as well as in the Lower Country, the fur traders were entrenched in the legislatures. A certain Rev. Father Edmund Burke complained, in a letter written in the spring of 1795, about the fur traders' old technique, apparently widely applied in these parts despite Simcoe's ban on the "selling or bartering rum or other spiritual liquors" among the Indians,[4] of swindling the Indians out of their skins or a reasonable price for them by means of those "spiritual" inducements, and adds: ". . . if the Indians be not our friends, they will be our most dangerous enemies. Can His Excellency strike out no mode of preventing the sale of spirits to them? Some of his Council and many members of the Assembly are, I believe, engaged in that contemptible trade."[5] As in the lower colony, so here, much of the land found its way into the hands of the fur merchants, and as the fur trade receded from the borders of the province, as land values rose with increasing settlement, and timber cut and flour milled reached exportable proportions, the economy of the two colonies became subservient to the timber and flour trade in the hands of the land monopolists, many of whom had come from the fur trade.

The fur trade entered a new phase in 1821 when the North West Company of the St. Lawrence was swallowed up by the Hudson's Bay Company which in the same year secured from the imperial Parliament a renewal of its monopoly in the trade, for twenty-one years.

The trade in the new staples, which rose out of a more highly diversified economy, required not merely a monopoly[6] grip on the

[3]*Ibid.*, p. 323.
[4]*Ibid.*, vol. V, p. 178.
[5]*Ibid.*, vol. IV, p. 23.
[6]I have labelled this stage that of "Monopolism" to distinguish it from the stage dominated by the fur trade, which I designated the period of "Monopoly", and have carefully traced the transition from the latter to the former in each of the Canadas in my thesis.

land (as had the fur trade) to check settlement, but also on shipping and road facilities, on banks and mills, on the community's purse strings, its schools and churches. In contrast to the fur trade, it was centred and directed from within the community. There was not, as in the fur trade, an integrated monopoly concern, but merely a minority group with common interests, who between themselves held an effective monopoly control of all the resources relevant to their trade (and speculation), in each province—the Family Compact in the upper and the Chateau Clique in the lower. In each it was the money and power derived from fur that vitalized the growth of the new social economy, but there were merchants from other spheres, though many of them in the supply trade of the peltry commerce, who had side by side with the McTavishes, the Frobishers, and the Todds of the North West Company fought for the Constitutional Act, and who, like them, benefited from that measure, upon which, as Mr. Stewart Wallace, in his *Family Compact* (p. 7) observed, the whole structure of Monopolism came to be founded.

By about 1825, the incubus of monopoly had fully matured and brought into prominence the acute social problems inherent in it, and progressively aggravated by its further development. The population of Upper Canada had reached 157,923, and over 13,000,000 acres of crown lands out of a total of 16,000,000 of surveyed land in Upper Canada had been granted or appropriated. Between 1825 and 1838, when the population had more than doubled, less than 600,000 acres were disposed of, chiefly by sales to speculators and settlers, including 466,742½ acres of clergy reserves and 100,317¾ acres of crown reserves. John Radenhurst, chief clerk of the Surveyor-General's Office, in his deposition before Buller, stated that "only one-tenth of all the lands alienated by the Crown were settled in 1838".[7] The "monopolists" had by 1837 ownership and control over approximately 10,000,000 acres in Upper Canada, of which 2,395,687 acres were in the hands of the Church of England; 2,484,413 in the hands of the Canada Company; and the balance, acquired by direct grant, or purchase at ridiculous prices, or grants to others, such as the 2,911,787 acres of the lands granted to the United Empire

[7]Appendix (B) to *Report on the Affairs of British North America* from the Earl of Durham (1839), p. 120, Minutes of Evidence, Q. 1083.

Loyalists. Hundreds of thousands of acres of Indian lands were in the hands of individual members of the Family Compact.[8]

The monopoly in land was merely the foundation for the comprehensive monopoly hold of the Family Compact on the economic and social life of the country. In William Lyon Mackenzie's enumeration of these various monopolies in 1832, there is scarcely a sphere of life omitted:

1. The House of Assembly; 2. The Legislative Council; 3. the Executive ditto; 4. and 5. the York and Kingston Banks; 6. the Law Society Incorporation; 7. to 11. York, Kingston, Niagara, Amherstburgh, and Brockville Town Incorporations; 12. Eleven Sets of District Magistrates; 13. the Canada Company; 14. Eleven District Courts; 15. Court of King's Bench; 16. Upper Canada College; 17. Clergy Incorporation; 18. Welland Canal Company; 19. Desjardin Canal do.; 20. Grand River Navigation Co.; 21. and 22. Cornwall and Sandwich Police; 23. The Lieutenant Governor, or agent of the Colonial Office. There are about 25 other chartered or incorporated monopolies. . . . I might also have added Education, which is the worst monopoly of all.[9]

The yeomanry suffered from scattered settlement, the resultant of the trichotomous division of the land sections and the holding up of land for speculation, which made it impossible to build and maintain adequate roads for communication and the marketing of produce. The Family Compact poured huge portions of the public treasure into the construction of canals to cheapen the rates on its lumber and flour shipments, and to enrich individual contractors. The small merchant or trader, and the master craftsman, found the avenues for personal advancement barred, the former because of the Compact's monopoly hold on profitable avenues (including, incidentally, those of the professions, especially law), and both because the internal market was kept from healthy expansion, and what is infinitely more important, because the colony's external trade was adjusted merely to serve the needs of the lumber and flour merchants, without any heed being given to the hardships and needs of the small merchant and craftsman. For example, because of the high duties on all goods imported from, or shipped *via*, the United States, British goods had to be shipped through the St. Lawrence. But since this channel was closed by ice for six months during the year, the merchant and the

[8]*Cf. ibid.*, pp. 11, 97-9, and 118.
[9]*Sketches of Canada and the United States* (London, 1833), p. 493.

manufacturer had to "submit to an injurious delay in his business, or must obtain his goods in the autumn and have his capital lying dead for six months",[10] or pay exorbitant prices for his stock-in-trade, and for his raw material. The tea monopoly of the East India Company was permitted up to 1838 although the British Parliament had revoked it for the company's trade to India in 1813. Finally, all the lower classes suffered from the burdensome taxation which they had to pay and from which only the Family Compact seemed to derive substantial benefits. The yeoman even had to shoulder the tax burden which should have fallen on the land in his district kept unoccupied by his speculating landlord. The chronic instability and insecurity of the colony's currency were largely results of the Family Compact's banking monopoly and its reckless and unrestrained manipulations which further aided in repressing and paralysing the growing trade and industry of the colony.

As early as 1806 Judge Robert Thorpe, William Weekes, and Joseph Willcocks organized a Reform party under the suggestive name of "Jacobins", but by 1808 they succumbed to the vicious onslaughts of the Compact, with Willcocks behind the bars. In the measure that the social problem grew in extent and intensity, so also did the militancy of the masses under Robert Gourlay from 1817 to 1819, William Lyon Mackenzie from 1824 to 1837, and the autocratic propensities and repressive reactions of the ruling class.

The Reform parties demanded the smashing of the Compact's hold on the reins of government so as to secure a voice in state affairs to legislate and direct in the interests of the yeoman and small entrepreneur instead of in those of the small band of mercantile monopolists. This they sought to achieve mainly through an elective instead of the appointed Legislative Council of the Constitutional Act, and a responsible Executive in place of the arbitrarily appointed Executive Council which had no responsibility to Parliament. The land question was to be solved by secularizing the clergy reserves and by consolidating the clergy and crown reserves with the rest of the land in each section under one administration—the disposal of land to be regulated by law. Other measures proposed were government construction of roads, and attracting of settlers, especially from the United States. All these land reforms had been suggested as early

[10]Durham, *Report*, p. 67.

as 1817 by the settlers in answer to Gourlay's questionnaire. Mackenzie, in 1824, was unaware of some of the problems and advocated the inclusion of all the other denominations in the policy of endowment through clergy reserves, then a monopoly of the Anglican Church, the spiritual partner of the Family Compact. It was not till 1831 that we find him advocating secularization, which alone could remedy the sectional withholding of land for speculation. There was a demand for absolute free trade (Mackenzie never tired of singing its praises and of applauding the smuggler) and for its seeming corollary, the break-up of monopolies.

The Reformers at first planned to achieve their programme by enlisting the help of the imperial Parliament. In England the "Radicals", party of the manufacturers and traders in arms against the agrarian interests and their mercantile monopolist twin, were becoming an ascending force in Parliament as the class they represented had long been in the social economy. And in 1832 they had wrested from the agrarian parties amid threat of revolution the first Reform Bill which fully enfranchised them and their hitherto unrepresented emporium, Manchester. It was shortly thereafter that Mackenzie went to England to lobby for his party. He was well received, and fairly rewarded. Goderich at the Colonial Office sent a dispatch to Colborne, then lieutenant-governor of Upper Canada, instructing him to refrain, with his councillors, from interfering in election contests, to lay all public accounts before the Assembly, to dismiss Archdeacon Macdonnell of the Legislative Council and Bishop Strachan of both the Legislative and Executive Councils from office, and to limit the number of government placemen in the Assembly. Nothing very revolutionary in this and far from the goal and aspirations of the Reformers, but it proved enough to send the Family Compact into a violent rage. Its mouthpiece, the *Upper Canada Courier*, in recording the Compact's reaction, incidentally laid bare the roots of its long-proclaimed "loyalty":

Instead of dwelling with delight and confidence upon their connections with the glorious empire of their sires, with a determination to support that connection, as many of them have already supported it, with their fortunes or their blood, their affections are already more than half alienated from the government of that country; and in the apprehension that the same insulting and degrading course of policy toward them is likely to be continued, they already begin to "cast about" in "their mind's eye", for some new state of political existence, which shall effectually put the colony beyond the reach of injury and insult from any and every ignoramus whom the political lottery of the day may chance to elevate to the chair of the Colonial office.[11]

But the Family Compact was prematurely pessimistic. It ignored the essential instructions in the dispatch with impunity, and thereafter, and until 1846, except for the interlude of 1838, was not again to be troubled by any "ignoramuses" in the British government.

When it had become plain to Mackenzie that nothing could be hoped for from the British Parliament, that the Family Compact was becoming ever more arrogant and violent in its repressions, and the social problem ever more acute, and that nothing could be achieved "constitutionally" within the political framework of the colony, he changed his *tactical* programme to anti-imperialism and sounded the call to armed revolution. Sir Francis Bond Head's about-face from the reform sympathizer, as which he had been sold to the province by Glenelg, Goderich's successor at the Colonial Office, to the most uncompromising and demagogic champion of the Family Compact, and his blunt dissolution of the Reform Assembly on May 28, 1836, as an answer to its non-confidence vote, drove the Reform leadership to this reversal of *tactics*. When the financial and economic crisis of 1837 seemed to have made the objective situation ripe for the seizure of power, and when the critical moment had arrived early in December, only seven hundred and fifty fighters marched behind Mackenzie's banner, to be vanquished on Montgomery's Farm on the seventh, three days after bullets were first exchanged.

Sir Francis held one card with which the constituents permitted him to trump any in the Reformers' hands, and that was his stand on imperial connection. When he flung the charge of disloyalty to the Empire against Mackenzie's party, it touched a very tender spot in the hearts of his listeners, for, economically, they were a complement to Great Britain. The merchants might profit most from the lumber and flour trade with the mother country, and the continued flow of these staples to British ports was, to their minds, the very condition of their existence. The part of the United States to the south of them was agrarian, and the thought of annexation meant to them material deterioration and dislocation, if not annihilation. Mackenzie threw his broadsides against the "English Parliament

[11]*Ibid.,* p. 58.

[which] have interfered with our internal affairs and regulations, by the passage of grievous and tyrannical enactments". Lord Durham's analysis of the 1836 election results was correct: "There seems to be no doubt that in several places, where the Tories succeeded, the electors were *merely* desirous of returning members who would not hazard any contest with England, by the assertion of claims which from the proclamation of the Lieutenant-Governor, they believed to be practically needless."

The history of Lower Canada from 1791 to the revolutionary uprising in 1837, ran almost identically along the same general lines. It was complicated by the feudal problem and the so-called "racial problem", but differed from the western province only in the more deeply rooted foundation of the Chateau Clique, the counterpart of the Family Compact, and the longer, stronger, and more continuous history of its reform movement embodied in the *Patriotes.*

The feudal structure, apart from barring the enterprising French peasant from profitable commercial pursuits in the fur trade or in the growing towns and cities, became, in addition, intolerably oppressive to most of them, through greedy exactions. The movement for emancipation already manifesting itself under French rule gained in momentum and came to eloquent expression in the American Revolutionary War. Even though the appeals of the revolutionaries were successfully impeded by the feudal structure from penetrating to the peasantry, nevertheless sympathy with them was expressed by the latter in a number of ways, most of them, however, primarily directed toward their own liberation. Thus, when, following Montgomery's second invasion of Canada in 1776-7, Carleton ordered the French peasants to render fealty to their seigneur, the response of the former was startling and significant. Francis Maseres reported active opposition by many to the seigneurs. On M. LaCorne's seigniory the habitants refused to be led by any but "English" leaders. On the Richelieu, three thousand habitants armed themselves against threatened reprisals by Carleton's troops for refusing to take up arms under their seigneur Deschambault. But many English seigneurs fared no better. Cuthbert's habitants refused to arm at his, or even at Carleton's and Lanaudière's, commands.[12] The opposition was apparently

[12]*Cf.* W. B. Munro, *Documents relating to Seigniorial Tenure in Canada* (Toronto, Champlain Society, 1908), pp. 241-6.

not to the French or the English as nationalities, but to feudalism. General Burgoyne complained of repeated desertions and insubordination, and believed them due "principally to the unpopularity of their seigneurs, and to the poison which the Emissaries of the rebels have thrown into their minds".[13]

The passage of the Constitutional Act of 1791 basically represented a victory of the St. Lawrence merchants over the imperialistic Hudson's Bay Company, a victory to which the peasantry in no small measure contributed. With the growth of population accompanying the westward retreat of the fur trade, the English merchants, who with their French counterparts and the feudal nobility, many of whom had taken to the trade, became entrenched in the government of the lower colony. With the Catholic and Anglican clergies, they appropriated to themselves a monopoly of virtually all the land henceforward distributed, precisely as in Upper Canada, to become the Chateau Clique, a land monopolist and merchant ruling class profiting on land values and feudal dues, and on their monopoly in the trade in fur, lumber, and flour staples, as well as the banking and all other economic and social institutions which were subserviently adjusted to that trade.

The merchant group sided with the seigneurs with whom it largely coincided. This shows itself most clearly in the struggle for commutation. The reform measures (largely offered as concessions to the Reformers) in 1822 and 1826 were voluntary measures and were rendered nugatory by being boycotted by the Clique. By 1830 there had been only two commutations! The execution of the more progressive report of the Commission of 1842 was again impeded by the same class, and in 1854 Beauharnois was still a seigniory and Edward Ellice (lord of the fur trade) still its seigneur. Finally, the French Roman Catholic clergy, the spiritual prop of the seigneurs and of the whole merchant clique, proved at least as deadly a weapon against the rebels of 1837 as the militia.

For the rest, though the split on the issue of imperial ties came a little sooner and expressed itself more distinctly than in the upper country and the revolutionary fighting had more the aspects of a civil war than in the sister colony, the aims and the course of the

[13]A. Shortt and A. G. Doughty (eds.), *Documents relating to the Constitutional History of Canada, 1759-1791* (Ottawa, 1918), p. 677, n. 1.

revolutionary parties in each province were much the same. The small merchant and financial class elements were even more prominent in the ranks of the fighting *Patriotes* than in those of the Reformers. Among eight hundred and eighty-five fighters and partisans arrested after December 7, 1837, while the yeomen and artisans predominated, yet small merchants, master craftsmen, and professionals were represented in due proportion to their strength in the community.

The union, or rather reunion, of the Canadas in 1841 was an event of utmost significance, in its essence, as a stepping stone (or rather milestone) *en route* to Confederation. It was an *imperialistic* coup, in the full sense of the word, executed by the merchant-financial group of Montreal and their long-established connections in England. With the development of financial institutions in subservience to the mercantile trade in lumber and flour, under the preferential patronage of the British mercantile and agrarian classes, the capital from the fur and land monopoly flowed into, and monopolized, the new and eminently profitable channels. The field in Lower Canada was limited and restricted, and the monopolists' agitation for reunion became ever intensified. Union would permit them to apply most of the customs revenues (consolidated through union whereas they had to be divided between the provinces before) and the other financial resources, to the perfection of the St. Lawrence canal system, which held out high premiums for them in contractors' profits and cheaper rates on their commercial shipments. It was for the very reason that the St. Lawrence improvements accrued exclusively to the benefit of the monopolist group, while expenditure on them meant neglect of the road and other improvements to the settlers, at the same time strengthening the monopoly hold of the mercantilists over the province as a whole, that the Reform Assemblies in both provinces, but more decisively in the lower one, had obstructed passage of the St. Lawrence improvement bills. Finally, the Montreal group cast jealous eyes on its weaker monopolist counterpart in the upper province.

Durham indisputably came under the influence of the Montreal group, and his union proposal earned him the fiercest hatred and abuse from the Family Compact. When the Union Bill, which had been urged on the imperial government in vain in 1806 and 1810, and which through the clandestine manoeuvres of Edward Ellice almost passed after 1821, was finally rushed through the legislature in Great Britain, where "official opinion" had for many years been "strongly supporting the union", all classes in both provinces, save only the merchant group of Montreal and their allies, were uncompromisingly hostile to it. Their "allies", it was worthy of note, were none other than the seigneurs and officials, their complements and supplements in the Chateau Clique. When the agitation had become particularly strong, there came from Quebec a "Petition of Seigniors, Magistrates, members of the Clergy, Officers of the Militia, Merchants, Landholders and others"; and a similar one, specifying "British birth or descent", from Montreal, praying the imperial government for union on the usual rationalization, viz., to heal the "spirit of dissension and animosity" between the provinces over the division of customs revenues.[14]

In 1840 the socio-economic and political machinery evolved within the country from the fur trade, had become fully mature for imperialistic expansion, and the "Union" was its first effective expression. When union had become a fact, the Family Compact found its worst fears justified. The "Farmers' Joint Stock Banking Company", among numerous other Family Compact banks, was swallowed up by the Bank of Montreal directly after union. The "Bank of the People", founded by the Reformers in 1835, was taken over and became "practically an agency" of the Bank of Montreal, "which, prior to the Union, had no agency in Upper Canada".[15] The Canada Company of Upper Canada was brought into closer co-operation with the British American Land Company of Lower Canada in 1842 with the appointment of A. T. Galt to supervise the affairs of the Lower Canadian concern.

For the first Assembly, the Montreal group succeeded, through effective racial propaganda, and Sydenham's reshuffling of the Montreal constituencies, whereby some two-thirds of the city's French Canadians were disfranchised, in electing as many government representatives as there were Reformers returned from Canada East. The Executive Council was, of course, irresponsible (except to Montreal) and its strength lay in the Legislative Council, among whose members was Peter McGill, president of the Bank of Montreal.

[14]W. P. M. Kennedy (ed.), *Documents of the Canadian Constitution, 1759-1915* (Toronto, 1919), pp. 318-26.

[15]Sir Francis Hincks, *Reminiscences of his Public Life* (Montreal, 1884), p. 11.

To their sorrow, the Montreal group found the combined strength of the Reformers from both provinces in the House strong enough to elect a French-Canadian Reformer as speaker.

Sydenham, the first governor-general of the union, had brought with him a guarantee for a £1,500,000 loan to complete the St. Lawrence canal system; but the political fruits of the union were not quite so sweet as the Montreal clique had anticipated. To make matters worse, upon Sydenham's death in 1842, Bagot, who had been sent out as his successor, committed the indiscretion of calling on Baldwin and Lafontaine to form a representative Executive Council. The harm was quickly enough repaired by the immediate recall of Bagot, and the dispatch of Metcalfe, trained in the East India civil service, to succeed him. Metcalfe arrived in 1843, and before the 1844 elections, had everything in such order again that a slight government majority was secured after a campaign closely paralleling that of Sir Francis Bond Head in 1836. But, as in Upper Canada after that event, so here, the muffled voices of the Reformers were rising to revolutionary heights. In 1846 the British industrial *bourgeoisie* asserted its final triumph over the agrarian and mercantile class, in forcing passage of the Acts repealing the Corn Laws and the colonial preference on corn as well as on timber. The sudden death of the mercantilist class in England was followed by the collapse of its colonial partner. This class in the colonies, however, felt itself much stronger than its imperial parent did at home, and after many indignant but vain demands that these repeals be retracted, they did what the Family Compact had done: they decided that a mother country that threatened to stop feeding them profits through the old established channels was not one fit to be connected with, and signed the Annexation Manifesto.

With the arrival of Elgin, sent out to succeed Metcalfe, the era of responsible government (limited, of course, by an appointed Legislative Council) may be said to have begun. The 1847 elections returned a Reform majority, and Elgin summoned Baldwin and Lafontaine to head a Reform Cabinet. There followed years of long-fought-for liberalizing and constructive measures. Baldwin's bill of 1849 freed the University of Toronto from its Anglican sectarianism; but far more significant were the measures relating to trade and industry, the secularization of clergy reserves, and the commutation of feudal tenure. In 1849 the General Amnesty Bill was passed on behalf of all the rebels of 1837 still in exile, and the Rebellion Losses Bill to indemnify all for losses suffered during those turbulent days. A good many Reformers thus came to share in the £100,000 voted by the Act, which thereby tended to vindicate the armed uprising of 1837. This was too much for the scotched monopolists. They geared up their race propaganda machine to its highest pitch in Montreal. Typical of the viciously inflammatory opinion against the bill and those who passed it is the following cited by Elgin in his letter to Grey: "We are glad of it,—the sooner the cloven foot is made visible the better; the obvious intention of that majority composed of Frenchmen, aided by traitorous British Canadians, is to force French institutions still further upon the British minority in Lower Canada . . . when French tyranny becomes insupportable we shall find our Cromwell. Sheffield, in olden times, used to be famous for its keen and well-tempered whittles—well, they make bayonets there now, just as sharp and just as well-tempered."[16]

Strangely enough, it was not a Frenchman, but none other than Lord Elgin, against whom that maddened group, displaced from its seat of power, directed the incited mob. The stoning of Elgin's carriage may have soothed the hearts of the group that saw in him the symbol of the British power that hastened its fall, but it did nothing to readjust and rehabilitate its members. The path for their readjustment and rehabilitation was, however, opened by the same government that passed the Rebellion Losses Bill,. and in the very same year of its passage. For it enacted in 1849 the Railway Bill, offering public credit for railway enterprises up to half the amount actually expended. It soon became clear to the old mercantile oligarchy that this newcomer in Canada might well prove as profitable a field for exploitation as the old monopolist trade. The capital from fur and land, trade and bank, now began to pour freely into railway construction. The legislatures of the two provinces had indeed granted over a dozen railway charters between 1832 and 1845, but until the fatal blow of 1846 the railway had not yet demonstrated its feasibility as a reliable means of communication in Canada, and certainly did not seem a promising rival to the lucrative St. Lawrence trade. Hence its progress in Canada was stunted, in spite of the settlers'

16Kennedy (ed.), *Documents of the Canadian Constitution*, p. 580.

grave need for improved communication, and Canada, in 1848, had no railways except a summer portage road stretching for sixteen miles between Laprairie on the St. Lawrence, and St. Johns on the Richelieu.[17] Now, however, with their old foundation swept from under them, the mercantilists saw the iron horse in a new light, and with it also the new factories producing textiles, boots and shoes, and agricultural implements, that sprang up like mushrooms, following the introduction of responsible government. These new industries promised to be potential sources of profit, perhaps as good as the land and mercantile trade had been; and while it was not possible to get a monopolistic control of them through the simple device of a Family Compact or Chateau Clique machine, yet financial power held out the same promise—while even a more representative Parliament and government might be assimilated and wielded in a way similar to its predecessors: and it was.

A. T. Galt at once plunged into railway construction and secured a charter for the St. Lawrence and Atlantic line from Montreal to Portland, and soon had his hand in almost every charter issued. Meanwhile, the British firm of Peto, Brassey, Jackson and Betts, who had built a third of England's railways, and had powerful connections in the British Cabinet, had stopped the British railway loan guarantee of £7 million promised to Nova Scotia and New Brunswick for a line from Quebec through Saint John to Maine and secured from the union government a charter to build a line from Lake Huron to Portland, beginning with construction of the section from Hamilton to Montreal, on the terms of 1849, and the right to buy up outstanding charters along this line. Galt, Macpherson, and Holton, who held most of the charters, amalgamated with the contractors to form the Grand Trunk Company, which secured from the province a guarantee of £3,000 per mile of road. The contractors, who owned over £3½ million of the company's stock, went to work at once, utterly oblivious of cost or expense. The directors of the company, voting themselves fanciful salaries and engaging in specious financial operations (such as the buying of Galt's St. Lawrence and Atlantic Railway at "cost" while its stock was selling at 50 per cent on the market) time and again applied to the provincial government, of which, incidentally,

[17]H. A. Lovett, *Canada and the Grand Trunk, 1829-1924* (Montreal, 1924), p. 2.

they had become an integral part, for additional grants, such as that for £900,000, which was followed by the government's assumption of interest payments on the company's seventy-five million dollars of bonds, in 1857. The legislature became a charter exchange bureau, where members voted each other charters. Municipalities, too, were caught in the railway fever, and by 1861 some thirty of them in Upper Canada alone had floated $5,594,400 in loans, on which they were $2,359,406 in arrears on interest payments to the provincial government. The representatives of all governments, local as well as union, meanwhile piled up huge profits, through jobbing and log-rolling in charters, grants, and loan guarantees, for themselves and their financial associates. Yet the communication-starved communities benefited by the leap in railway mileage from 60 miles in 1853 to 1,881 in 1861.

However, the union Assembly by 1861 had been pumped dry and the Grand Trunk Company, which had meanwhile begun to hesitate about the wisdom of the originally proposed terminus in Portland, came to a standstill and its London bond and shareholders in 1862 took the line out of its contractors' hands. Watkin, its new president, had been sent out as commissioner to Canada, and had found the management an "organized mess". He conferred with representatives from all the provinces on the amount each could contribute to an Intercolonial Railway. The solution lay in getting greater assistance from the Canadian government, a Canadian sea board terminus, amalgamation of competing and feeding lines, together with expansion to the logical western limit on the Pacific, and the development of settlement post haste. In 1863 the company bought out, or rather absorbed, the Hudson's Bay Company and agitation for the union of all the British North American provinces was intensified.

The difficulty lay with the Maritimes. Their economy still rested largely on extractive and other primary industries. Federation with the industrial and financial Canadas would not merely mean subservience to the latter, but complete dislocation and ruin of their economy through high tariffs and economic divorcement from the United States. But the Grand Trunk interests needed the additional revenues of these provinces, while the manufacturing and financial interests saw in them new markets, if they could only be shut off from the United States. The Grand Trunk Company was the consummation of monopoly in the fur trade (Hudson's Bay Company) and in land (A. T. Galt), fused by railway financing. It had to swallow the Maritimes completely, had to bring them under absolute central control of the Canadas, alias the Toronto-Montreal-London axis, to serve their interests. This idea, conceived in the fever of railway financing in Canada by men, the end products of a chain of centuries of conditioning, forged link by link, was finally clothed in material reality in 1867. And unlike the constitution of the United States, there can be no doubt as to what the drafters of the British North America Act *really intended*[18] to be the form and power of certain institutions of the state. At least as far as the balance of power is concerned, they meant it to rest as concentratedly as possible within the hands of the federal government.

The way in which the Maritimes were inveigled into this imperialistic scheme, of whose essence and significance to themselves they were fully conscious, and whose consequences showed their fears justified, is common knowledge and need not be here detailed. It will suffice to recall that Nova Scotia returned an overwhelming majority of anti-unionists to the first Dominion legislature, in a ratio of nineteen to one, while Prince Edward Island, whose Assembly still showed an anti-unionist majority in 1870, was forced into the union in 1873 by her threatened railway bankruptcy.

[18]See W. B. Munro, *American Influences on Canadian Government* (Toronto, 1929).